THE
EDWARD
HOAGLAND
READER

THE EDWARD HOAGLAND READER

EDITED AND
WITH AN INTRODUCTION
BY

GEOFFREY WOLFF

RANDOM HOUSE · NEW YORK

Library of Congress Cataloging in Publication Data
Hoagland, Edward.
The Edward Hoagland reader.
1. Natural history—Addresses, essays, lectures.
I. Wolff, Geoffrey, 1937-   II. Title.
QH81.H68   500.9   79-4776
ISBN 0-394-50742-8

Manufactured in the United States of America
24689753
First Edition

CONTENTS

v

INTRODUCTION

GEOFFREY WOLFF

"How long will these readers continue to miss walking in the woods enough to employ oddballs like me and Edward Abbey and Peter Matthiessen and John McPhee to do it for them? Not long, I suspect. We're a peculiar lot: McPhee long bent to the traces of *The New Yorker,* Matthiessen an explorer in remote regions that would hound most people into a nervous breakdown, Abbey angry, molded by what is nowadays euphemistically called 'Appalachia.' As a boy, I myself was mute for years, forced either to become acutely intuitive or to take to the woods. By default, we are the ones the phone rings for, old enough to have known real cowboys and real woods."

There's Edward Hoagland; I'd know the author of that paragraph from a mile off. It comes from the middle of an essay titled "Writing Wild," and like a wolf pissing along his trail, its author lets you know whom you're following. The breezy "oddball" is a Hoagland signature, and so is the confident placement of his own work with McPhee's, Abbey's and Matthiessen's. The outburst of candor—"As a boy, I myself was mute . . ."—is vintage Hoagland, together with the audacious transition to and from his confession.

We are speaking here of an original, and I am here to advertise him. In the course of an essay on the literary situation, Hoagland hit upon a truth relevant to his *career* (a word he doesn't like): "There are writers' writers and readers' writers, and though each group is inclined to envy the other, the writers' writers envy the readers' writers more and cross over if they find they can. After all, writers want to be read."

Of course they do. Hoagland has written that while he could easily set limits on his appetite for fame and fortune, he'd happily have readers in their millions with their noses stuck in his pages, finding something they need or want. He deserves them: he has range, tenacity, intelligence, special knowledge, comic gifts, invention, an intimate proximity with his reader.

God knows the critical attention has been extravagant: Alfred Kazin has called Hoagland "a writer born, a writer obsessed." Philip Roth has chimed in, Archibald MacLeish, Saul Bellow, John Berryman, many heavyweights. Hoagland's essays are accessible: about how we live, love, marry, die, divide, replicate, suffer, celebrate . . . essays about the circus, boxing, New York, bears, tugboats, turtles, country fairs, dogs, taxidermy, bad luck. One of my favorites is "A Low-Water Man," about a man who dives from an ever-increasing height into an ever-decreasing depth of water, a paradigm for the "writers' writer," who continues to do what he does, like the diver, because "this is what he is good at."

When I suggested in a review that Hoagland is a kind of low-water man, he bristled; he is a *hell* of a bristler. "Why not a high-water man?" he asked me. Why not indeed? It's past time for this gorgeous writers' writer to dive deep into a great abundance of readers, who have for too long missed too much.

Hoagland was born in New York, four days before Christmas, 1932. His father was a lawyer for an oil company, and life was comfortable, education at St. Bernard's, birthday parties at the St. Regis. Hoagland grew up in Fairfield County, Connecticut, and was sent away to "a kind of Yeshiva called Deerfield Academy" and then to "sumptuous Harvard," graduating in 1954. As a boy he was made to take golf lessons, which he hated, and allowed to tramp the woods, which he loved. He had tough, character-building summer jobs fighting fires with Indians out West, tramping back and forth across the country, riding the rods, working for a circus with the big cats. He joined the army as a draftee, married, divorced, remarried, had a daughter, wrote and published three novels, traveled. . . .

No: it is so much more complicated than this. The data I so casually summarize is released, sometimes under great pressure and explosively, in myriad essays. Hoagland is often categorized as a naturalist, but in fact he is of the tribe of Edward Abbey, who describes his own books as belonging to "the category of personal history rather than natural history." Still, as strong as the personal impulse may be in Hoagland, it is very nearly blocked by the man's reticence, a reticence that sends him alone to the woods, an inwardness that sends him five months out of twelve from his home on New York's Lower West Side to a small farmhouse in Barton, Vermont, two miles up an unplowed dirt road, without electricity. So he tells of himself obliquely as well as abruptly, getting word of himself in edgewise among lore about bears and tiger trainers.

Sidewise speech and the explosive outburst are facts of his life as well as the manner (if not provocation) of his art. He stutters; Hoagland's debility is obtrusive: "I strangle; I can't speak at all . . ." He shakes his head side to side, choking. His words come, finally, in sobbing bursts, till he unaccountably, temporarily, relaxes. His stutter arrived as a mystery (he remembers mocking a stuttering boy at summer camp, catching speechlessness as a punishment), and occasionally departs the same way.

Hoagland understands the consequences of his stutter. When he was a boy, on holiday in the Rockies, daydreaming of finding a mountain lion, climbing through wilderness rocks with his eyes peeled, he saw what he wanted to see, a miracle. The moment is captured in one of his finest essays, "Hailing the Elusory Mountain Lion," and so too the moment after, running down the mountain to bring the news: ". . . I knew my real problem would not be to make myself believed but rather to make myself understood at all, simply in reporting the story, and that I must at least keep the memory straight for myself."

Thus, a writer. Elsewhere he puts the progress bluntly: "Being in these vocal handcuffs made me a devoted writer at twenty. I worked like a dog, choosing each word." And meantime, not only his stutter placed him apart. Scattered throughout his essays are hints of his father's disapproval of Hoagland, and of Hoagland's work. At Deerfield he was assigned to a special corridor populated by "incorrigible maladroits and known informally as The Zoo." At Harvard he hoarded the *Daily Worker* and "attended meetings of a Trotskyite cell in the theater district in Boston, and then perjured myself when I entered the army by signing a statement that I never had." In the army he tended bodies in a morgue, and perhaps from this experience, or hitchhiking, or taking down circus tents to move along, he learned to like saying good-bye, "believing that we are alone to begin with anyway, and that the good-bye only returns us to our original state."

An outsider, then. A man who expected, when he was called for jury duty, to be rejected by the lawyers on both sides of a case, because he was an "oddball," a novelist and stutterer, "a little askew," as he has written of himself. In the course of his essays he has doubted his own mind, thought for a while he was homosexual, referred to his "accustomed neurotic self," reported that during one particular year of courtship "my feet smelled terrible . . . like a forest fire." He writes that he's a voyeur, and briefly a sadist, beating with a belt or hairbrush a woman who liked sadists.

And more than an alien: a naysayer. His mother told him never to bargain, so "if I had some object to sell, as when I got rid of my trumpet, I enjoyed bringing it to a pawnshop and bargaining diligently with a Jew." It is not difficult to imagine Hoagland's effect on his father, a clubman who liked the conventions and fine clothes. But, again, the facts come out odder than our expectations, and Hoagland hints at reconciliations and mysteries, his father's disappointment in his own career, his father's end, after he "drifted, wrote poetry, and went to Kyoto," death by cancer. And then "my mother saw horses with blowing manes climbing the sky for weeks after he died."

In the woods Hoagland learned attention, and rhapsody. His stutter threw him back on the power of his eyes to record a scene, and he communicated best with animals who had no need to hear him speak. (He claims to be able to talk with tigers, bugling a kind of fluty raspberry to which they'll reply.) He calls himself a "brassbound optimist by habit—I'm an optimist in the same way that I am right-handed, and will always be." He divides writers, perhaps too simplistically, between those who "prefer subject matter that they rejoice in or subject matter they deplore and wish to savage with ironies . . . I'm of the first type . . . I'm a merry-go-round fan . . ."

And a tugboat fan, circus fan, old-man fan, tall-tale fan, Updike fan, boxing fan, turtle fan, "Jack-of-all-trades, not too interested in anything, but interested in everything." As a kid "the out-of-doors was everything to me," and he haunted ponds near his Connecticut house studying turtles and snakes, keeping reptiles as pets because he suffered from asthma. He is still allergic to fur, which I learned deep into *Notes from the Century Before: A Journal from British Columbia* (1969), a remarkable travel book that turned him away from fiction (at least temporarily), toward personal journalism. "In the cabin I'm in, a grizzly skin is pinned to the wall like a spread-eagled moth. I should probably note that I'm allergic to it."

The rueful, confessional note, a reminder of what's really what in the world, is pure Hoagland. At a small settlement way up a wilderness river: "Don't let me escape admitting that I got rather scared in the bush." His work and preoccupations take him into rough country, but he likes as well to leave it—"to get home to [a] soft house and fortifying dinners"—as to reach it; "I do tiptoe about this matter of roughing it," he wrote in *Notes from the Century Before.* "I curl in my sleeping bag daintily and I'm awfully fastidious as I wash at the creek, and never quite do my share of the jobs."

Hoagland's life is artfully balanced—or divided, depending on your perspective—between the wildness of New York and the wilderness of places unsought by most people. Sometimes he is at home either in New York or in Vermont's Northeast Kingdown, and sometimes he is torn between them, but always he's alive to the distinction, and often in his personal journalism he remarks it. "Wildness is a relative term," he wrote in 1968 from British Columbia. "The last time I lived in British Columbia I saw two bears shot and several drunken Indians skidding their cars around Hazelton on Saturday night. But in the first week or two after I had returned to New York, I saw a man shot on the street—he sat on a stoop holding his stomach. And I was on the subway when a man jumped underneath, giving a desolate, memorable scream. And the boiler exploded in my building, setting a fire and blowing the floor out of the apartment below me."

Perhaps it's the theatricality of the city's wild violence that inspires Hoagland's cocksure opinion that New Yorkers are tougher than the toughest country people, suppler, quicker and (when sane) "the sanest people on earth." He loves tramping the city, and writing about its variety. The voyeur in him is drawn to crowds, a bracing sense of solitude thick in a mess of strangers. Swept up by a subway rush hour "I liked losing control of where my feet took me, I liked swimming against the tide and with the tide." (Two-way swimming is one of Hoagland's great subjects.)

The city can provoke his most rhapsodic apostrophes, like this, from the deck of a tugboat in "Knights and Squires: For Love of the Tugs": "The spray plumed like cream at our bow, and the water was like crinkled tinfoil. The lights of the city were like jubilant news. They were flung out so far that what can one say? They're not man-made; they're the work of some several millions of men . . . As we went down Manhattan from 23rd Street, every light in the office buildings was on—ranks and ladders of lights like a thousand trombones. All Harlem was there; the cleaning women were working. And the whole city stood on end for me, the light pricks of darkest Brooklyn, the whole grandslam cacophony."

But there is a critical distance here from the particular people who comprise that "grandslam cacophony," and if one of the malign characteristics of our age is "the common benevolence we have . . . for the race but not for the in-dividual," it is a preference Hoagland sometimes shares, as he shows by his use of the first person plural. His distance from particular people, sometimes verging on truculence, I'll take up presently. For now I'll merely note that there are limits to his love of city life, and the same essay that inspires such a dazzling, light-shot stream of prose from the river also acknowledges that by spring this writer becomes "something of a menace to myself. Spring fever isn't the word for it; I want to get to the country."

He keeps the country with him in the city, plays whale songs and wolf howls on the phonograph at night, leaves on his air conditioner all year to drown out the street sounds. And then, "when my native iconoclasm builds up in me until I want to knock people's hats off, I pile into my car and drive away with the window open, and soon find myself singing 'God is good, God is great!' at the top of my lungs into the roaring wind . . ."

But wherever he fetches up, there's the immutable fact of solitude, another of his great subjects, and of all his subjects the one that has most deepened his judgment. He writes of crying jags when he's alone, looking for wolves: "Instead of growing less susceptible to the debilitations of solitude, as I get older I am more so. It's a peculiar life: Tuesday hurrying along Sixth Avenue in New York, Wednesday, after a flight, exploring Dog Canyon in the Big Bend country near the Rio Grande, startling the vultures off a lion-killed deer in a dry streambed . . . Air travel and the telephone, too, make for hysteria. A few spins of the dial and we can talk to almost anybody in the world, and in towns like Hackberry or Buras, Louisiana, or Alpine, Texas, at the first strong pinch of loneliness I've known that I could jump into my Hertz Ford and hop a plane for home. The trouble is, at home I've often wanted to catch a plane for Alpine . . ."

Hoagland writes now and then of his childhood worship of heroes, and our need and lack of them. He's not the banner-waving fan McPhee is, but he likes to hang around people who do well what they do. There was a British Columbian, a woodsman named Willie: "He was a doer, he was the best in the country, grotesquely slowed down though he has become, and since his manner still carries the certainty of this, I call him Willie as people call Joe DiMaggio Joe, for instance, from meeting him once." And another woodsman and pioneer, Jim Morgan: "He's like Willie Campbell. He's the very best, the obscure common hero. He's the man you want to see mountains named after, and yet he leaves it at that, he's antidramatic . . . He splits firewood with a few quiet taps with one hand, holding the axe head. He keeps a blaze in the cook stove throughout the day, though our weather is up in the eighties, and he also wears long underwear: let the temperature change instead of him."

While Hoagland reserves a special affection for old men, especially old men who have done difficult things they'd prefer to keep to themselves, he also celebrates flamboyance. One of his most ardent subjects is the circus cat trainer Gunther Gebel-Williams, who loves to spend money on flash, but maintains dignity and reserve at his craft. For all his rebellion against his parents' snobberies and proprieties, Hoagland has his own notions of good taste, and he can be a hanging judge of people who violate them. Many people, that is, fail to measure up to this writer's exacting values, and this is in large part why he so often feels the tug and pain of solitude, wanting in Alpine to be home in New York, longing in New York to be back in Alpine.

Hoagland has the gift of fine discrimination, distinguishing between this and that style in a matter so seemingly elementary as the gutting of a deer: One hunter "goes at it like a soldier who is stripping a foe, and the other rather resembles a woman poking through her purse, examining what it contains, although she knows what everything is." At his best Hoagland, like anyone telling us what we didn't know, is eagle-eyed, and keen-eared, listening for peculiarities and particularities of speech, for the Maine guide who'd "sell December awfully cheap" and the Vermont livestock judge carrying on about a winning cow's "terrific set of legs, her whole top-line, and her dairy promise, the shapeliness of the udder and teat placement, the mammary system—she's just so very *dairy* with that udder promise!"

At his worst he is merely astringent, uncharitable, too quick to assume he has a stranger's number. "I have yet to like anyone who wears a string tie," he says, and I believe him, and wish I didn't. Jealous of his own privacy, he is nevertheless intrusive, a journalist, after all. As a child and young man he got the treatment he sometimes cruelly gives: "The family dinners, occurring whenever there was a visit, intimidated me; the questioning was bluff, immediate and intimate, as if blood were thicker than water." Now, despite his stutter, he asks the questions: "As for me, I'm very brisk. It's a cold profession, this new one of journalism. I skimp on and rather snub everybody near my own age . . . Towards the older people I'm full of affection, but am all questions, all smiles and no give. They know nothing about me when I leave and I know a great deal about them."

This is how a writer as good as Hoagland works. No free lunch for anyone, for sure, and he's smart enough to know this, honest enough to say it. Sometimes he's honest to a fault. His tolerance is stretched past the break-point by credulous tourists, the Yukonese, "without exception . . . heavyset, conscious of how heavy a punch they can throw. Goodness knows when they throw it, though; they seem so tame." In the same Yukon town "one sees lots of ground-monkey faces among the women." Tree monkeys can be attractive, but "the ground monkeys, best represented by the baboon, have close-set eyes and a broomstick nose." He's also hard, in *Notes from the Century Before*, on "young knuckleheads" he met here and there on his travels, people without the gravity of age. During a canoe trip on Maine's Allagash Hoagland shares camp with a suburbanite whose "pouchy face . . . looked as if he had laughed at his boss's jokes about five thousand times too often, a face that looked as if maybe he had been served up one of his kids at a business lunch once and had gone ahead and eaten it anyway."

When Hoagland judges people fecklessly, and calls for hanging, I don't much care for him. (Though I should mention that the man judged capable of eating his daughter had tried out some campfire anti-Semitism on Hoagland, not much of an audience for that kind of thing, and that when he is cruel he is often very funny.) So much for Hoagland's vices, and my reservations: the rest is trumpet voluntaries. And even his occasional sourness is the fruit of a brassbound optimist's vision of the night-side of things, his apprehension that "life is lonely. Some are sinkers and some are floaters."

For the floaters there is compassion. Hoagland takes care to call barge commanders—"the fallen men" of New York Harbor, boozers mostly—*Captain*, and to call them Captain "every sentence or two." He's shrewd enough to remember suburban angst, the commuter running his grim constitutional, trying "to get his emotions under control." He writes, with bleak precision, about the fate of turtles, painted for the Times Square novelty market, whose shells once they were painted ceased to grow—but whose bodies did not: "Gradually, invisibly, they would be crushed. Around us their bellies—two thousand belly shells —rubbed on the bins with a mournful, momentous hiss."

People die, and death is accepted, almost casually, "unless our noses are rubbed in it." What is more shocking is how casually people observe their friends' lives. Hoagland is resolved, it seems, to watch life exhaustively, intrusively (if need be), and to judge how well or ill his fellows spend it. He is a social critic. Writing of how we live, Hoagland writes of change—of course—and of loss. He writes of hectic, purposeless motion, the jitters. Of the erosion of codes: if the hunt was once the stalk, now it is merely the kill. "Whatever was being done well finally was overdone." Everyone wants more of the less that is left, or else he does not want any of it enough: "Despite all the fuss about wilderness, people nowadays don't really want to be in the woods all alone. If they did, there would be less wildness in the woods and in the end there would also be more of it. Even faster than the woods go," he writes in "The New England Wilderness," "people are losing their taste for the woods."

As an essayist Hoagland is a conservative, hanging on for dear life to things still here, about to vanish. That's why he prefers old-timers to young knuckleheads; he wants to conserve their stories, the lore in the attics of their memories. So up in British Columbia, digging for the stories that weren't "threadbare from handling," up in Vermont asking questions "that soon won't be asked at all," Hoagland had a vision of himself: "Talking with the various old men, each one with a heart condition, I some- times felt the need for haste in gathering information: even a sense that if the fellow should suffer a stroke before my eyes, I would bend over him, urgently asking, *Where was that cave? Who was it that you said lived there?*" He's not merely, as he himself wonders, an "antiquarian." He feels no compulsion to record, for himself, what he has already experienced. Neither does he write, like a polemicist, to reverse the world's processes. "Lament the Red Wolf" is a long essay about a dying species; an interviewer asked Hoagland if he wrote about red wolves to save them, and Hoagland said, "No. There is absolutely no hope for red wolves, and my article didn't do a thing for them." He writes for generations to come, as all writers with reach write, and his ambition is precisely articulated: "It's as though the last bit of ocean were about to become more dry land, planted and paved. The loss would be not to us who have already sailed it, who have no wish to be sea-men, and who can always go back and relive in our minds what we've experienced. The loss is to people unborn who might have turned into seamen, or who might have seen it and loved it as we, alive now and not seamen, have seen it and loved it."

If Hoagland's purpose is to conserve, his method is radi-cal, inventive, often audacious. Except for occasional book reviews, he does not write to order, on "assignment." If he feels like writing about the Golden Rule, so he does, and hopes when it's finished someone will want to publish it. In this he's had the good fortune his work deserves, with publication in such periodicals as *Harper's*, *The Atlantic Monthly*, *The Village Voice*, *The New Yorker*, *Sports Illus-trated*, *Commentary*. His first novel, *Cat Man*, was accepted while he was still at Harvard, and published in 1956 by Houghton Mifflin, which gave it a Literary Fellowship Award. *The Circle Home*, about a boxer, followed four years later, and in 1965 *The Peacock's Tail*, a New York novel that Hoagland has called a "failure, critical, artistic," that came just as he was splitting up with his first wife, an experience that caused so profound a "rip" in his life that he came "at sea" and "floundering"—as he told an interviewer—to the journal form, and from there to the personal essay.

Hoagland began his writing life as a "bleeder." He has said that he gave about an hour of work to every ten words published in his novels, working "like a dog," writing "two

full-length novels in iambic meter and a firehose style."
Now he works differently, essaying a truly rough first draft,
learning as he goes where he means to end up. The looping,
almost loopy, design mapped on some of his pieces remains
through the final draft, and the most radical quality of his
architecture—especially in his most recent work—is the de-
tour. Like his precious wolves and bears, he needs range
room; his many and often abrupt transitions cannot survive
excessive constriction, which is why his longer essays seem
to me so much more successful than his short performances.

Look at "Other Lives," the final essay in this collection.
It disregards commonplace syntactical, logical and epis-
temological transitions; Hoagland lights and flies, lights
and flies again, on through an entire alphabet of postulates
and preoccupations. At a first, casual reading it is impossible to know (but easy to feel) what the essay is "about."
It touches on the following subjects, among others: wis-
dom, playfulness, vulnerability, resilience, divorce, expectation, risk, ambition, leisure time, the social efficiency that
places a New York penitentiary next door to a neighborhood drug exchange. The essay is set in New York, but
bound only by its author's meditation as he walks from his
apartment to the waterfront, and sits on a pier, thinking of
mortality, cruelty, his dog, flux, the clergy, communards,
the institution of the family. "Half the battle," the essayist
knows, "is knowing what matters." Hoagland lets so much
matter to him; he sits on the dock watching other lives pass
within the range of his acute vision, and his memory. The
other lives are not just like his own, and this he welcomes:
"Somehow the more the merrier. I'm grinning. It's like

swimming in the ocean . . . one rides above it all. It can all be absorbed." In sixteen pages, absorbed.

He likes the figure of the swimmer, likes to describe the writer—his kind, at least—as an upstream swimmer afloat "in a sea of paradoxes." And the conceit of the sea satisfies Hoagland's sense of community, the many to whom he will speak, if they will listen. "The essay is a vulnerable form," he has written. "Rooted in middle-class civility, it presupposes not only that the essayist himself be demonstrably sane, but that his readers also operate upon a set of widely held assumptions. Fiction can be hallucinatory if it wishes, and journalism impassive, and so each continues through thick and thin, but essays presuppose a certain standard of education in the reader, a world ruled by some sort of order . . . where people seek not fragmentation but a common bond."

Hoagland is never impassive, sometimes uncivil, often hallucinatory. His diction, seldom gratuitously or strenuously bizarre, can, at the necessary moment, astonish like a dream. A whore "pushed a wallet-like breast out of her brassiere" at his adolescent self. Deer "snort with the sharp sound of a box dropped." Billiard balls "seem to enjoy themselves. Painted brightly, they seem to revel in the zigzag sociability of the table, crowding together, then flying apart." Hoagland encounters by the Osalinka River two young men, "as skinny as icicles." A half-breed's swollen lips have "baked into testimonial form, or a sort of art form, like the curve of a fish backbone on a beach." In Texas, where "oil wells pump like nodding grasshoppers," a real wolfer "walked from his hiding place to scalp [dead

wolves] and strip off their skins in an act quick as sex." An
iguana's face is "really a great double-take . . . a face like
a trumpet blast." A mountain lion treed by dogs will sometimes fall from a limb upon one of them, "as heavy as a
chunk of iron wrapped in a flag." In Alberta, when Hoagland encounters a bighorn sheep "I felt as natural in his
company as if he were a friend of mine reincarnated in a
shag suit." A boxer's nose "looks doubleparked." A moose's
heart, seen at the taxidermist's, "was as big as a cannonball."
Tigers "smell like rye bread smeared with Roquefort
cheese," while bears make "a blowing sound," when they
are annoyed, "like a man loudly cooling soup."

Humor, the wise wink and city shrug, runs through
Hoagland's work; it's as much his style as the unexpected
confession, radical locution, winding progress through the
things on his mind. He's not above the merely colloquial:
a bear is "goofy" or "a poor fatty." Winter puts "hair on
their chests." A deer is "just a joker like oneself." A man
alone in the woods can get "the willies." Hoagland writes
of "old-timers" and "runts." And "wolves love to cross into
the territory of another pack and leave their mark to razz
the residents, like kids painting their colors on a rival
school."

Hoagland loves to assemble lists. Bear-hounds are "Blue-
ticks, Black-and-tans, Redbones and Plotts; and Airedale
blood is sometimes bred into a pack for extra grit." Here
are some songs and marches enumerated in one of the circus essays: "Quality Plus" and "World Events," and "The
Entry of the Gladiators." Also: "The Crimson Petal" and
"Royal Bridesmaids" and "March Ponderoso" and "Colos-

sus of Columbia" and "Bull Trombone." Here are Indian names in British Columbia: "Deaf Dan, Billy Fan, Packer Johnny, Taku Johnny, Chili Johnny, Long Jimmy, Dease Tommy, Bear Lake Billy . . . Cigar Willie, Yoho Joe, Lame Dick . . . Bummer Jack . . . Broken Arm Jim, Sambo, Johnny Quash. Also Ah Yack, Ah Clem, Ah Que, Ah Sing, George Jap and Frank Jap." Inventories of weeds here and berries there, the roll of names and places and things has the feel of weapons counted and described in *The Iliad*. Hoagland looks for the things that have stuck around in people's minds for many years.

He likes tall tales, the story of the British Columbian so tough he cut off his own frostbitten toes, one at a time, with a jackknife. Not because they hurt, but because the sound of his skinless, fleshless bare toe bones scraping against a hardwood floor annoyed him. Hoagland celebrates the minute detail, reporting to those who didn't know that white birch, because it is odorless, is used to make Popsicle sticks. Like his acquaintance, who has taught himself to look for eagles—"look up much farther, deeper and higher than one is accustomed to, but if you do this, in the course of an afternoon spent along a major valley like the Penobscot or the Kennebec, you will see an eagle cruise by"— Hoagland has taught himself to look sharp, and see.

He notices a country-fair stripper with "the flushed look of a college girl—stoned, loving the evening, yet about to cry." That about covers most of what he sees, leaving aside the rhapsodies and celebrations. But the rhapsodies and celebrations are his specialty. I like them because they're felt, and because they're manageable, no rebuke to novices

and stay-at-homes. In Hoagland's stories, obsessions, however wild, have a domestic—shall we say human?—character. A bear expert's wife wears shirts with bear tracks
painted on them. Hoagland has a particular partiality for
a friend who married the same woman twice: "Although it
didn't work out either time, she was well worth marrying
twice, and to my way of thinking this showed that he was
at once a man of fervent, rash, abiding love, and yet a
man of flexibility, ready to admit an error and to act to
correct it."

Perhaps best of all, I like why Hoagland goes to the
circus, and why he's glad to see you and me there, too. It's
because it's one of the last places left, or so he believes,
where a crowd will watch someone teeter on the wire of
death and not yell "Jump!" So he writes in "Splendid, with
Trumpets," and so he repeats, with a variation, in "Tiger
Bright": "In a day of casual death everywhere, we are rejoicing *he lives! he lives!*"

Hoagland's essay on taxidermy, "The Moose on the
Wall," concludes with a young boy in a Vermont bank,
looking at a moose head fixed to the bank's wall. The boy
"tried to go through to the other side so that he could see
the rest of the animal. To begin with, they had to tell him
it wasn't alive." I've read that essay, and the rest, many
times now, and I still try to walk through them to see more,
and they can't tell me the damned things aren't alive.

Selection and sequence have been my responsibility.
While I am partial to Hoagland's long essays, for reasons
of space I have not included some of his longest: "The

War in the Woods" (from *The Courage of Turtles*), "The
New England Wilderness" and "Walking the Dead Diamond River" (from *Walking the Dead Diamond River*),
"Lament the Red Wolf" and "Virginie and the Slaves"
(from *Red Wolves and Black Bears*). From fifty-three
essays published in these three books I have selected
twenty-one, in addition to three short passages from
Notes from the Century Before, the last of them an extraordinary tour de force about salmon blocked by a rockfall
from their upstream spawning grounds.

The progress of my selections is eclectic but not random. "Home Is Two Places" and "On Not Being a Jew"
are autobiographical in effect if not intention, so I set them
first to establish Hoagland's history and received preoccupations. I have scattered essays about animals through the
book, progressing from turtles (Hoagland's earliest interest, closest to his boyhood haunts) to dogs to mountain
lions to "Bears, Bears, Bears," a particularly warm-hearted
and exhaustive essay. Hoagland has had a special place in
his attention for bears from the beginning, when I stumbled
on his observation in *Notes from the Century Before* that
grizzlies, "like the French . . . have the merit of being just
as hard on their own race as on foreigners." Like Hoagland,
"they are solitaries, they are property owners, and they
are virtuosos." Years later, when Hoagland became my
friend, I thought of him when he wrote of their "prickly
egos"; he himself thinks of bears as "a kind of shadow of
man, a tracery or etching of him—as mutes and schizo-
phrenics and idiots sometimes are . . ."

I have mingled city pieces—"City Rat" and "Knights and

Squires" and "The Problem of the Golden Rule"—among wilderness essays. Rhapsodies about boxing ("Heart's Desire") and the circus ("Tiger Bright") have not been neglected, nor such sour and bleak meditations as "Fred King on the Allagash" and "A Run of Bad Luck." I close with the twined, looping complication of "Other Lives," but earlier selections—"Home Is Two Places" and "The Problem of the Golden Rule"—anticipate some of its radical transitions. Among all these I have a favorite, but I'll keep its name to myself—for good luck—and let newcomers to this remarkable writer get on with the important pleasure at hand.

THE
EDWARD
HOAGLAND
READER

HOME
IS TWO
PLACES

Things are worse than many of us are admitting. I'm a brassbound optimist by habit— I'm an optimist in the same way that I am right-handed, and will always be. It's simpler to be an optimist and it's a sensible defense against the uncertainties and abysses which otherwise confront us prematurely—we can die a dozen deaths and then usually we find that the outcome is not one we predicted, neither so "bad" nor so "good," but one we hadn't taken into consideration. In an election, though, for instance, where it's only a question of No. 1 or No. 2, I confidently assume that whoever seems to be the better fellow is going to win. When sometimes he doesn't, I begin to feel quite sure that perhaps the other man, now in a position of responsibility, will shift around to views much closer to my own. If this doesn't occur either, then I fall back on my fuzzy but rooted belief that people of opposed opinions at least do share the quality of good-heartedness, of wanting good things to happen, and so events finally will work out for the best.

The trouble is that they're not working out for the best. Even the cheerfully inveterate sardonicists, whose chirpy pessimism is an affirmation of sorts, are growing dispirited and alarmed. And it's not just the liberals; the unease emanates from everybody, Republicans and Christian Scientists—the lapel buttons and bumper stickers and decal figures imply a kind of general clamming-up, a sense of being beleaguered, maybe a panic at the great numbers of people we each pass in a single day—this with the hardening of sects of opinion which have despaired of conversing with one another but only holler out code words and threats. Many people think about finding some peaceful holing-up spot, which may be in the suburbs, or if the individual has already opted for the suburbs, may be up toward Mount Katahdin. As soon as he can afford it he starts wanting a second home, a place to recuperate from the place where he lives while he works, and though it used to be that such a home was frankly a luxury, now nearly everybody who makes a middle-class living starts to think about buying a cottage in the woods or a boat at the shore, if just for the sake of his health. The thirty-hour week, so heralded, may mean three hard ten-hour days of work in the city and then a fast retreat for everybody (in shifts) to what will pass for "the country" in twenty years, there to lead the leisure life, building canoes and greenhouses and picket fences.

I grew up in the suburbs. My father left for New York City every weekday morning and got home about 7 P.M. The commuting was grueling and he liked a change of scene on his vacations in later years, but we didn't need to have a country cottage, since we saw deer in the evening and grew a Victory Garden during the war; there was a feed store in town, painted with checkerboards, where the local farmers talked about chicken diseases and trapping weasels. A man named Frank Weed trained pheasant dogs professionally, and my sister when she was growing up went across the road and watched a calf born every spring. Both she and I spent part of our childhoods developing a special sympathy for the animal personality. There was a magical fullness to my perceptions when I was with my dogs, a heat-lightning shiver and speed, quicker than words. Of course to rule is a pleasure, and yet as happiness, as intimacy, these interludes are not to be dismissed, and the experience of sensing other wave lengths in the world besides the human gabble needs woods and fields and isn't found as easily now.

The out-of-doors was everything to me. I spent the summer mornings on Miss Walker's big estate, vaulting the brooks, climbing the pines, creeping along the rabbit paths. Then I made lemonade for the afternoon heat wave and lay on the screen porch listening to Mel Allen broadcast the Yankee game. There'd be a thunderstorm and I would lie in the backyard for that, watching the black clouds brew, feeling the wind. Soaked, grinning, I'd go and sit inside the chicken coop for the clubbiness of the chickens, whose pecking order I knew all about. Later I traveled to prep school carrying my alligators wrapped in a blanket to protect them from the cold. But I loved Tommy Henrich too; I was a hero-worshiper. And at night, when I was jittery, I returned to the city, where I'd lived earlier; in the most frequent dream I jumped off the Empire State Building and flew with uneven success between the skyscrapers by flapping my arms. Winters were spent in galoshes, fooling on the schoolbus. Those bus rides were the best part of the day; we had no teacher accompanying us and the driver put up with anything. There was a boy who kept a Model A to tinker with when he got home; another was the quarterback who won our football games; another the school mathematician or "brain." The mechanic has since turned into a clergyman, the quarterback works humbly for General Electric, the mathematician is mad. One nondescript goof-off has made a million dollars, and his chum of the period is a social worker with addicts. Of my own friends, the precocious radical has become a stockbroker and the knockabout juvenile delinquent journeys now in Africa. The same sea changes seem to have affected even the houses that I knew. Mrs. Holcomb's, where I took piano lessons, is now the Red Cross Headquarters; Dr. Ludlow's, where I went for inoculations, has become the town museum. Miss Walker's woodsy acres are the Nature Study Center, and the farm where my sister watched the calves born—Mr. Hulendorf's—has been subdivided into a deluxe set of hutches called Historic Homes.

Wherever, whoever we were, we've been squeezed out of the haunts of our childhood, and there is no reason why we shouldn't have been. The question is only whether we are gradually being squeezed out of all possible homes. To the fear of dying of the ailments that killed our fathers, of angina or driving badly, we have an added, overlying trepidation that life may be shortened anyway for all of us. Old age seems not to exist as a possibility culturally, in any case, and the generalized future seems incomprehensible—exploding, crazily variant developments to be fitted together. The more successful and propulsive a man of affairs is, the more freckled and browned he usually looks, so that when he finally folds up in exhaustion, he must correspond to a tree which has turned to punk inside the bark invisibly and which suddenly crumbles. Aging used to be a slow process involving wasting less and less of one's energy as well as having less energy, and so, for a long while at least, the pleasure in one's increased effectiveness just about balanced the sadness of winding down. And as a man lost some of his youthful idealism, he lost, too, some of the brutality that goes along with being young: a balance was maintained there also. Now he's either young or on the shelf, and if he's on the shelf he's savage.

When my father was dying I had a dream which amounts to a first memory, brought up intact like some frozen fossil which the ice has preserved. I was diapered, lying on my back in his hands, well before I could talk. By comparing my size in his hands to my daughter's right now I would guess that I was about ten months old. I was struggling, kicking, and he was dandling me, blowing in my ear, a sensation too ticklish, too delicious to bear. Squealing, powerless to prevent his doing it, I loved it, though at the same time I was dependent upon him to stop before it became excruciating—I was waving my

7

arms in the air trying to protect my ears. But the best, vividest piece of the memory is the whirring, vital presence of my father, with deep eyes and a humming voice, in the prime of life; I remember his strong hands. Even his early baldness seemed to add to his vigor because it made for more area of skin. He was several years younger than I am now, and so the continuity of seeing him then and myself now, and seeing him die, is startling.

This memory feeds on to the pinpoint events of a train wreck in Nebraska a year later, and to the familiar jumble of childhood. During the Depression we lived in the city; there were singers at the bottom of the air shaft whom the maid and I threw dimes down to, wrapped in toilet paper so that they wouldn't bounce too far. I pulled the bow of her apron to tease her twenty times a day, and she took me to Catholic church, whose mysteries I remember better than the inside of our church, though once recently when I was hurrying along Lexington Avenue I was brought up short by the sight of a mnemonic worn brick wall that shook me: Sunday School. My parents reappeared in youthful roles, and I could remember something about that whole extraordinary masquerade which one plays as a child—pretending to learn to read, as if we didn't know already, pretending to learn to tell the time, as if we hadn't known all about clocks for years and years.

My father was a financial lawyer. At first I went to an English-type school called St. Bernard's and to birthday parties at the St. Regis Hotel. I remember, too, watching King George pass in a cavalcade on Fifth Avenue from a

dowager's wide windows. But Eisenhower, another war-
time eminence whom I saw feted from those windows,
represents much better my father's style. The side of
Eisenhower that wasn't glamorous like Clark Gable re-
sembled my father—the grin, the Kansas accent, the
Middlewestern forehead, the level-headed calmness or
caution, the sanguine and good-tempered informality.
Each was a poor-boy democrat and a Republican; each
stood out for rural, old-time values, though personally
preferring to hang out at the golf club with industrialists;
each was softer in manner than the average soldier or
lawyer; and each had a Chinese face lurking behind the
prosaic American bones which materialized inchmeal as
he aged and died. My father worked in Eisenhower's
administration, and Ike was the president he most ap-
proved of—an internationalist abroad, a gentle-minded
conservative on the home front, who started, however,
from the assumption that most people deserved to be
liked.

Once when my father was leaving a Mario Lanza movie
he stopped to hear one last aria again, and collapsed with
emotion on the floor of the theater when it ended. And,
if he hadn't much sense of humor (or it came hard to
him), he laughed a lot, loudly, every chance he had. He
thought that exercise, music and friends were the cure
for mental illness: in other words, it terrified him. He
thought homosexuality "sinister" on the occasions when
he recognized it, and never drank much, and probably
was sexually faithful, although I think he fooled himself
about the nature of certain avuncular relationships he

had; when one young woman married he tore her honeymoon picture in half. But his marriage wasn't unhappy. Quite often he ended his friendships with men who got divorced on what he considered frivolous grounds; he didn't swear or like swearing, although he liked vitality and a masculine air in his friends. He had the chest of a track man and may have read more passionately as a man of sixty than as a college boy, which is unusual—he was especially partial to translated classics and to looking at Renaissance art. Mother married him partly because of his idealism, she says, though naturally I didn't think him idealistic at all. I even went to a different barber in town as a means of delineating the difference between us. Mine was the Town Barbershop, which had *Liberty* magazine beside the chairs and a proprietor nearly eighty years old, wonderfully wiry and tall, with black hair, knotted hands and a sharp nose. For the many years I went to him he knew me as "Peter"—in the beginning I'd been too shy to set him straight. The Colonial Barbershop, which my father patronized, did a smoother job, and the owner, who was a worldly man, tried at one point to break out into the wholesale barbering-supply business but went bankrupt and soon was right back in the local shop. After that, he spent his weekends in New York, wandering reflectively among the skyscrapers, musing on the enigmas of fortune and wealth.

My father was battling for advancement at the same time, trying to rise from the position of a hired attorney to a directorship in the oil corporation he worked for. He wasn't an original type or a sparkplug—he seemed awfully

meticulous—and so he lost. He went into retirement angry,
though several offers came his way thereafter, such as to
go to Hong Kong as consul or head a graduate school.
Instead he drifted, wrote poetry and went to Kyoto. When
the World's Fair played on Long Island he drove out
and roamed the cheerful pavilions, scanning the Midwest-
ern faces, delighted by the accents, reminded of his boyhood; like the Fair itself, he was hopeful. In manner, he
was so deliberate some of the other commuters had called
him Speed, and yet late in his life he traveled round the
world, pulling my mother after him when her enthusiasm
waned. He returned to Rome and Paris ten or twelve times,
and he loved Florence—nothing that a thousand other men
don't do but with as much intensity as any. Dutch Reform
by background, he shifted towards agnosticism in middle
age, joining the Episcopal Church as a form of neutralism.
He liked to sail, sailed rather daringly, not with the caution
that exasperated some business associates. He sent money
to relatives who had hard rows to hoe and liked uninfluen-
tial people as well as the strong. For instance, when I was
a boy he made me aware of a fellow at the oil company
whose function was to meet transatlantic ships and speed
the debarking of company bigwigs and guests—a tall,
prudent, intelligent-looking man of mature years whom
one would see standing among the crowd of passengers'
relatives and friends as the ship docked. Noticeable for his
banker's dress and for his height, he would step forward
through the multitude and fix upon the personage he was
supposed to meet (I suppose he studied photographs),

THE EDWARD HOAGLAND READER

bring over a Customs man, somehow accelerate the inspection, get porters, flag down a taxi, and see the mogul whisked away before most of the passengers were even off the boat. My father was touched by his plight.

When it was possible to procrastinate, my father did so, being a dreamy man, but he was decisive at the end. He went for a sail alone overnight in his little sloop before turning himself in, exhausted, to the doctor, with cancer signals, and while he was waiting to die, still ambulatory, he journeyed to Sarasota with my mother. She could scarcely get him to leave before it was too late for him to go under his own power, but then he settled into the house in Connecticut for the last siege with gallantry and gaiety, so that the big busty nurse, accustomed though she was to seeing men die, actually fell in love with him and became inconsolable. He enjoyed the ripening spring weather, the phonograph, the house he loved, and kept hold of his self-command (what, after all, can one do with one's time in those last weeks except to be friendly?). He talked on the telephone, blinked in the brightening sun—to overhear him in the final conversations he had with friends was piercing. And he did want the Church to fulfill its appointed duties, so when a cub minister was sent to visit him he wasn't satisfied with the small talk they were able to muster. Then an old senior minister, a tippler with a crumpled face, came and told him that he faced "a great adventure," which he accepted as being probably about as good a construction as anybody was going to be able to put on it. My mother saw horses with blowing manes climbing the sky for weeks after he died.

If we are to contrive to lead two lives now, one in the city and one near Katahdin, we can draw some quick assurance from the fact that our backgrounds individually are even more diverse than that. I've got millers, tailors and outdoorsmen in mine, real outdoorsmen to whom the summer soldiers' Katahdin would be a tasty canapé. Though the two names, Morley and Hoagland, fit together neatly for me because I'm so used to them, the families—my mother's and father's—stretch back in complicated, quite disparate fashion, the Hoaglands to early Brooklyn; later they lived in New Jersey. They came out badly in the Revolutionary War—the branch of them I know about. A skirmish with the British a few minutes' walk from their farm put several of them out of commission for the rest of their lives. The ones who weren't too demoralized moved west and south shortly afterwards to Lexington, Kentucky, where they did fairly well, except that again my own ancestors after a generation or so migrated on by boat and wagon to the farming country of Bardolph, Illinois, where they spent the Civil War. One who had marched with Sherman creaked on from Bardolph by wagon to Hutchinson, Kansas, where he farmed a Soldier's Land Claim, kept a hotel, and worked with team and wagon on the construction of the Santa Fe, and wound up as the county agricultural agent and a Freemason. Though there were proud Eastern Hoaglands who belonged to the upper crust, and other Hoaglands who split away to seek lonelier, unknown destinies, most of my branch of the family were farmers consistently for two or three hundred years, right back to Brooklyn,

13

and they appear to have filtered away into the soil finally, or else to have wound up in Los Angeles with the rest of the prairie farmers who scraped together a few thousand dollars, there joining the middling middle class.

One early pale fellow loyally fought cholera in the Kentucky epidemic of 1823, dying at his post, and my grandfather, who was a doctor too, died abruptly of meningitis in the 1930s after a bumpy career, mostly practicing obstetrics in Kansas City. He was a husky-faced, square-set man with a red complexion, certainly a kindly doctor, but he found it hard to make a living and for several interludes went down to the bayou lumber camps in Louisiana to work as a company physician. His oldest child died of a fever on one of these tours of duty; his youngest died in his arms after being hit by a trolley a little bit later. His wife, too, died young. I have the impression that his happiest years were while he was in the Medical Corps during the First World War. He and my father got along quite well, and my father, despite his successes and travels later on, would have gone to the state university and presumably stayed in Kansas City if at the last minute he hadn't noticed a scholarship competition for Yale on his school's bulletin board. Being a lawyer and the son of a doctor, he thought of us as a family of professionals and hoped that I would enter one of the professions—if not either of those, then what he called "the cloth"—rather than be a businessman. When I wound up a writer he was utterly taken by surprise.

The Morleys, by contrast, were merchants instead of farmers for as far back as I am aware. They arrived in the

New World after the Hoaglands did, and whatever matters they applied themselves to when they first got off the boat, they were in upstate New York for a while before settling in Painesville, Ohio, in the nineteenth century. The Morley burial plot is still in Painesville, along with a rambling white house with long porches and a poppy and gentian field in the rear—a sort of family "seat," which the Hoaglands lack. It was partly the Morleys' clannishness that put me off them when I was a boy. By 1900 they were worthy people with fat family businesses, big family weddings—the marriages were patriarchal; none of your warlike American ladies there— and they kept right on flourishing, until by the time Franklin D. Roosevelt campaigned through town, some of them wouldn't even walk down to the railroad depot just to set eyes on the man. Since I'd been brought up among the comforts my father's breadwinning had earned, these shrewd breadwinning businessmen from Painesville, and Saginaw, Michigan, and Aberdeen, Washington, seemed like vaguely unsavory bores to me. The family dinners, occurring whenever there was a visit, intimidated me; the questioning was bluff, immediate and intimate, as if blood were thicker than water. Yet I remember that when my Great-uncle Ralph came east for the last time, knowing he was soon to die, he rented his suite at the Biltmore, invited my father up, and spent that last interview with us reading aloud with relish the notebook notations he kept in an inside pocket of what his stock-market portfolio was. My father, who had nothing to do with handling the Morleys' money, was astonished. This stingy or mercenary quality afflicting many of the Morleys is in me also, but they were a florid, varied crew whom a less Protestant person than myself would have found fascinating from the start, and next to whom we of the present tribe are insipid fellows. The Morleys are following the Hoaglands into modest extinction, part of the Johnny Carson family.

My mother's family's pride and principal vocation during the time between the two world wars was Morley Bros., a department store and statewide hardware dealership located in Saginaw. Before opening that, her grandfather had had a saddlery business in Chicago, after leaving Painesville as a young man. While getting his Chicago operation going, he married a packinghouse heiress, a Kelley (the family had sold out to Armour). Later, in Saginaw, he founded a bank as a kind of a sideline. Banking intrigued him, but during the 1929 boom he sold the bank to a big Detroit bank that was looking for mergers. He happened to be in New York City on a business trip in October during the first black days of the Crash. Realizing the seriousness of the situation, realizing that the Detroit bank was over-committed and might have to close, he hated to think of his own town's bank collapsing along with it, and so he caught a Pullman home. The panic was spreading west, the officers in Detroit already saw the handwriting on the wall, and hurrying to rally the help of a few other Saginaw citizens, he was able to buy back the bank and save it, in a fine hour. Banks were still a centerpiece in the post-Victorian era and banks do figure on this side of my family; this same ancestor's daughter-in-law, my grandmother, had grown up in Homer, New York, the child of the local bank president. But they'd had to sneak out of town in sudden disgrace during the 1893 Panic when their bank failed. Her father's health foundered in the aftermath; he died, and she weathered some very hard years.

At any rate, Morley Bros. prospered. My great-grandfather toured the world with his beautiful chestnut-haired Kelley, leaving Ralph in charge of the Saginaw business and A. J., my grandfather, based in Chicago running the older saddlery firm. There were two other brothers, Walter and Paul. Paul was a Peter Pan type who loved combing my mother's hair when she was a young girl (it was the Kelley hair). An esthete and idealist, he hobnobbed with landscape painters and portrait artists and married a girl of nineteen who was so very demure and Alice-like that she proved to be feeble-minded. He died at only forty-six, welcoming death, so it is said, and leaving behind five blighted children who suffered from St. Vitus dance, and worse. Walter, a more earthly man, was a gambler and womanizer, a failed writer and, later in life, a Presbyterian minister, who lived in relative poverty, exiled by his father to the Wisconsin woods after some early miscues. However, Walter was the first of the Morleys to venture out to the state of Washington. He got mixed up in some kind of woman scandal and went badly into debt to the sawmill promoters of Aberdeen, and A. J. was sent west to buy them off. After Walter had been extricated, though, A. J. went to work investing in timber himself. Bored with Chicago saddlery, he became a pioneer businessman in the Gray's Harbor woods. When his first wife died in childbirth, he married my grandmother, whom he met in a tiny town where she was schoolteaching and where he'd missed his train. Soon he had three trains of his own for hauling logs, and a house on the hill, a yacht, a mistress in downtown Aberdeen (also a schoolmarm, oddly enough), a burro for his children, and a manservant, Tom. Land that he bought for $7000 and logged was sold recently for $3,000,000. He was a careful, decent man with no archenemies, although he fought the Wobblies, and he and Ralph had pleasing sons. Both he and Ralph partook of the Morleys' honest but griping conservatism about money, which ultimately prevented them from getting big-time. Back in Michigan, Ralph turned down a neighbor named Henry Ford who wanted him to invest in a motorcar company, while out in Aberdeen a decade or two later A. J. declined the chance to buy a new corporation called Boeing. His eldest boy had been killed by a falling tree, but he and his other two sons put their resources into timberland in the Oregon Coast Range instead. One was a financial man, at ease with the business community in Portland; the other, silver-haired before his mid-thirties, could deal with the loggers and union men and drove around through the mountains all day in his pickup truck. Unfortunately, the financial son dropped dead in church in his early fifties. Immediately the hard-nosed investors in Saginaw got scared that my silver-haired uncle would not be able to manage the business alone, and they made him sell out. He did enlist the ladies in the family, who were also stockholders, to help him stave them off when it came to a vote until he'd delayed long enough to get the proper price.

There is much to the Morleys that I don't know about and much to be said for them. Two women of Northern persuasion wrote action-filled, observant diaries during the Civil War, for instance—all about guerrillas and the battlefronts along the Mississippi. But for a long time, certainly throughout my teens, it was my wish to start from scratch and make my own way in the world without the help of relatives. The Morleys were always boosting each other, some were slightly-Babbitt-like, and they assumed, aggravatingly, that any relative was fair game for their gregariousness. Besides, my socialist sentiments leaned more toward the Hoaglands on their dirt farms— they were pleasingly faceless to me, the few I'd seen having just been the Los Angeles transplants. Of course I'd traveled through enough Kansas farming communities to know how little tolerance people there would show for an oddball like me if they perceived my true colors, so, glad to let them remain faceless, I simply liked to think of myself as anchored—in theory, at least—in the heartland, in the Wheat Belt.

Lately it's become the rage to ridicule young radicals from middle-class backgrounds who pretend to themselves that they are black or are blue-collar, when actually all they need to do if things get tough is reach a telephone to raise bail money or be invited home. The ridicule has been a political weapon because what most bothers people about these young persons is their accomplishment in challenging the nation's stance. I was in their shoes in the 1950s, and we weren't challenging anybody successfully; we kept our heads down, lived privately, and we were few and far between; perhaps the troubles of the present time may owe a little something to our ineffectuality. But like these activists, I'm sure, I was aware of the inconsistencies in my own position—being only too eager to give my parents' suburban address to officialdom if I edged into a jam instead of my grubby Lower East Side street number. Despite the inconsistencies, it seemed to me then that I had the choice of either going out in the world and seeing what was foreign and maybe wretched, having experiences which were not strictly necessary in my case, and *caring*, however uselessly, or else of spending my summer on the tennis courts and terrace at the country club, as some of my schoolmates were doing. The head start they supposed they had on people born into different surroundings has often proved illusory, and anyway the effort to make a beginning on independent lines, not piggyback on one's father's achievements, seemed admirable, even traditional, in America until recently. It's just lately, with the exasperated warfare between the generations, that attempting to make a new start for oneself is ridiculed.

Apart from the fuss of being political, the reasons why I was so agitated as a youngster, so angry at my parents that it amounted to a fury lasting for weeks on end, are difficult to reconstruct; I was a bunch of nerves. My mother, who besides being impulsive and generous was a strangely warm woman at times, would ask me to eat dinner without my glasses on so she could look at my uncluttered face, and tried to insist that I move down from the third floor to the room next to hers. Sometimes after my father and I had had a conciliatory talk, she'd give me a quite opposite report of what he thought, or thought of me, as though to revive the quarrel. Later, in my twenties, looking back, my chief complaint against him was that he hadn't shielded me from some of her eccentric whims and decisions; yet I'd fought with him rather than her, especially when I was in earnest. She was my cohort, guiding me most directly, and now, when I put first things first and respond quickly to the moment, it's her influence. What I learned from him was not the Boerlike sobriety and self-denial he espoused but the qualities that I saw for myself: his gentleness and slow-tempoed soft gaiety, his equanimity under pressure. I liked the way he ate too; he ate like a gourmet whenever he could.

Although I would have been willing to ignore most facets of the life of the town where I grew up, luckily it wasn't possible for me to do that. So I have the many loose-leaf memories a hometown is supposed to provide— of the Kane children, whose father was a gardener and who threw jackknives at trees whenever they were mad, which, living as they did in other people's garages, was a good deal of the time; of setter field trials and local football; of woebegone neighbors and abrupt marital puzzles —a wife who rejoiced when her husband died and buried him before his friends knew there was going to be a funeral. There were some advertising people so rich that they lived in one large house by themselves and kept their children in another a hundred yards away. There was a young architect struck into stone with polio, and a lady who collected impoverished nobles in Italy after the war and whose husband, left sick at home, made the maid disrobe at gunpoint when he finally got lonely. On the dark roads after supper you'd see more than one commuter taking a determined-looking constitutional, walking fast for miles, as if to get his emotions under control.

After my father's death we sold our house and set about looking for new places to consider home, not an easy task. The memory was of twenty rooms, artesian water, a shady lawn, a little orchard and many majestic maples and spruce, all situated where an old crossroads stagecoach inn had stood. None of us came up with an arrangement to equal that, but my mother has an apartment in the city and a trim pretty house on Martha's Vineyard. My sister married and, with her husband, found a farmhouse in Connecticut near his work with five or six acres on which she put ten horses, in order to start a riding stable. These were snake-necked, branded horses that they'd brought in a van from California, right off the range, with a long winter's growth of hair. The neighbors, who believed that life ought to have a dual, contemporary character, rushed to the zoning board to express dismay that in a fast-developing, year-round community the regulations hadn't yet been revised to bar such activities, which seemed more appropriate to a *summer* home. They were right to think it surprising, and yet the board was awfully reluctant to declare once and for all, officially, that the era of farms and barns had ended. A compromise was struck.

I married too and live in western Greenwich Village, which is an ungeometric district of architecture in a smorgasbord and little stores. There is a massive wholesale meat market in the neighborhood, a gypsy moving industry, many printing plants and bakeries, a trading center for antiques, a dozen ocean-oriented wharves, and four or five hundred mysterious-looking enterprises in lofts, each of which could either be a cover for the Federal Narcotics Bureau or house an inventor-at-work. I like the variety (the mounted police have a stable two blocks away, the spice industry's warehouses are not far south) —I like the low nineteenth-century houses alongside bars with rock jukeboxes and all the swoosh of à la mode. The pull or the necessity of living in the city seems only to grow stronger as every sort of development is telescoped into a briefer span of time. We can either live in our own period or decline to, and to decline revokes many other choices we have. Mostly what we try to do is live with one foot in the seventies and one foot in an earlier decade— the foot that doesn't mind going to sleep and maybe missing something.

I've just bought a house of my own in Vermont, eight rooms with a steel roof, all painted a witching green. It's two miles from the nearest light pole and it was cheap, but it's got forty acres, extending in a diamond shape, that back up to 5000 acres of state-owned land, and stands in a basin just underneath the western-style peak of a stiff little mountain, Wheeler Mountain, that curves around in front. The Wheelers, our only neighbors, live next door on a 300-acre farm, growing up in aspen, balsam, birch and pine, just as our land is. Mr. Wheeler, in his eighties now, was a fireman on the Grand Trunk Railroad for much of his life but grew up here and returned during the Depression. His father had pioneered the land; the Butterfields pioneered mine. The Butterfields built a log house close to that of old Mr. Wheeler, for whom Mr. Butterfield worked. There was a sawmill, a sugar house and even a granite quarry on Wheeler's place. The log house was really more like a root house than living quarters, to judge from the photograph we have, so in 1900 Mr. Butterfield and his three sons built this new home out of sawn spruce and big granite foundation blocks and plaster mixed from sand from the Boiling Spring over the hill. Their lame old horse did the hauling and pulled the scoop when they dug out the cellar hole, and young Wheeler, a schoolboy then, helped nail the laths.

Butterfield was a rough character, he says, "part Indian," as the phrase goes, but you could depend on him to do a job. His mother-in-law lived with the family, constantly fighting with him. She called him dumb and crude because he couldn't do sums, for instance; she wrote a column of numbers on the wall and watched him fail to add it. About 1909 he shot her, took his remaining relatives next door for refuge, and shot himself. There are bullet holes, stopped up with putty, and it is claimed that

that nagging column of numbers on the parlor wall had finally been added correctly. Newspaper reporters buzzed around, the property soon passed to the Stanley family, and Burt Stanley, who was a stonemason, farmed it in his spare time until his death in the 1930s. Then a tax bill of $13 came due. His widow, Della, was unable to pay it (some say she paid it but got no receipt), so the town tax collector, a fellow named Byron Bundy, foreclosed and sold her home to a crony of his named Gray, who quickly reconveyed the place to Bundy himself. Bundy died, the house stood empty through World War II (the porcupines chewing away like carpenters at the corners and edges), and his heirs sold it to our predecessors at a joke of a price.

So I'm getting a grip on the ground, in other words—gathering the stories of what went on and poking in the woods. It's certainly not an onerous chore; I've explored so many wood lots which *weren't* mine. Up among the mountain ledges is a cave as big as a band concert shell, and a narrow unexpected swamp with pitcher plants growing in it, very lush, a spring that springs out of a rock, and a huge ash sheltered in a hollow which has disguised its height and kept the loggers and the lightning off. Not far away is a whetstone ledge where a little businesslike mining used to be done. And there are ravens, bats, barred owls, a hawk or two, phoebes under the eaves, and tales of big bears in the pasture and somebody being cornered by a bull. Delphiniums, mint, lemon lilies, catnip, wild roses and marigolds grow next to the house. Storer's snakes live in the woodpile, as well as garter snakes, brick-colored and black. In the spring dogtooth violets come up, and trilliums, Dutchman's-breeches, box-flowers, foamflowers and lady's slippers, and in the fall the fields fill up with goldenrod and brown-eyed Susans, aster, fireweed. Raspberries grow in masses; also black-berries, blueberries, wild cherries and wild plums. The apple orchard is complicated in its plotting, because these farmers wanted apples in late summer—Dutch apples, Yellow Transparents and McIntosh—and then another set of trees which ripened in the autumn, perhaps Bald-wins or Northern Spies, and lastly the hard winter apples, which weren't sweet and which they canned or cooked as applesauce or "sulphured" to keep till spring. An orchard was a man's bequest to his children, being something that they couldn't promptly create for themselves when the land passed to them. I've got more going on on that hill slope of apple trees than I know about, and when the fruit falls finally, the deer and bears eat it—the bears when they have grown impatient waiting have bashed down whole limbs.

In New York my home *is* New York; nothing less than the city itself is worth the abrasion of living there, and the alterations go on so fast that favorite hangouts go by the boards in a month's time; the stream of people and sensation is the thing. But in the country the one word is exactitude. If you don't like the barn behind the house and the slant of the land and the trees that you face, then you're not going to be happy. The Canadian climate of north Vermont makes for an ideal second home because in four months three seasons can be witnessed. June is spring, September already is autumn. The moonlight is wheat-colored in August, and the mountain rises with protean gradualism to a taciturn round peak. On the east face is a wall which, if you walk around that way, can look to be nine thousand feet; the granite turns ice-white. The trees puff in the moonlight to swirling, steeplish shapes, or look like ferns. During the day sometimes a fog will effect the same exaggerated trick. High up, the wind blows harder, gnarling the spruce and bringing clouds swiftly across like those in the high Rockies; you seldom have a sense of just what altitude you're at. Every winter the deer yard under the cliffs in a cedar copse, and on the opposite side, the valley behind the hill that lies behind the Wheelers' house and mine has never been farmed and is so big it is called Big Valley. Vast and thick with trees, it's like an inlet of the sea, sending off a sheen in midsummer as you look down on it.

Mr. Wheeler, the youngest in his family, went to school with the Butterfield children in what is now the Wheelers' house, remodeled and enlarged. He is a broad-shouldered, white-faced man, a machinist at one point, until the dust bothered his lungs. Now he tinkers with his tractor and the power mower, listening to the Red Sox games, although the only professional baseball he ever saw was when he lived in Montreal during the early 1920s. He's a serene, bold man who has survived heart trouble and diabetes and says little but appears full of cheer even when he's angry. Mrs. Wheeler is a dignified, straight-backed woman, quite a reader, and formerly a psychiatric nurse. She once wrote a column for the county newspaper, and used to brew a thousand pounds of cottage cheese during the summer and peddle it among the vacationers, along with strawberries, butter and cream. She keeps a diary and a record of the visitors who come to climb the mountain that we look at, and keeps a calorie count of what her husband eats. She is his second wife, ten years younger. They have a walkie-talkie for communication with the world outside, and extra stocks of food, and a 280-gallon tank of kerosene for heating, so that the snows don't threaten them. The road plugs up but eventually it's plowed; the snow in the fields gets five feet deep and lasts so long "it mosses over—you always get six weeks of March." Being a vigorous walker still, Mrs. Wheeler is even less intimidated than her husband, and in the country style is reticently generous, as realistic as a nurse and farmer's wife combined.

In the old days there was a local man who could run down the deer and knife them, he had such endurance— he could keep up with their first dash, and as they porpoised through the woods, could keep going longer than they could. He hung the meat in a tree by his cabin to freeze, and liked raccoons particularly also, so that by midwinter the tree was strung with upwards of thirty raccoons, skinned and dressed, suspended like white pineapples. Another character, whose complexion was silver-colored, made a regular business out of bountying porcupines. The town paid fifty cents per pair of ears, and sometimes he brought in a hundred pairs. He claimed he had a super-hunting-dog, but actually he was cutting out triangular snips of stomach skin to make a dozen

"porcupines" for every one he killed. He didn't do enough
real work to break the Sabbath, as they say, and didn't
lay in hay enough to last his cattle through the winter,
so that by the end of February he would be dragging
birch trees to the barn for them to scrape a living from.
For spending money, he gave boxing lessons at night in
the waiting room of the old railroad station at the foot of
the hill. Roy Lord, who lives across from where the
station was, learned to box from him. Lord has shot
seventy-three deer in his lifetime. He lives with a sneezing parrot fifty-six-years-old, and a bull terrier who lost
an eye in a fight in the driveway; he points out the spot
where the eye fell. He can recite the details of the
murders and suicides in the neighborhood going back
forty years—all the fights with fenceposts, all the dirty
cheating deals and sudden strange inheritances. He's
learned the secrets of more than one suspicious death because he's made it a point over the years to get right to
the scene, sometimes even before the police. Or they'd be
gathering reinforcements, distributing riot guns and radio-
ing for instructions in front of the house, while Lord
would sneak around to the back door and pop inside and
see the way the brains were sprayed and where the body
lay and where the gun was propped, and damn well
know it wasn't suicide. There was a family of Indians
here, who'd murdered somebody in Canada and buried
him in their cellar and moved across the border. They
slept on a pile of old buffalo robes laid on the floor. The
daughter, a half-breed, went back into the woods in a fit
of despondency and found a cliff and jumped. Then when

the men had died as well, the last of them, a white-haired old woman, stretched out on the railroad tracks with her neck on a rail and ended it that way. (Lord tells these stories while watching the TV—sheriffs slugging baddies and bouncers punching drunks. His son was a sniper in the Pacific theater, stalking the Japanese like deer; is now a quiet bachelor who works in Massachusetts, driving home weekends.)

I'm transplanting some spruce and beginning to clear my upper field of striped maple and arctic birch. I'm also refashioning a chicken coop to serve as a playhouse when our baby is four or five. The barn is sturdy, moderate-sized, unpainted, built with used planking fifteen years ago. Although the place where I grew up probably had a better barn, I took that one for granted. Now I stand in my own barn and look up at the joists and rafters, the beams under the hayloft, the king posts, struts and studding, the slabs of wood nailed angularly for extra strength. It's all on the same pattern as the other barns in town, and yet I marvel at it. The junk inside consists of whiffle trees, neck yokes and harness, a tractor and a harrow, neither functional, and painters' ladders, milking stools and broken stanchions. In the attic in the house are smaller memorabilia, like fox and beaver traps, deer antlers and tobacco cans of clean deer lard, an old grindstone, an old bedpan, a pair of high green boots, a pile of *Reader's Digest*s, which when matched with our assorted miscellany and childhood books, stacked up, and different boxes of letters and snapshots (snapshots of the prairie Hoaglands seventy years ago, posed in joky insouciance—Hoaglands who would have felt at home here), will be the attic our daughter grows up to know.

Freight trains hoot through town; there is a busy blacksmith, a Ben Franklin store, and a rest home called Poole's, whose telephone is the night number for all emergency facilities. People say "the forenoon" and say a man whose wife has left him "keeps bachelor's hall." Our predecessors in the house, the Basfords, ate groundhogs parboiled, on occasion, and deer in season and out, and, though we're easier on the game, we cook on their wood stove and light with kerosene, and just as in the platitudes, it's a source of ease and peace. Nothing hokum-yokum, just a sense of competence and self-sufficiency. Everything takes time—when it's too dark to read we cook supper, hearing the calling of the owls; then maybe I take the dogs for a walk, playing the part of the blind god. Of course I wouldn't want to get along with wood and kerosene all *winter*; nor do I want to turn the clock back. It's simply doing what is necessary; there is one kind of necessity in the city and another here.

The Basfords only moved around the mountain when we bought their farm. The stove is one Mr. B.'s father bought in 1921—the salesman drove up with a team and wagon piled with iron stoves and told him that if he could break the lid of any of them he could have the whole stove free. The spring we pipe our water from Mr. B. found himself, using water-witching procedures. The first time that he dug a catch-hole he tried enlarging it with dynamite. One stick—detonated with the tractor engine—worked all right, but when he got greedy and wanted still a bigger source, he put in two more sticks and blew the spring away, tipping the base rock so that the water flowed by other routes. He had to go dowsing again, farther from the house, but found a new spot underground where three trickles joined together in front of a tree, and dug more modestly this time, although the overflow was sufficient for Mrs. B. to raise beds of celery there. She's English, once a war bride, now a giggly and seductive woman of about fifty. He is slow-speaking, sharp-witted, rather truculent and rather endearing. He doesn't vote, doesn't get along in town, doesn't work especially hard, doesn't look up to anyone, is an iconoclast. But she admires him. They seem to love each other in absolutely current terms. They're always having coffee, sipping wine, and talking endlessly.

I might as well have begun this essay by saying that things are better than we think. In the public domain they're not, and we can't glance ahead with pleasure to the world our children will inhabit—more than us, perhaps, they will have to swim for dear life. But middle age is the time when we give more than we get—give love, give work, seek sites. And sites can still be found, at least. You may discover you need two houses, but you can find your homes and set to work, living for the decade.

O N
NOT BEING
A JEW

My girlfriend is trying
to decide if I was an Auschwitz guard in order to know
how seriously to regard my attentions. She is somewhat
old-fashioned, of course, a quality I respect her for, but I
don't believe that I was. I believe, in other words, that the
Auschwitz guards were Germans, not gentiles. I'm Dutch,
as far as that goes. One of my ancestors, a girl of sixteen,
was publicly whipped in a market square in New Am-
sterdam for fornicating with a married man (he was
fined). Another, a burgher of the same period, was murdered in a revolt of his slaves. I, for my part, was once
fired from a good job for climbing into a mountain lion's
cage. I took care of a row of retired MGM lions at the
World Jungle Compound in California. MGM adopts as
its own one particular lion every year, the year of his
clinical prime, which is three to four, and then retires him
to the row of cages that I took care of. There was also a
mountain lion, a female in heat who called to me at night

in my boarding house across the fields with a sound like a pigeon's coo. When I crawled through her door, she went to the back of the cage, turned, and then sprang at me; I simply froze. She darted her football-sized paw into the pale bull's-eye of my face with the claws withdrawn, like a lady's muff. (This was in 1953 and Trader Horn, who was the boss, happened to be passing by and fired me.)

I went to school at various times with Charles Lindbergh's son, Gene Tunney's son, Nelson Rockefeller's son, David Selznick's son, Joseph Kennedy's son, the Aga Khan's son, Henri Matisse's and James Joyce's grandsons; with a Dupont, a Mellon, a Cabot, a Phipps. So what do I have to complain about? Nothing really. I had my lumps to take too, naturally. I spent a great many nights in flophouses in Boston, Pittsburgh, St. Louis, and so on, making up for all this, where an alarm bell rang at nine in the morning and everyone had to be out of the building until five o'clock except for the corps of clean-up trusties. I wrote a term paper at college about one skid row, going to a couple of dozen missions, sitting on the bony benches with the bums, and eating a thin jelly sandwich after the hymns. The Catholics were more generous and easygoing, but I fell for a Grace and Hope nun, a timid hillbilly soprano. At home I'd been required to take lessons in golf at the country club, but I stopped, partly in social revolt and partly because I was on the golf course when a friend of my father's, a liquor company executive, got struck in the groin by a wild ball. He lay on the bench in the locker room as though he'd been hit by a car. The next summer I was traveling with Ringling Bros. and Barnum & Bailey, sleeping in the heap of straw in the giraffe's wagon with a number of battered fellows. When I walked in my sleep they were panic-stricken, thinking the giraffe must have gotten loose and was trampling them. The proprietor's name was Heavy, and because I stuttered he thought that I couldn't understand English, so he would yell, "No sleep, no sleep!" to me, as if to a Chinaman.

My stutter made my teens eventful even on ordinary occasions. Storekeepers were always shoving a paper and pencil at me and then suddenly, deciding I wasn't a mute after all, running around from behind the counter to push me into the street, supposing I must be an epileptic instead. I went to a kind of Yeshiva called Deerfield Academy, which had the oldest headmaster in this hemisphere. He had started the school in 1911 and was an astute power broker, hard on the faculty but a good man, in fact. We called him The Monger; I can't remember why. He gave those of my teachers I especially liked a free hand with me and the years passed quickly enough. One of my friends there is now a traffic manager for Pan Am and I would be at a loss to say what either of us got out of the place, except for straight schooling. We were taught to pick up any scraps of paper we found on the grounds (I don't know who dropped them, but we always seemed to be picking them up), and to look at the sunsets on the western hills.

Sumptuous Harvard was next, where I learned that Pepys is pronounced "peeps" and studied with several extraordinary teachers—MacLeish, Wilder, Ciardi, Kazin, for instance—though I spent an inordinate amount of my hours hanging around Fish Pier and the East Boston docks and the Revere oil refinery. I went to the railroad bridge above the Charlestown State Prison to be enveloped in diesel smoke, and to Copp's Hill, where there was a red-light whorehouse next to the famous burying ground. I used to scuttle past it three or four times in an evening, never able to nerve myself up to go in, until the girls gave up calling to me. As jittery as I was, I needed more rest than my roommate, so I went to bed earlier. I'd masturbate and shortly afterwards he would come in. I'd pretend to be fast asleep so as not to disturb him. He'd masturbate and go to sleep, and then I'd go to sleep.

At Harvard during my freshman year I got to know my first Jews. I tried eagerly to make friends with all that I met, as long as that idea remained plausible, and sometimes their Jewishness was the best thing about them, when, soon after, they turned into bland, buttoned-down types as the sense of being in a minority left them. I had grown up in a suburb of New York where it was next to impossible for a Jew to live. Once, a real estate agent, a red-haired widow, sold one a house and was virtually bankrupted and forced out of business as a result of being ostracized. Another Jewish family somehow contrived to acquire a piece of land, but the neighbors hired a bulldozer to come in and dig a trench around the property to keep their children penned in. It was a strange town. A wealthy elderly lady attempted to leave the community her estate on the noblest-looking of the avenues

36

for a new high school, but this was prep-school territory and in a perfectly open town meeting, New England style, the proposal to accept her gift was voted down. Instead the school was built in a swamp alongside the Merritt Parkway. At the Country Day School we used "jew" as a verb, gigglingly. There were two store owners whose names we recognized as suspect: a Mr. Rosen and Mr. Breslow. Both worked seven days a week (a notion of endless reverberations), and when they retired, the local newspaper confirmed that indeed they'd belonged to the Hebrew faith. Rosen operated a grocery store, so it was our parents who dealt with him, but Mr. Breslow, whose shop was for knicknacks and comic books, we took for our own, some of us stealing, some making phone calls at midnight to him. I myself hung up without saying a word because of my stutter, and then would go to the mirror to look at my nose, which had been described by somebody as Jewish: the thought thrilled me insidiously.

These memories retain the same impress on my mind as being told that it's bad for the eyes to wear rubbers inside the house. They are luminous, permanent. "Never bargain," I was taught at home, and so if I had some object to sell, as when I got rid of my trumpet, I enjoyed bringing it to a pawnshop and bargaining diligently with a Jew. By the age of thirteen, nevertheless, I had picked up two rather remarkable labels: I was a member of the American Society of Ichthyologists and Herpetologists, and I was a socialist. I had known, I think, only one socialist, a humorous man named Gray who lived with his many children in a thirty-room house near us. Actually,

I'd never spoken to him, but I knew that he was a socialist and I stuck to my guns against all argument, although called a commie at school and though every week I spent an absorbed afternoon in the company of *Time* magazine. At Deerfield in 1948 they ran a straw poll. Dewey won something like four hundred thirty-one votes. As for the other candidates—this I'm clear on—Henry Wallace got eight, Truman got three, and Norman Thomas my single vote. An incredulous whoop went up when I gave it. But Deerfield was a sweet-natured 1910 place by comparison with my hometown, where I fought many tearful, furious fights. They might be on unionization or the minimum wage, but anti-Semitism was generally detectable in the discussion. Though Negroes were only a laughing matter, Jews were not, and quite correctly so, because in a few years Leonard Bernstein was to be the New York Philharmonic's conductor, publicly kissing the President's wife (this was the worst), and Arthur Goldberg would have caught Kennedy's ear instead of the silly Bernie Baruch. Even the town itself, as a bastion, fell when the developers built too many houses for the sales to be closely controlled. Today the population has tripled from the hometown I knew, and if there still aren't many such outright and shameless stark names as Cohen or Gould in the telephone book, a number of ambiguous forerunners—Wolfs, Millers and Whites—have appeared.

Meanwhile, I was out in the West fighting forest fires in a hotshot crew, or mopping the basement of Madison Square Garden when the circus was there. Lindbergh's son, I used to hear, was paddling a kayak on Long Island

Sound, camping out winter and summer. Another boy I went to school with went up to Fairbanks, Alaska, and became a world authority on grizzly bears. My college roommate, having read Thoreau, was solving our masturbatory difficulties by sleeping rolled up in a khaki blanket on the floor of the sitting room. On the other hand, my best friend at Deerfield had made the unfortunate mistake of reading a lot of late Tolstoy, had quit school to live on the Lower East Side, and was giving the shirts off his back to every addict who asked for one, until he wound up in a mental hospital.

I was a bit Tolstoyan too. I lived in that neighborhood later on, watching the games of stoop-ball, the kids swimming off the piers downtown, the beatniks who lived overswept by stray cats with a sign in the window: "Have you ever owned a painting?—20¢." On the street I would lean down and feel the pulse of a bum who was lying unconscious to make sure his problem was liquor.

The lives led by the very poor are not very much more harassed than the lives which middle-class people lead. It's the crampedness, the developing paranoia, that make poor people so wretched—never getting away for a trip, never enjoying any real relaxation, new scenes, new distractions. Wagner and Lehman campaigned through the Lower East Side with apologetic, uneasy expressions, looking like older men than they did uptown, like men who wished to retire and let somebody else try to fix these problems. Once when I'd sprained my ankle I realized how dangerous the neighborhood could be, because I couldn't run—couldn't even walk briskly through the most depressing streets like Third Street, which was spattered with puke and broken glass, where the Emergency Home for men was located. But it was also where hot-dog push-carts loaded up, and you would see the full-bearded patriarchs who did the pushing extinguishing their char-coal at the end of the day to get some use out of the coals tomorrow. You'd see a police car cruise by and a boy on a tricycle peddling as fast as he could alongside with his arm raised in greeting. I lived next to an artisan locksmith who taxied all over the city to jobs or else worked in front of our building on a succession of cars, having the driver lock him in the trunk, where he could pick his way free. Sometimes he seemed superbly human, sometimes scarcely human at all because he worked so hard. He had a slouchy Z posture, gnarled blocky fingers, the earnest face of a clever groundhog, and a fat chest he folded his arms on when he was talking. His main tool was just a tap-hammer, and he could have walked into any bank and begun to work on the locks without being asked to show his credentials; he looked like an incontrovertible lock-smith, an honest master.

We alumni of the Lower East Side pour out stories when we get together as if we were at a college reunion —especially those of us who are in a position to go to college reunions. Plenty of girls from my sort of back-ground were there, girls metamorphosed into wan social workers; and some went overboard and married a sandal-maker of thirty-eight or a man obsessed with clocks and axes. I was too much of a waffler to turn into a drastic Tolstoyan, and besides I'd been out in the fresh air for years, learning the truck drivers' language of headlight flicks and benedictions conveyed with a roll of the hand.

The first girl I kissed was an innkeeper's daughter in Pittsfield, Mass. (I wrote her a letter of self-abasement afterwards which her mother steamed open.) The second girl lived next door to me in a hotel in Cleveland. Three days before, she had escaped from a coal-mining town in the Appalachians where they spit on the floor of the fire hall, watching the weekly movie; and she crossed the clattering streets holding my hand as if we were wading into big breakers. We went to the Palace Theater, with its chandeliers, mirrors and thick pile rugs, as if we'd inherited a mighty sum.

It wasn't until my mid-twenties that I could volunteer where I was from: until then, I said "near Stamford" or "from Connecticut." But all this adventuring, the clumsy penance of living in Negro hotels on upper Broadway, makes me a confident WASP nowadays without any apologies for what I am. As a matter of fact, I'm not a WASP—my name is Americanized Dutch—but I'm lumped with the Anglo-Saxons as carelessly as we in that bedroom suburb would have classified an Armenian with the rest of the Jews. WASP is a pejorative word, a sociological equivalent of dago or kike. W.P., for white Protestant, certainly can have a legitimate meaning, but the A.S. in the middle has been added gratuitously for kicks. Everyone took to the word at first, but lately, oddly enough, the people who use it the most are themselves WASPs, often boot-me's who relish the sensation of turnabout, or else those like myself who say it ironically, as a black man will say he's a nigger. Usually Jews, sensing its disparaging connotations and remembering kike, avoid the word as non-U, though they may be content that it exists.

Anyway, as a WASP, I found that my tearful battles when I was thirteen on behalf of social justice, or whatever it might be considered to be, were wholly beside the point, to put it mildly. I saved no householder his house, and history was marching swiftly along. No doubt some of my classmates who remained placidly anti-Semitic until they were of voting age are freer of the memory of those early catechisms than I. Recently my mother asked me why so many of the writers interviewed on TV appear to be Jews; I said because probably most writers are Jews. It was a new world for me, New York in the late 1950s. To be a Jew must have been like being a Yorkshireman if you were a young English writer— the vigor was said to be yours; the eyes were on you. I found I was kind of an Ibo, an ornament, in some circles, though welcome enough. My fair skin and glossy hair were commented on by every girlfriend. That scene from Saul Bellow's *The Victim* must have been enacted two dozen times—someone would reach out and touch my hair in the midst of an unrelated conversation. Of course I was no victim; I was doing quite well for myself. The girls thought sex might be better with me and I thought sex might be better with them. They would try to decide what to cook for me that I would feel at home with, and end up doing Indian pudding; afterwards they would marvel, practically catch their breath, at the literal cross the hair forms on my chest. It was fun and tender and serious too, no longer mere experimentation. I did grow a bit bored at being taught *chutzpah* and *mensch* and *shlepping* so regularly; no one seemed to realize that everybody was teaching these words to people like me. Usually the teacher herself had only just learned them, but they were ethnically hers, and the idea was that some of their extraordinary vigor might be imparted to me if I ingested them. A person who knew how to say *chutzpah* could develop *chutzpah* even if he weren't Jewish.

I could make a good many obvious jokes about all of this, but later when I spent a year in British Columbia, where the whites were either Scottish or Irish, I would have embraced anybody who'd walked up to me whispering in Yiddish. And in New York I was learning, meanwhile, about the slaughter of six million Jews. During the war we gentiles had heard in detail about the Japanese concentration camps but very little about the German camps, and although some time along in my teens I had figured out for myself the astounding information that Christ was a Jew, this other news was not news you could figure out. There were large and terrific reasons for the surge of Jewish identity or pride, and maybe those Jews who had never wondered where they wanted their roots to be needed more patience than I during the process of self-discovery. People who had changed their names wished that they hadn't done so. Jews my age simply were saying the word "Jew" a great deal, as if they had never said it before, trying the sound of it in their mouths. The most Protestantized Ivy League fellows began to teach me *chutzpah,* and everybody in New York who wasn't a Jew was marrying one, just as everybody who was a Jew was marrying a gentile.

One way or another it was as intriguing to be a Jew as it was precarious. I was walking on Broadway on the afternoon Jack Ruby shot Lee Harvey Oswald. You could breathe the hushed, gingerly triumph. One old man of the many who'd hastily rushed out to the street came up to me. "Did you hear Oswald got shot?" I said yes. "Yeah, a Jew shot him!" he said gleefully. *Now they'll have to respect us!* Before he began to imagine horrible pogroms, Ruby's logic is reported to have been the same. A liberal people who have been belittled become confused, the intellectuals too, as when Israel achieved her lightning conquest in 1967 and suddenly sat astraddle so much territory. She'd had to win but now she was *bigger.* Being bigger, and the prowess of victory, supplanted having to win, like a shrill bugling.

During the fifties, at the same time as my work was beginning to be published, there was a historic coming of age of American Jewish writing. Malamud after *The Natural,* Bellow after *Dangling Man,* Kazin after *On Native Grounds* went out and wrote much more than brilliantly; they wrote differently, establishing a new tradition, indeed a new establishment. To a young writer three establishments were apparent. The Southerners, leaning heavily on the greatness of Faulkner and on their own social graces, didn't especially interest me, except for Faulkner himself. *The New Yorker* paid its contributors lavish honorariums but seemed a dying institution. It had the phenomenal John Updike, a brilliant throwback prodigiously equipped, and the admirable workhorse John Cheever, and the frail, phosphorescent J. D. Salinger, who wrote as if he were chipping mica. I had grown up reading Melville, Whitman, Dreiser and Faulkner, and the next in line for me was Saul Bellow. Malamud, slightly less gifted, pulled even with him in certain short master-pieces because of the clarity and incandescence of his themes, but when Bellow had a theme going for him, as in *Henderson the Rain King* and in *Seize the Day*, I read him most avidly. We were finally introduced by the affec-tionate poet John Berryman, and took to each other, he becoming a friend by correspondence and a faithful reader, so that as far as I could see there was no question of this establishment being exclusive (as Gore Vidal has complained). Other than Bellow, the novelists I en-countered who went out of their way to make kindly gestures to me were people like Philip Roth and Harvey Swados.

The burst of concentrated enthusiasm for writers con-sciously Jewish couldn't help having an effect, however. I think that Cheever received less attention than he deserved for several years while he was at the height of his powers, and maybe the recognition due other writers was also delayed. For youngsters like Updike or John Barth it didn't matter as much. The push of their talent was only beginning, and a lean fox catches more rabbits. In my own case, my first novel came out about the same month as Sam Astrakhan's *An End to Dying*, which was about immigrant family life, shifting from the Ukraine to the garment center. Both were pretty fair books, he was a friend of many of my friends, and I remember being startled and disconcerted by how completely they gave their immediate attention to him. Being reviewed well, though, I was happy, and, in any event, the only bad effect of non-recognition to a writer at that stage of the game is when he can't publish what he has written while it is still important to him, a trouble that generally I didn't have. I dealt with a couple of magazine editors who expressed surprise when I mentioned Bellow's liking my stuff ("You? He *does?*") and who turned their moo-cow eyes on me intently when I allowed as how I felt an affinity for him. "But he's so *unhappy*," one said, meaning in his role of suffering Jew.

In the meantime Philip Roth was having problems quite the reverse. After the howl of hosanna for *Goodbye Columbus,* which is a splendid book, he was able to publish practically anything and would sometimes wonder whether he should. He'd done the first widely read satire of a genre of Jewish-American life, and so the false expectation was raised that each of his succeeding books must be a first. It seems to me that along with Barth and Updike he's the best writer now in his thirties we have; I think he knows the most about people. But he was penalized in the responses to *Letting Go* and *When She Was Good* for that initial hosanna. Some critics say that Henry Roth should have received an instant hosanna too, in the 1930s, for *Call It Sleep,* and regard his career as pitifully blighted. I agree that his book deserved cymbals and clangor, but writing is a spartan, bloody profession and I think if he'd had further books in him they would have come out—like Nelson Algren's, which were just as neglected, although his first two books are nearly as gracefully written as his middle two; like Nathanael West's; like Faulkner's, who in 1944 is said to have been listed only twice in the central card catalogue of the New York libraries.

One thing *did* matter to somebody like me, classified as a WASP writer. This was being told in print and occasionally in person that I and my heritage lacked vitality, that except perhaps for a residual arrogance the vitality had long ago been squeezed dry—if in fact it had ever existed in thin blood like mine. I was a museum piece, like some State of Mainer, because I could field no ancestor who had hawked copper pots in a Polish *shtetl*. Obviously talk like that can grow fur on a stone! I looked up old photographs of my great-grandfathers in Kansas, their faces unsteady and mad as John Brown's, and recognized an equivalent rashness in me. I had a riverboat captain on the Ohio for a relative; another, a naval cook in the Boxer Rebellion, sprang ashore from his ship and was the first man shot dead.

But the decade is past when even the zealous take note of which writer is Jewish and which is not. Instead, the question has shifted around to who is a writer at all. We go to the movies now, or read the lyrics on the back of the Beatles' record albums. It's certainly quicker than reading a book; and we all go to poetry readings because we can catch a taste of the young fellow's personality without actually needing to bite a chunk out of his work.

47

Allen Ginsberg is the new Carl Sandburg. Blessings on both: Sandburg was quite a stage man himself. But the concept of taking a poet's vocal abilities so seriously we've borrowed from the Russians, forgetting that they hold their readings as a dismal if defiant substitute for a free press. Hardly two years ago novelists who were having trouble with their work, the talented but chronic under-performers, were going into book-length journalism, which was supposed to be the form of the future. Now it's the Easy Arts that are in—easy for viewer, easy for artist. Who wants to read books any more—unless it's zany pornography? *The Graduate* replaces *Bonnie and Clyde* replaces *La Guerre Est Finie* as Book-of-the-Month. We writers are told that the novel is moribund, that we're working in a dead language; time is short, people are listening to glugging guitarists and aren't going to spend it curled up with a book. I doubt that we're going to be told this for long, but if I am wrong, if we do find that our language at last is certified dead, then I think that we will draw strength from our privacy, as Isaac Bashevis Singer has, and precisely because of that privacy, some of us will irradiate and transcend translation.

IN HAZELTON
AND FLYING NORTH

Am reading *Pickwick Papers,* which I once thought egregiously trivial. One is always a fool disliking a classic. Like disliking a nation one visits, it's the result of a blind spot, which goes away and leaves one embarrassed.

I'm staying in a plaster-and-plastic motel, getting back the use of my knee. I watch TV and bask in the shower. Smithers, founded fifty-three years ago, resembles a California town three years old except for a few pleasant relics. This is elbow-grease country, this is the young man's land of which we hear mention, where all the young men one could hope for are busy with loans from the bank, getting in on the ground floor, scrimping for the bonanza. Six years ago the Hazelton-Smithers highway was a corkscrew dirt road where old men sat sunning in front of the homesteads they'd cleared, their children having gone south to greener pastures. Now it's three straight lanes, and the pastel lunch stops being put up are set back to allow an expected expan-

49

sion. Cars go by with canoes on top like New Year's hats. The nature displayed is human nature—there is always that. After some seventy-five years of pioneering in the valley, the stage has been prepared for money making.

Yesterday I drove to Hazelton with an English girl, a freckle-faced, spunky, runty type whom I picked when I left the hospital in preference to a girl from Manitoba, although the latter was much sweeter and took poetical strolls at dawn. I wanted the British astringence and the seven-seas stuff—the brother in Hong Kong, the mother in Cyprus. And I made a mistake. The girl is on a seesaw with lesbianism. She lives with a hefty Australian butch who drives the neighborhood roads at eighty if we go to the movies, suffering frantically, and she is herself changeably contrary. But she's appealing, too—breezy, sleepless, tough on herself. The saving fun for the moment is just in the fussing, the courtship, going through the time-honored motions that get nowhere.

I was afraid I'd be spotted by one of the people I'd known in town who would ask where my wife was. It didn't happen, however. The tiny pre-fab shack by the river where we lived looked suitably dingy. All of the buildings we lived in look dingy now, whether in New York or here, and we slept in atrocious single-sized beds. Skirting past, I winced as some of my arrogances of the period came to mind, but mostly the memory was of two people living together like two ticking clocks: unaware. I was, anyway. I didn't even realize I loved her, which naturally made her feel inadequate to the job of forcing me to realize. The shabby house gave me pangs. Without wanting to stay long, I hurried about town to see what I could. For one thing, the museum has gotten quite grand, with decorative masks, headdresses, eagle-beak rattles and dignified ceremonial garments of which the Tahltans have no equivalent. Outside is the big totem pole the kids used to climb. When I lived here, the manager of the Royal Bank branch was helping establish the place, in lieu of a scout troop to work with or a charity fund to direct. Unfortunately, he was in competition with the owner of the gas station, who also had founded a "museum." Each of them drove out to one or another of the sites on Sunday and searched for relics scattered through the grass. The gas-station fellow kept his discoveries only until he could sell them to tourists. They probably didn't last long after that, as he said, mocking his rivals from the committee.

I was struck by how much like Telegraph Creek Hazelton is. There are lopsided churches of missions that failed and went home, and ghostly, ramshackle novelty stores with antique lettering on warbled windowglass. Or *Lee Chong's, LAUNDRY and BATHS.* A few sled dogs still roam between the eccentric log houses and haphazard gardens. The cemetery with its wax flowers and infants' graves is up on top of the same sort of nettly bluff standing alongside the river. Although the road leading into Hazelton is a clamor of jerry-built housing and government compounds—Forestry, Hydro-Electric—the inner village, ringed by the Tsimshian reserve, has been left unaffected. The senior Indians sit on the street corner instead of wandering rootlessly around, as they do in Smithers or on the Alaska Highway. Nobody runs over their feet if they stretch them out. Most everyone carries a dash of their bloodline, and they can consider the town is theirs. Their houses are either

blue frame or log brown, while the old-timer whites', tilting idiosyncratically, are painted red or are whitewashed.
On the beach traces of the old steamboat landing remain,
beside the rig for a bucket-seat cable.

The Skeena is a remarkable twin of the Stikine. It's a
spiky raw river, a swift silt-yellow with a great deal to do,
yet managing somehow to leaven the town with history
and leisure at the same time, as perhaps every river, by the
nature of rivers, will. Speeding by, it's so raw that you wait
for it to switch its course while you're watching, or to sweep
a floating mastodon by. It's so new you feel like a gazing
explorer; yet the town on its bank is made to seem ancient
and wise and tried and true.

The helicopters land and take off with that peculiarly
concentrated jet-age whine combined with an old-fashioned drumming which has become the identifying sound
of all of these settlements, however. The horses that used
to graze free down the street are fenced into buttercup
fields, growing fat, not like the snake-necked, flat-flanked
bush horses. After the houses and pastures end, a thick
cottonwood woods runs alongside the river to a sand point,
full of well-beaten paths through the hazel bushes and full
of children. An adult must creep and stoop, but the paths
are centuries old. The logs on the ground are worn like
benches, the trees written on. An especially attractive family, the Sargents, have dominated Hazelton since riverboat
days, when they had the *Inlander.* They are still represented by a son who operates the principal hotel and store,
a fancy, luxurious, graceful structure architectured into the
village with understatement. He has a penthouse he lives
in and an excellent restaurant downstairs. He's a silent,

haunted-looking, inconspicuous man who fixes the kids' bicycles on the patio on the fine summer days, kids from far and near. He soft-foots along, carrying most of the Indian band on his credit rolls like relatives down on their luck—immense sums; I remember the banker agog. Like Steele Hyland, he's an heir who has relinquished the wheeling and dealing in lumber or silver ores to the new entrepreneurs. Instead of a toolshop and forty machines, or instead of keeping a hundred wild horses, he has his book-lined penthouse looking out on the mountains and his crabmeat supreme. He flies a plane once in a while, and his wife is the mover and shaker of the town.

My friend and I missed in our aim whenever we tried to speak pleasantly to each other, but were overly accurate if we leveled and fired. Both wearing prissy ironic smiles, we bumped north fourteen miles in her red sports car to the Kispiox to see the totems, a good many of which have been restored. They've been put in two rows. The very top figures—bears, ravens, porcupines—poise themselves uneasily on their perches, peering off as if they had been asleep when it happened and don't know how to climb down. They're like cats who have gone to sleep under the hood of a car and woken up after the car is in motion. Other larger totem poles lie bedridden in the grass, patiently grimacing, too old to restore. They mark where the snowplow should plow and they furnish the children with elevated paths. The children have gotten blasé in the past six years—not a head poked out of a window for our benefit. The village is spacious and clean, with white farmlike houses and barns. The Skeena slides over wide gravel bars along one side and the flossy Kispiox cuts a square channel on the other. Eighty log trucks a day go by now—200,000 board feet of lumber. A handful of eagles continues to patrol the salmon runs, but the moose have been drastically shot off. There are twice as many whites and twice as many hunters, so that it looks like another green, God's-country valley, like the upper Hudson or upper Ohio—nothing paganly tumbled or tangled about it.

We said good-bye, she and I. I hitchhiked fifteen miles further in a log truck, being somewhat ungracious to the driver. I've gotten snotty about how long the person I am talking with has been in the country. Most of these young knuckleheads I ignore. Coming from a world where everyone is young, where any old man on the street is virtually a freak, the great thing is to be where a man's achievements can be guessed at pretty well just by his age. I was hoping to see Jack Lee again, and even my bushy-haired host was interested in that.

Lee answered the door. "I remember you, but I don't know who you are," he said with a smile. He's sallower, hollower, and his wife Frances looks bigger and more competent than ever. The garden is like a flower show and the vegetable garden like a state fair. Wet green fields spread to a pond five hundred yards away. "Look at all the dead horses," he said. When he whistled, the sleepers raised their heads; those awake went on yanking grass. Horses eat forever, eat twice as much as a cow, he says. He has a hotbed where he starts his cabbages and tomato plants with horse manure—cow manure doesn't heat. When he retires he's going to live up on the Duti and the Kluatantan in the summer, he says. He still has his phenomenal woods-stomp to cover the ground.

We talked rapidly, catching up to date. They were brimming with their guiding successes and I was asking questions about the demise of the game. Last fall through field glasses Frances was watching her son in snow costume hunt high above her on a slope. He shot a mountain goat. A snowy, man-shaped figure, it rolled and dropped, slamming and bowling over and over, rump over head and head over rump, down, down, as if it were he who had fallen. Jack has been hunting the very head of the Kispiox lately with bow-and-arrow clients. The river is so fish-rich it becomes a sort of bear kingdom, though at the same time you can actually hear the earth-moving equipment at work on a part of the highway that will connect through to Eddontenajon. The machinery pounds in the distance and the bears promenade, mostly grizzlies, grizzlies two to one. There are so many bears his description sounds as if a bear had climbed into a tree in Central Park and concealed himself, taking note of the people who ambled by. Big bears, little bears, laggards and hungries. There is a fairy-tale surrealism to it. Last year the party of hunters was strung along the river in different trees miles apart, so that instead of ambushing a solitary animal, each of them meekly witnessed a series of set pieces: Papa after youngsters, Mama intercedes; Fatty tires of ants' nest; shy lad loses female. Jack had a mean bear under him for a while, whimsically destroying the fish. It would half kill them with a gentle bite and paw them. Straddling a log, it patty-caked the surface of the water. Another bear napped nearby and finally woke up, tripping on the windfalls as it went off drowsily into the brush. Strollers strolled, frittering the day away. They greeted each other or dodged aside. They whacked the rotten logs and licked the grubs. Upwards of twenty bears.

While I was with the Lees their garden was visited by several families new to the valley who hadn't had an opportunity to plant a garden of their own as yet, though Jack wasn't sure why in every case. We went for lunch to his mother-in-law's, who lives with her brother, who dropped in for Christmas nine years ago, had a stroke and has stayed. Dinner was three vegetables, roast beef, rolls, potatoes, salad, milk, saskatoon berries with cream, and pie and tea. "Sit in," they say.

Marty Allen, the other man I'd wanted to see, was next to me. He's her other son-in-law and may be the northernmost farmer in our hemisphere. He was telling me what he'd said to the Governor General of Canada when the Governor General inspected Kispiox, and what he'd said at the most recent wedding of the Wookey family. The Wookeys are the Snopes here. His own wedding was marred when the bull they'd been given pulled the ring out of its nose on the way home. His wife's puppy, tied to the wagon, got its rope twisted in the wheel and almost choked. Although the ride between farms was day long, they used to do it every second week then. Now, with their trucks and cars around the yard, he says, they never bother stopping by unless it's to borrow something.

I was made much of—this idea of my having come four thousand miles to lunch again with them after being in Norway and Spain. The conversation frisked easily. Marty is a burned-faced fellow with sloping shoulders and a Roman nose, an Alberta nose. When I was in Hazelton last, he was driving his eldest daughter seventy miles to her piano lessons Tuesdays and Fridays. She's seventeen now, not quite ready to accept a steady boyfriend, but pouring coffee for the lonesome loggers who show up, and pestered by their pinching. He took me to his house afterwards, where I fell for his blond daughter, ten, instead. She was up on a black mare, whizzing around, directing it with digs of her little big toe. A rope looped about its nose for a halter. She hauled herself up and down by two handholds of mane, and they flickered across the yard like a pair of fish, trembling and fluttering. The boys were enmeshed with an improvised sawmill resembling a Ford, surrounded by sawdust and leaking oil. Every few minutes it went up in flames and they took off their coats and beat them out. Mrs. Allen, a serene, squared-off woman with attractive small features, was cooking fifty-three cans of salmon that the Kispiox Indians had given her in exchange for the beaver meat which her boys turn over to them in the spring and the steer tripes Marty gives them.

Marty, flattered that I'd remembered him, was ready to open the gates of his memory for me: how he'd finished the war in Holland on a burial squad, marched across the George Washington bridge with twenty thousand other Canadians, and headed for the Yukon to make his fortune. He wound up in Whitehorse as a mechanic instead. One night his partner and he got drunk in the Legion Hall. They sniffed the cold air, and squirrels were selling for a dollar a skin, so they quit. They came south to the Skeena and trapped in the Groundhog Range, priding themselves on making the one hundred miles home in a single day, putting the tarpaulin up alongside a tree and catching an hour's snooze, perhaps.* His partner counts fish at the head of the Babine River every summer in a lean-to, living the rest of the year on the government rations he hoards. But Marty bought the ranch of George Byrnes, the man who had been the packer at this end of the Telegraph Trail, working a huge string, until at last he went crazy and dug a grave and killed himself at the edge. He was "bushed," they call it. They named one of the mountains after him.

So was I bushed. I was enjoying the Norman Rockwell sing round the piano in the next room, the larder of cakes, the spoonfuls of cream like liquid marshmallow, the round family table. Even more than the Lees', the place was loud with visitors and unofficial orphans—a logger with a hook for a hand, a dried-out drunk from Santa Barbara. Lee is the old-timer, but Allen is the valley's chief citizen. Like any early settler, like the people who built my parents' house in Connecticut in the first part of the nineteenth century too, he built right next to the road. The traffic was horses and wagons, perhaps twice a day, and the contact was welcome. Recently, though, when the road was re-graded, the supervisor obliged him by bending it to go around in back of his property, out of sight. Tom Black, in founding Eddontenajon, has begun with a house site a hundred yards back.

I was interested to hear about my friend who agreed to walk me over the Telegraph Trail and who would have

* This Groundhog Pass could be a killer after a snowfall. Two Indians were taking fifty-six horses to Caribou Hide for George Byrnes to winter them, got a rather late start, got caught in four feet of fluff and had to shoot every one.

made it, with or without me. He "seemed to be worth so little that I thought we ought to take him out and shoot him," according to Marty. Then at thirty-three he advertised in the *Free Press Prairie Farmer* for a wife, signing himself "Black Beard." He said she should be able to live on lynx pie and skunk stew and he got a good many answers, including one from a girl from a family of eleven sisters. He went east to look at the others as well, but stuck with her. They've broken a plot of ground a dozen miles beyond here and are living on turnips and moose meat. Their food bill last winter was $5, for the baby's Pablum and orange juice.

Chasing the kids out, arranging himself on the settee for an interview session, Marty kept wanting to see me write things down. After all, when somebody is the northernmost farmer in Canada, it's about time! On the other hand I was relaxing for a change. The household in its prime of life, the civilized hustle, delighted me. Though there wasn't plumbing and though the original log-house walls were barely disguised behind paneling, it was more like Connecticut than Telegraph Creek. It's odd how superabundantly I exulted on the Stikine, and yet how flatly my preferences are here. I'm like a person whose passion is the violin, who haunts all the concerts, yet doesn't attempt to play himself.

Marty dangled facts before me. He walked me about the garden, where Swiss chard, pumpkins and pole beans were growing—anything you can think of. The harvest season gets too wet and cold for crops on a commercial scale, but the only limit on the number of cattle he raises is the acreage that he can keep in hay. Nearly half the year they're out on their own in the burdock and wild June grass and the timothy meadows of the old homesteads. Besides his main hay cutting, a second growth has time to spring up a couple of feet before he mows it for silage. It steams and ferments all winter and the cattle are crazy for it.

For most of us now, simply to be on a farm is exhilarating, to be let in on the humble logistics of dealing with eggs, to walk past the sheds of tall red machines smelling of greenery. The details of making a start seem intriguing, as the finances of putting a dry-goods business on its feet do not. In the Rockies in 1960 I had seen a gaunt family of five and a humpy miscellaneous huddle of animals passing the cabin where I was staying on their way to homestead land which was across a bridgeless, strong river, beyond the skimpiest road. My wife and I were boarding with a woman who was living on goats' milk, principally, with her young son. I remember her tugging those goats, morning and night, on the end of their tethers, and doing the wash for the town, but of course she was quite an established citizen compared to the tattered outfit who passed.

Marty began with several horses left over from the Byrnes' pack train, then bought an old tractor, a baler, then an old car, then an old truck, then another tractor for his wife to use. He borrowed $20,000 and paid back $30,000. "Isn't that a corker? Lots of people have moved in and moved right out again; had a little hard luck, you know." To avoid lengthy rotation schedules he needed to buy fertilizer also. Some of the swampier patches took years and years to clear and sow. He'd get the worst of the brush off during the winter when the ice had brittled the wood, but the beavers would flood out his seed afterwards in the warm weather. He sold cedar poles to the telephone company and balsam and hemlock logs to a fellow located in the Empire State Building. By last fall he had worked up to the point where he mustered sixty-six beefs to butcher, "long yearlings," eighteen months old, including the heifers who hadn't managed to get themselves pregnant. He takes the meat door to door, cut and wrapped, at forty-five cents a pound, though his regular customers buy in quantity. He can tell what he's giving them by the way that the hide comes off. Tough beef is tough to skin; good meat announces itself with a hide which practically skins itself.

I wouldn't have wanted to be the death of a cow, but he was killing an infertile animal anyway that afternoon, so I watched. Since I'd just inaugurated the highway between the Skeena and the Stikine with its first injury, and since I was revisiting a house where I'd known happier days, my mood was suitably sober. In fact I felt as if I were watching a quite random death, as if the rifle at the last moment might swing towards me. I noticed from how the farm dog slunk around that he did too. My memories of marital twists and follies ran into memories from earlier still, which for silliness put even my marriage into the shade.

Judging by the situation in the pasture, the whole lot of them had been tipped off. Besides the victim, the heifers as a group bounded into a poplar woods as soon as we entered, while the cows with nursing calves kept perfectly placid and quiet. With the heiferlike lope which farmers develop, Marty followed the fugitives, his face beet-burned except underneath his large nose. I got into the truck again in the premonitory silence. When he had driven the runaways back into the field, they bunched for self-protection. He walked around and around them with a pump-action short 30-30, resembling a light BB gun. When he scattered some hay they separated hesitantly. As the others left her, the cow fixed her eye on me over her shoulder, while he took aim. He shot her below the ear in order "not to kill her too dead." She fell as though axed, without any bull-ring delays, and he dashed and cut her throat quickly with sudden professionalism as she lay stunned—a small, exact man, instead of gangling and lanky. With apt, jerking, upward motions he sawed the hole until it gaped, as if he were crouching, tying a swift knot. Then he drove off the rest of the herd. They'd bolted at the shot, but had turned and come back, lowering their heads to look lingeringly, whether from fellow-feeling or out of curiosity. The heifers bounded into the same woods, but the cows who had calves were calm and unresponsive. When he was shooing the others they didn't consider that his advice applied to them. "Yes, you too. On you go," he said, friendly.

The cow lay in shock, sometimes conscious, sometimes anesthetized. Her legs pumped, and he squatted beside her throat, superintending the flow. If she stopped threshing he jabbed her feet with the knife or else got up and manually swung her legs with a kind of comradely sympathy, like helping someone to finish a job, giving his attention to her hind legs as well. None of the other cattle were anywhere in sight. Once they left us there was a finality to it. The relationship that exists with them is such a strange one. They live with us: we live off them. They were deciding not to know. The cow on the ground groaned and gasped, pawing from the horizontal position. And yet it wasn't so much an act of suffering as of dismay and regret—

all was over. Because she ignored Marty she seemed to me remarkably impersonal, but the pawing was redolent with woe and sharp frustration—all was dissolved.

I still wasn't convinced that this was the end of the deaths for today, that this wasn't the first of a chain. And the dog skulked subduedly, swallowing, feeling exposed in the open field, full of his own mortality, though he was smiling, too. He licked his chops rather guiltily, so as not to arouse or offend us. He was waiting to lick the grass where she now lay, but he was also afraid of being shot. I was thinking that the event had become irreversible; we were stuck with it. If we should change our minds, however much we might try to save the cow, it was too late. She kept rallying, fighting for air through the hole in her throat, her face a contrast of red and white, but it had gone too far.

When she was dead, Marty severed her feet and head and hung her from the fork lift of the tractor by her ankle tendons. He began to loosen and strip off the skin, mainly by pushing down on it with his elbows. Opening the body, he sawed through the brisket, handling the organs familiarly, turning them over, examining the uterus to confirm that she had been barren, and let them slide down on the ground in their dull, various colors. He was gently respectful about this. He might have been going through an old person's last possessions; the sense was the same. A neighbor boy rode up, kicking his horse close to the pile of organs, and tried to make him smell them. He told Marty his sons had caught three big salmon, and he laughed because the cow's bowels had moved when she was shot, and at the dismal-sounding exhalations from her dead lungs. Marty chased him away, saying he was insulting the horse.

Cutting carefully, he reminded me of the bush professionals working on a moose, with the skin spread out like a table. The tail was saved for soup; the liver and kidneys were placed on the skin, which was inside up. Globs of fat were put aside for suet for pies and cooking lard. The rib cage looked like a red accordion. Nothing of life or remembrance clung to it, though the flesh on the steaks continued to twitch. The impression was of a burden surrendered, an assignment completed—the stomach left for the crows to peck. Onerously, the body was sawed lengthwise and left to hang. The skin was dumped in a lump on the head. And that's where the cow remained, on the ground, as a Hereford-colored wad of hide and a meek head upside down, reduced to the size of a newborn calf. I thought of the pulverizers that convert an automobile to a modest bandbox of scrap. But its character as a cow did remain. It was like a costume taken off, tossed aside, that contains more of the character in the play than the actor does as he disappears. The character lies there behind.

I've forgotten to mention the Fish that flies over Smithers from atop a pole in a Chinese man's yard. He's had it since the New Year, and it's a great, fat, elongated Fish, more of a fish than all these caught salmon.

THE SPATSIZI
COUNTRY:
JIM MORGAN

If you moved Morgan back seventy-five years, he would fit like a beard. He would not be a leader of any kind; he would be like what Joe Valachi called the "soldiers" of gangsterdom. He's fussy if crossed, but quickly forgiving, and right now he's in the midst of doing what I've been hearing everybody else tell me they did in the past. He's ripping the Arctic willow out, laying in a good wood supply, exploring a fierce little river and digging and timbering a garbage hole, which is set into the hillside to drain easily. If he has a mainspring it is curiosity, and yet, elusive and reticent as he is, when I corner him to make him answer my questions, he does so with lifeless dutifulness, as if we were filling out forms. The best description of him is the bare facts.

I asked if any of his friends had walked over the Telegraph Trail. He said one took twenty-six horses through to Atlin in 1934, losing only two of them. Any adventures?

No, just a regular trail drive. I asked what he himself used to carry on his back when he went trapping from Ootsa Lake. He said a piece of canvas eight by ten to put up as a lean-to, and a light sleeping bag, an axe, a few traps, a .22 pistol to kill what got caught in the traps, or a rifle for procuring food on long trips. The food he carried would include baking powder, flour, rice, sugar, salt, tea, a little bacon or dried venison, and maybe a box of powdered potatoes or powdered milk. Scurvy takes months to develop, he said when I mentioned that. It comes from a limited diet of salt pork and so forth. A little lime juice brought along to mix with your tea will keep it away. The 30–30 is the ideal meat gun because it doesn't smash or hemorrhage the meat. The 30–06 was for trophies, with more powder behind the bullet, although nothing like the modern hunting rifles, which ruin half the animal in order to assure that it's downed when it's hit.

In the winter Morgan puts dry grass under his outer layer of clothes if the wind turns unexpectedly cold. Only a small fire is needed at night if it's kept within reach and is built against a rock that reflects the heat. The lean-to is faced against the wind, which generally blows up a mountain during the day and down the mountain in the chill of the night. He stamps the snow down on the tent pegs, so that they get encased in ice. When we talk about trapping, he adds a bit to what Frank Pete told me. Muskrats, for instance, push wads of moss through the ice as it forms to preserve their air holes and they can be trapped alongside these. Otter in a small creek can be caught by fixing barriers of sticks which funnel them to the spot where the trap is located. For fisher and lynx you build a "cubby," which is a cat-sized hut, with catnip or greased beaver castor inside, or a rotten fish. Beaver behave like a dog going to a post if the scent of another beaver is put somewhere around, so that trapping them is easier still. The main danger in the winter is falling through the ice, which he says he's done three or four times. Each time he went under a live spruce after extricating himself, and built a fast fire from the protected litter of needles and boughs (he keeps his matches in a bottle). There is always kindling under a live spruce, just as there is always dry wood inside a dead tree, although an axe, not a hatchet, may be needed to get it out. He packs an axe first of all, even before a gun, and generally he lies low in brutal weather, moving only if he has run out of food. The worst spell of that sort was once when it was 30° below and he had to go fifty-five miles in a storm. It took him three days because the snow underfoot was so fluffy and soft.

It's been watery again today. We've greased and tarred our boots, and here we are, two teen-age boys, one mild, accomplished, patient old man, and one dithering writer. Far from being in a time machine, we're very representative, it seems to me: just the line-up that one would expect for the place and the age.

This afternoon a drowned coyote washed past with an ugly, foiled grin on his mouth, as if at the joke on himself. We chased him in the boat. In the evening I walked downriver, watching the sky clear. At the end of each island the current added a whine to its noise. The forest stood in a thick mad mass, an anarchy that I sneaked through.

JULY 19, TUESDAY:

I've been watching two horses romancing—rearing, cavorting around each other, so graceful they aren't to be believed. They aren't like horses at all; they nuzzle and flutter and flow in a *pas de deux*, spreading themselves like butterflies. They seem as at home on two legs as four. Slow-motion, and tall and curving, facing each other, they float for joy.

In the city when you go to the zoo the line between people and animals appears fairly narrow. To judge from the moods on both sides of the bars, the wonder is that the animals are kept separated at all. Dogs, too, become like their masters on a keyed-down scale, until they bustle about the whole day at make-work pursuits, since they haven't a job. But up here the difference is sharp. Even the horses ignore our existence, living by their own mirthful rhythms. It's not a matter of godliness or ungodliness; the difference is who is busy. I don't know who sleeps the longest hours, but we human beings are absorbed the entire day in setting the cook stove into a box of earth for fire-prevention purposes, or building a chute in the corral, or hauling firewood through the mud on a sleigh. Or else we're enjoying ourselves, which in my own case boils down to a business of standing, sitting, and standing up again readily, reading *Great Escapes* for twenty minutes or so, and busily strolling, patrolling around. The horses flirt at a slow and lascivious pace; the moose browse in the muskeg; some goats and a grizzly graze on the mountain above us at timberline. Compared to us, if they're not nerveless, they're motionless. We're bowling 'em over—the chain saw is rasping from sunrise to dark—and they quietly browse.

RIVER-GRAY,
RIVER-GREEN

Was lifted today by my fisheries friends to the slide on the Tahltan River where the salmon are blocked. The Tahltan is the main spawning tributary of the Stikine, which is naturally why the tribe gave it their name. Lately, most of the fish are being harvested by Alaskan boats on the coast and therefore the Americans are footing part of the bill. The operation has been a fiasco so far. The first plan was to have the men on the ground scoop the fish into barrels of water that the helicopter simply lifted upriver. The fish were traumatized by this, however, and the water in the barrels became toxic to them. At present, the helicopter only ferries the men back and forth and takes the foreman on tours. His dilemma is that if he blows a passage with dynamite he will kill all the fish who are waiting and perhaps precipitate a worse slide.

The canyon is a rudimentary steep V, the walls clay and silt. The river within looks slender and white from the air, but the damaged area is like an artillery range, pitted with

boulders, heaped with khaki-colored debris. Our arrival
sent up legions of birds—eagles, crows, gulls from the sea.
Being left to my own devices, I explored gingerly, completely alone once the pilot dropped me. It's only a little
neighborhood river but it moves with violent velocity. The
water gets through, all right; it has blasted a zigzag chute
for itself with the force of a fire hose. Just to sit in the
thunder and watch is awesome. There were so many fish
waiting in the slower water below the chute that half an
hour must have gone by before I was even aware of them.
I listened and looked at the gulls who had gotten the word
and had traveled so far. I thought the actual fish were
thickets of driftwood that the river had smashed together
and submerged; their fins stuck out like a welter of
branches. I was astonished instead at the carnage on shore,
the bear-chewed or beak-bitten bodies scattered about
everywhere. When I did see the living fish I gaped because
there were many thousands. The Tahltan was jammed with
them, flank to flank and atop one another, seldom moving,
just holding whatever position they'd gained, though that
took continual swimming. Hundreds of them were in water
which scarcely covered their backs. I thought of shark fins,
except that there was a capitulation to it, a stockade still-
ness, as if they were prisoners of war waiting in huddled
silence under the river's bombarding roar. The pity I felt
was so strong that I did everything I could not to alarm the
ones nearest me. They were in an eddy behind a boulder a
few feet away, and I wouldn't have dreamed of touching
one of them. Each had fought to attain that eddy, and at
any confusion or weakening of resolve he lost his hold and
was washed downstream. Like mountain climbers, the

most active fish would wiggle twenty yards further on and gain a new cranny. It might require a number of tries, but they were the freshest fish, unscarred, and occasionally one would get into some partially sheltered corner of the chute itself, in one of the zigs or zags. These dozen desperate niches were so packed that they were like boxfuls of crated fish set into the bullet-gray water. The salmon who were able to battle upcurrent did so by shimmying and thrusting more than by leaping, although they did leap now and again. This was the cruelest sight of all, because they were like paper airplanes thrown into the hydrant blast. The water shattered and obliterated the leap and then banged the limp, tender body down the same stretch of rapids that it had been fighting its way up for perhaps the past day and a half.

Most of the salmon were quite catatonic by now. They just held their own in whichever clump or eddy they'd reached, unless some pathetic impulse moved them again. They might try to better themselves, only to be dislodged and lose fifteen yards. For me, walking back and forth on the bank with absolute freedom, it was eerie to watch a spectacle of death that was measured in feet and yards. I could lift a fly out of a spider's web but I couldn't assist these salmon. The swimmer who drowns is surrounded by fish who scull at their ease, and I suppose there was something in it about spheres of existence and the difference between being on water and land. But I felt like a witness at a slow massacre. Thirty thousand fish, each as long as my arm, stymied and dying in the droning roar.

These were sockeyes. Their bodies have a carroty tint on top of the back at spawning time, often quite bright, and their heads turn a garish green. They wear a lurid, mascaraed look, a tragedian's look, as if they were dressed for an *auto-da-fé*. I could tell how long a fish had been waiting by the color he'd turned and also, especially, by the length of his nose. This was another delayed discovery. All of them were gashed from being battered on the rocks, but some, I realized in horror, had practically no nose left, as though a fishmonger had amputated it, as though he had thrown the poor fish on his chopping block and cut off the front end right by the eyes.

The Stikine is a very rough river. Permanent canyons shut off its upper tributaries to the salmon entirely. The Spatsizi, the Pitman, the Klappan have none. Tahltan Lake happens to be ideal for spawning, but this year only two individuals out of the umpteen thousands who've tried have been seen by the fisheries counters to have reached the lake. Salmon live in the ocean for four years or so before they return, by the grace of some unexplained recording device, to the fresh-water source where they were born. They lay their eggs, languish genteelly and die. Thus four generations are in the sea at a time, and when a rock slide occurs, three years can go by before the blockage *has* to be cleared. If the fourth generation is equally foiled when it tries to spawn, then the river ceases to be a salmon river because no other salmon are living with memories of how to swim there. Given that much time, the Tahltan itself, fire hose that it is, might manage to clear its bed of the debris of the slide, but in the meantime a lot of commercial fishermen will be going broke.

The seven-man ground crew, arriving on the opposite bluff, stood looking at me. I was reminded uneasily of what the Tahltans did to the early prospectors who trespassed during a salmon run: they stripped them and tossed them in. These fellows descended the bluff by means of a rope, put on rubber suits, took long-handled nets and commenced to dip salmon out of the niches and crannies along the lower sides of the chute, sixty pounds at a clip. It was a fisherman's dream until about the thirty-ninth netload, and then, as somebody said, you would never want to fish again. They'd constructed a rock-walled pool next to the chute with an exit into the river above, and in assembly-line fashion they dumped their catches in that, although it was such an onerous business one man was kept busy simply repairing the nets. They worked with care, hurrying the fish to the pool before they could smother, with the common benevolence we have nowadays, for the race but not for the individual. Yesterday they moved something like twenty-three hundred, so it seemed very promising, except I'd already been told that there is a second rockslide upriver which the fish are not able to pass and there isn't the manpower to lift them over that one yet.

The eagles were reveling in the air like bank robbers who had broken into the vault. All they could see below them was fish; the river smelled like a fish-peddler's cart. The gulls sat by the water, so fat by now that they ate only the eyes. The river raged by like a forest fire, while the living fish in it, as silent as climbers, clung to the eddies for their very lives. The level had fallen, draining several of the pools on the edge. There fish lay in the sand in spoke patterns where they'd been trapped, with gaping eyes and their gills aghast, like victims stretched in a common grave.

Walking downriver, I met grizzly tracks; also coyote and

fox tracks and tracks of black bear: then more grizzly tracks
—little bears, big bears and cub bear tracks. Blood and roe
were smeared over the rocks. A lynx had been licking at it.
Immense fish heads stared up. But the salmon still in the
Tahltan were much warier and less fatigued here. They
were newcomers and were alarmed when they blundered
into the shallows, instead of resting in exhausted droves.
This far downstream it became like a regular salmon river,
the fish dawdling along in a placid if cautious manner,
keeping a decent distance from one another, though their
fins filled the river and they were obviously unaccustomed
to such constricted circumstances after their free-swim-
ming years at sea. When one of them leaped, it was a
superleap, a fat-bellied, splendid, classic leap, not over-
whelmed. They looked startlingly large and maneuverable,
as if they would not be easy to catch despite the glut and
congestion and the squeezed gauntlet that they had to run.
When I matched my boot with a grizzly's paws, our hind
feet turned out to be the same size. His forepaws were
about as broad as my boot was long. His stool consisted of
nothing but berry seeds, so yesterday he was up in the
meadows and this morning he was down biting salmon in
half.

On my way home, I stopped at the Wood family's smoke-
house above the main river to see some salmon who had
come to a different end. It's an ambitious structure, like the
one at Tahltan. Water from a spring flows by on a series of
wooden flumes, where the fish are washed. Mr. Wood, a
gentle fellow from Casca, has a couple of pickling barrels
for the fish that he wants to salt. Most of them are split and
hung inside, however, spitted on long poles so that they

look like tobacco curing, on two levels. The smoke comes from small piles of fireweed burning under two washtubs with holes punched in them, but the red fish make the whole barn seem on fire—salmon from floor to ceiling, as thick as red leaves.

Of course there would be no salmon if every time a creek was blocked by a slide all of its spawning stock died futilely, butting the rocks. Suppressed and feeble under the instinct to return to the single site at all cost is a counterurge. After taking a terrific beating, some very few of those Tahltan salmon will let the current wash them downstream into the Stikine and down the Stikine to the Chutine or perhaps the Katete to search for another spawning ground.

AMERICANA, ETC.

In 1969 we were engaged in experimenting with ourselves in groups, in getting along in groups, particularly the younger people, who are the ones who need to face the future with more than curiosity. Thus the vast Woodstock Festival and the peace March on Washington, as well as the group-grope contingents who hugged and parried in Encounters. It was a year for seeing whether we really could live civilly in the crowds that the world is coming to or whether the experimenters are right and, like penned rats, we will soon begin eating each other. We found that so far, anyway, we could; as with the other new sensations, we could even have fun. The year was also one in which marital infidelity seemed to become an epidemic, if it hadn't been before, and when a generalized bewilderment ran up and down the land in boots. Indeed, a good many people wore boots, and battened down, wincing at the news broadcasts, exhausted by leapfrogging vogues.

Most of the vogues were vogues in loneliness. Girls wore lonely-looking, dragging coats and fashions from the Okie era or the Civil War. There was a vogue in vibrators and stimulators, a vogue in pets, a vogue in chain letters and homey weathermen who talked the way the man next door might talk if neighbors in the city talked.

I used to love to get into the thick of crowds. I loved the subway rush hour, the crush at ticket windows, the squeeze of New Year's Eve on Forty-second Street, or the night street market in Boston. I felt enlarged, recharged by these mob scenes, much as I did when climbing on a mountainside. The tussling beefiness of everybody poured into me like broth; I felt exuberant, enhanced by the soul-mix. I liked losing control of where my feet took me, I liked swimming against the tide and with the tide. I liked feeling united with many, many other men, becoming all together as big as Gulliver, sprawled bulkily and uncoordinatedly along the street. And though I'd seen mobs behave savagely, some of my experience was of the moments when, on the contrary, a benign expressiveness, even a kind of *sweetness,* is loosed—when life seems to be an unmixed good, the more the merrier, and each man rises to a sense of glee and mitigation, alleviation or freedom which perhaps he wouldn't quite dare feel alone. The smiling lightness, infectious blitheness, the loose exultant sense of unity in which sometimes a mass of people as a whole seem to improve upon the better nature of the parts—this intrigued me. Figuratively it manifests itself for instance in the extraordinary quality that singing by a congregation acquires. The humdrum and unlovely voices gradually merge into a sweet, uniquely pristine note, a note angelic-sounding, hardly believable. Looking about, one can't see who in particular might have such a voice; everybody in the pew wears an expression as if he were about to sneeze, and squawks at least a little. It is a note created only when hundreds sing. It needs them all; no single person is responsible, any more than any individual in a roaring mob lends that its bestiality.

Just as with other natural wonders of the world to which one relinquishes oneself, instead of feeling smaller, I often felt bigger when I was packed into a multitude, and taking for granted the potential for mayhem of crowds, of which so much has been written, I was fascinated instead by the clear pealing gaiety, the swelling savory relief and regenerative power that sometimes overrides the anxieties we suffer from when we're alone and lets us stand there beaming on the pavement with twenty thousand other people. It's like riding in surf, it's like a Dantean ascent one circle up. Suddenly we *like* all of these strangers—even the stranger in ourselves—and seem to see a shape to life, as if all the exertions of the week really were justified and were a source of joy.

On the other hand, my daydreams at this stage usually involved triumphs of solitude, like Lawrence riding in Arabia, because great open barren spreading space was necessary for any true victory. Since such space had already ceased to exist, I settled for the idea that moving around a lot was freedom enough: a bleak and friendless start in a new place would furnish the leeway of space. The reaction is a common one, and so we have our job shifts and change-of-address routines, moving from Delaware to Phoenix. Young men move and move and move again, enjoying their invisibility, enjoying being lonely (crowds in this case are a desert). Circus and carnival life attracted me especially and much of the allure was on this same basis—to be anonymous, a traveler through thickets of cities, to be nearly as alone as if in Arabia and yet surrounded by huge crowds daily. It was winy to me. I dipped into the two sensations: the solitude (while I was working in the circus, quite literally I took care of the camels), and yet the comradeship of immense crowds, renewed in every town, crowds which began forming at 4 A.M.—maybe two or three thousand people right at the railroad yards as we pulled in.

The circus provided universal entertainment for anyone with eyes to see. First the procession to the lot, with elephants and painted wagons and caravans of flighty horses; the tents were slowly lifted; the cookhouse stovepipes started smoking. The Midway was public property, and then with the band music drifting through the sidewalls, a crowd sometimes almost as large as that inside the Big Top stood around the rope barriers of the "backyard" during the hubbub of the night performance. Before each spectacle, custardy ruffled frosted floats bearing lighted castles and ballet girls perched in them were hauled into position. The tumblers practiced flips, their voices as tense as barks as they prepared themselves, and horse-holders and spear-carriers ran around hitching the teams, adjusting the gaudy-looking carpets on the floats, grinning at the girls and giving latecomers a foot up. The elephants arrived, with their imperial howdahs on, galumphing, as ponderous as Hannibal's army but carrying the accumulated grace of twenty centuries. They took hoops in their mouths and more girls sat and swung in these, rocking gently as the beasts walked. The clowns got into line, and the jugglers, the costume mistress dressed as the Queen of Hearts, trained palominos drumming their feet, and several strange stalking ladies who released pigeons on signal. There was the racket of the tractors working, of generator engines; shrill whistles blew; and in the meantime the canvasmen, the cookhouse crew, menagerie men, prop handlers and ringstock roustabouts gathered around, wiping the crumbs from supper off their mouths and squinting at the leggy girls as into a spotlight. The splendor and the smells, the wealth and deprivation, the jammed exotic mass islanded in flooding lights, fairytale figures leaping to life in plaster masks and sequined frocks (Jack Horner, Goldilocks), and fleshly glamor girls, and pachyderms like African kings in thick brocade, swaying and heralding themselves with French-horn honks and waving trunks—we ragged Bedouin types darting in and out were the connective tissue of all this. Inspired as the circus was, we were its gristle and we made it so.

I'd stand as part of that—larger than myself, larger than life—and then I'd go to the Midway and mingle with the hordes of people there: the children and the hawkers and the gazing grownups who were shoulder to shoulder and pink and ivory in the lights. It was chil-

dren's night, lovers' night, a night for taking things at
face value, a night for smiling and for spending freely.
Finally when the grounds had emptied and the performers had gone downtown to their hotels, if we were staying another day, people in my position looked for a pile
of straw to make a bed on, under the stars Bedouin style,
or underneath the lions' cage if rain was falling. Of
course I loved the lions' roaring—it sauced my dreams—
the restless feet over my head. I dreamt adventurously,
and because robberies often occurred after midnight
among the gang of roughies sleeping along the ground,
to lie under the lions' cage was safer than most places;
their stringent smell, their paws that eloquently hung out
between the bars scared off the thieves.

Gloom and fastidiousness have diluted these pleasures
for me. The lions which are left have enough to do just
being seen. It would probably be necessary to organize
an unbroken line of spectators five abreast shuffling past
their cages in every zoo around the world in order to
give everybody alive a glimpse of one, and private experiences with them, such as I had, are not so easily
obtainable. I wouldn't like to live as a Bedouin now; I
haven't got the stomach for it; and I don't go looking for
crowds either—I extricate myself from random crushes
on the street before I'm pinned, being quite an expert at
foreseeing how they will develop, as a former aficionado.
Occasionally I do still steep myself in the few great incidents of herding that arise, however, because even now
there is more meaning in the unexpected exhilaration of
being a mote in a vast winding creature buoyed by itself,

rolling across a rolling mall, than one can account for. The sudden simplicity of joy is still puzzling, and if we are seldom able to settle on what we think of ourselves, at least we see the way we sometimes lift our heads and catch the beat of other people's good intentions, queue up with them for the sake of their company, and beam and grin as if we're glad to have been born—as if we even find it reasonable. Though most of us no longer feel inklings of an existence after life, we do somehow have to take into consideration this big mystifying infusion of euphoria which comes to us in crowds.

A crowd oscillates around its edges like a swimming skate, and by moving forward it's possible to experience the tight squeeze of Dunkirk or the hysteric press of the real claustrophobes who struggle at the center: then by backing away, the easy chummy nudging of people who do not know each other but seem to be in optimistic agreement anyway, who catch each other's yawns and jokes. The best crowds are made up of city people, who are used to close conditions, wise at the tactics and the etiquette. It's among them you see the sidelong, tacit, essential politeness, when the event is good-humored— a sense of space as being commonly owned. There is a silent, round-and-round and to-and-fro motion occurring in crowds, a sort of mesmeric Brownian motion which makes a sane participation possible. Each person strolls as though the space at hand were limitless, keeping counsel with himself, though constantly altering course in order to avoid collisions. It's like deficit high finance, where more money is used than actually exists because what does exist is out on loan in several directions. Turning, tacking to and fro, everybody borrows and reborrows space as from a common hoard. If they are enormous and purposeful and yet peaceable enough, such scenes give us a kick like the earth's other great natural sights—waterfalls, high wooded bluffs. We gulp them in, believe in them, without knowing exactly what it is that we're believing.

I wasn't at Woodstock or on the beach at Cape Canaveral for the Moonshot; my only crowd fest for the summer was the Orleans County Fair in north Vermont. But this was a hunk of the same phenomenon—exhilarating and exhausting, and somewhat of a mystery. Upwards of twenty thousand people attended; it's one of the large fairs, over a century old as a fete and an occasion, and I got headaches from going to it continually; squinting with relief, I watched the last trucks leave when the week ended. Nothing culturally explosive had happened, nothing that wouldn't have happened before the Second World War, for example, but I'd gazed on Americana by the acre, and steeped myself in the biscuity smell of people packed together, pacing through the dust, celebrating the short north-country summer.

Like other county fairs, the Orleans Fair serves to measure the energy of the local business groups who organize it and reassures everybody, even the summer visitors, that this neck of the woods is not just a watered-down vacation package but has a concreteness its own.

THE EDWARD HOAGLAND READER

Although the fairs do need some subsidizing now—the Orleans promoters get about $10,000 from Vermont's racetrack take—this only compensates them for the competition which more modern diversions provide. As in earlier days, circus acts, hell drivers and comedians must be hired; there are trotting races, raffles, craft and livestock competitions; and a carnival is on hand. So many events take place that nobody can see them all. The Fair Association's thirty-five directors are citizens whose own work usually relates to one of the specialties on the program. Farmers supervise the cattle judging; there are horsemen for the horse show, loggers to oversee the ox pulling, and a machinery dealer helps out with the tractor rodeo. The ticket manager is an insurance agent, and the State's Harness Racing Commissioner, who lives close by, arranges the racing program and books the grandstand show.

The president of the fair is a controversial, indefatigable auto dealer named Howard Conley, who has pushed operations out of the red the past few years. In July, at the dedication of the new Floral Hall, a kind of backlash love-in was held for him, with Vermont's governor speaking, because *Life* magazine had written up Conley as the father of a young man who shot into a Negro newcomer's house one night, vigilante-fashion, and then nearly got off scot-free. The state police are estimated to have lavished 2,256 man-hours on the case, mostly investigating the Negro. Conley is a fidgety, thin, Appalachian type, bony and acquisitive, and yet sometimes impulsively generous —loyal, down-homey, hard-driving and shrewd. He limps,

and looks personable enough, not like a civil-rights villain, unless perhaps when he laughs, and has a handsome,
strapping wife. The several Confederate bumper stickers
around town, certain writing on the walls of the telephone
booths, and the defensive, unhappy air in his office when
I went there to leave a note, indicated that the township
has divided into camps for and against him, but it was
hard to find anybody who would admit they were against.
The publicity about the episode seemed to have hurt and
amazed him, nevertheless, and made him hesitant and
shy. His pride in the fair as it got going, the vim he threw
into the jobs at hand, seemed an attempt at vindication,
and he was rather touching at times.

Three days before Opening Day the miscellaneous collection of vehicles comprising *Smoky Gilmore's Greater
Shows* began to arrive. Humpy, shabby trucks, long trailer
rigs loaded with numbered dismantled equipment, and
camper pickups and snug house trailers with blinds in the
windows and Southern license plates pulled onto the lot.
Parking in convoys until Smoky got around to assigning
space, the drivers dozed. Smoky, whose home base is
Strong, Maine, is a lumbering, somnolent-bodied fat man
with a wolf's bright eyes. He cast these over the stretch
of ground available to him and paced off a few distances, calculating where he'd fit the rides and games,
while munching a cheese sandwich from the food stand
which the Irasburg Grange was setting up. Meanwhile
his carny roustabouts in cowboy hats with Aussie brims
circled the lot with an Alsatian dog which had a glass
eye, surveying where they would be living for the next

week. The various Grange ladies were sprucing up the grounds, and the watchmen and handymen were shoveling mud out of the entrances to the grandstand. A bulldozer worked on the road in front of the barns, filling in potholes; some boys were tossing straw into the stalls. The carnival and grandstand faced the row of barns across the half-mile track. Inside the track was the announcer's tower, the stage platform, and a thriving expanse of grass where the thousands of cars would park.

For me, the fair offered a chance to taste again the delectations of my life of nearly twenty years ago—the uproar and the heat, the loneliness of slipping through a mob, the atmosphere of smothered violence—and yet go home to wife and child and mountain farmhouse in the dusk, leaving the hullabaloo behind. The circus hasn't fared well since when I knew it. Several unions began to menace it with organizing drives, the railroads which transported it started to founder, the public lost the fresh wide-eyed delight needed for itinerant extravaganzas. Temporary personnel could not be recruited so easily and the way of life came to seem punishing and grueling, even unnatural, to the circus types themselves: living mostly out of doors, traveling nearly every night, performing in a new place the next day with the wind currents jostling them. The pay was bad, the dedication required of a performer was almost monastic, so they preferred at least the comfort of week-long engagements indoors under the auspices of organizations like the Shriners, who guaranteed expenses. But once the tents were put away, more and more circuses folded, and often acts were booked individually for the arena shows. By contrast, a carnival is harder to dismember or to move indoors or subject to efficiency procedures, and carnival "jumps" are leisurely and infrequent compared to the continual peregrinations of a circus. The overhead is low; the show operates twelve hours a day; and the few jobs on the lot need no lifelong outlay of discipline or expertise on the part of anyone.

Usually a carnival is a collection of independent concessionaires who gather each year under the aegis of one energetic man who may own only a few of the rides himself but who does the negotiating for all the rest for a percentage of their take. Smoky was paying the Fair Association about $11,000 for the privilege of setting up shop during Fair Week, and Conley's group then distributed much of this money among the novelty and thrill performers who had been hired to do two shows a day in front of the grandstand. The carnival depended upon the fair to draw good crowds, in other words, and paid for the service, but the fair itself depended on the circus-style daredevil or variety acts to bring the crowds to the fairgrounds in the first place. The fair charged an admission at the gate and with this other source of income paid for the prizes, raffles and what not, breaking even when the State's subsidy came in, as well.

Smoky's show is fairly free of gyp devices, and I noticed that most of the hardies operating the rides were boys who were adventuring, or sturdy knock-about hoboes, not the lunatics and dazed fellows just out of jail and bitter-mouthed bad-luck-histories who work in many carnivals. A circus feeds its personnel, but a carnival is laissez-faire; every man eats whatever he can get his hands on. Staying longer in each little town, he and his cronies aren't as set apart and self-sufficient as circus men, churning along under their own power; they're linked to New England or the U.S. instead of to a self-contained, tradition-bound and death-defying fraternity which is rooted in Europe. A circus has a special whirlwind momentum and glory, the craft of a lifetime piled on the craft of previous lifetimes, whereas a carnival does not give performances but provides games and equipment on which the townsfolk may amuse themselves. The carny boys sit on stools beside the tractor engines that drive the machinery, shifting gears and watching for the wallets that are dropped or that fly off centrifugally. In the old days sometimes these boys did so poorly that they would let themselves be locked into the vendors' wagons to sleep when it was raining. The vendors didn't trust them but they would do them that much of a favor, and if it was slightly creepy to be behind padlocks, at least the boys were dry. Now they can afford to bunk downtown in a hotel and feast on London broil, instead of wolfing leftover pretzels and cream soda. And yet the tales survive of raffish, snake-oil carnies traveling through small towns and playing the hicks for fools. Most of us like to think of the carnies as triumphing—we take the viewpoint of Mark Twain—but up here in Vermont the contest wasn't seen from that angle. As the fair's opening approached, the stories told were just the opposite: of farm hands getting their money back, of young kids ganging up on the carnie man in righteous wrath and pulling his tent down.

The girlie shows appeared: Puss 'n Boots, The Dancing Dollies, The French Quarter, and Casa Kahlua. Each of the four consisted of a truck, a tent, two ladies in residence, and two or three hard-guy young touts to ride shotgun for them.

Guy Gossing drove overnight from Providence with eight tigers in a moving van. He had a broken hand, a hopping limp, forearms stitched with scars, a thousand lines in his forehead, a down-drawn mouth with wind-swept elements of humor behind it, and triangular, fatalistic blue eyes. He was short, blond and burned and looked like an old Africa hand, which indeed he was, although originally from Belgium. Driving the van was obviously not his idea of fun—he hardly spoke enough English to ask directions if he had to. He was dismayed and depressed upon arriving and sat in a camp chair in a feminine artistic grump because no chute or proper facilities for his act cage to stand on had been built. His wife was cooking a Continental-smelling lunch, however, and Conley came over, agreeably chatty and cosmopolitan for the moment, not rawhide-hillbilly, and set the carpenters to work.

The Cyclonians, Charlie Van Buskirk and wife, also showed up, Buskirk with a sprained ankle sustained at his last gig down in Pennsylvania. He looked more like an emperor's footman than a unicyclist, being statuesque, with waxed mustaches, and yet as shuffling and happy-go-lucky onstage as a college dropout, but he said that his father had had a troupe of unicyclists and had trained him from babyhood. His wife was a former adagio dancer, so their act blended both trades. A pleasant fellow, Buskirk has a rundown farm outside Rochester that he gets to about one month a year, and says he likes the alternation of performing outdoors in the summer and indoors in the winter.

Other performers rolled in, driving from different points: the Manuel Del Morals, two tumbler brothers who look like the President of Mexico photographed twice, and the Gutis, small German strong men with wizened skin, almost dwarflike, who play gorillas in costume and enact a bullfight. They're impersonal and polished, longtime veterans of circus life. The Sensational Leighs, acrobats, had hurried through bad weather from Milwaukee (he with a temperature of 102, stopping along the way for shots), where they had seen a big top blow down next to them in a windstorm. Nodding to the rest—most of them had met before—they pulled their trailer into the covered-wagon protective square where everybody parked behind the stage. The agent who had booked the groups was on hand too, a tiny, clever, barber-like man who sat reading *Billboard* when there weren't any little flare-ups of temperament to be smoothed over—he'd rise and walk quickly to Floral Hall, telling jokes softly but rapid-fire, and then withdraw, refusing me an interview, much like a boxer's cornerman.

To be successful a country fair needs a rural county to draw on for its events and spirit—yet not a county that is so rural it is empty. By Wednesday, when the gates officially opened, the crowds were on the scene and growing. Lithe slender trotters exercised on the racetrack, going by like gala ribbons, shining with well-bred sweat. The cattle judging was under way, a slow, quiet proceeding with few spectators but a great many animals, who were being looked at by three men hired from outside the state. A slim cowboy in boots judged the beef breeds only, the Anguses and Herefords, and spoke into the microphone diffidently to explain each decision ("clean in the neck, strength of loins"). The Anguses were muscly, black and squat like boars, with a low center of gravity and square wide ears; the Herefords looked like orangutans, their legs a bit longer, their bodies blotted with orange and postured as solidly as a large ape's. The Holsteins and Guernseys—big pro milkers that feed America's schoolchildren—were judged by a tense lyric man with a kind heart, who practically sang his summations. "She won by her spread of rump, depth of body, and that terrific set of legs, her whole top-line, and her dairy promise, the shapeliness of the udder and teat placement, the mammary system—she's just so very *dairy* with that udder promise!"

Calves, yearlings, two-year-olds, mature animals, fat hornless bulls with testicles like udders, and assorted combinations, the get of one sire or one dam, were displayed. Watching the gradual fleshing out of the heifers, the fickle distribution of natural gifts, and then the aging, it became like watching the march from birth to death of all creatures, as the contests, successively involving older

91

and older classes, went on late into the afternoon and the next day. The Jerseys appeared overshadowed by the bigger specialized dairy breeds, but they were as dainty as does and the same pretty color, and they interested me because they were the cows of my boyhood. They and the Ayrshires were judged by a Canadian cattle breeder, a natty white-haired man with a sharp Scottish nose, level-eyed and dry in mood, who wore a sport coat and a crew cut. He tilted his fedora against the sun, and as he studied the animals, signaled the owners with brief, somber gestures to turn them or to line them up in orderly fashion for a march-past, not speaking till the end. He gave his verdict in a low, easy voice. "I'm placing number one over number two because of her balance and walk, her flesh, which is neater up front, laid in more neatly in the shoulder and the rib, her glands, and the attachment of her teats." Between shows he drives all night—from here he was going to Three Rivers, Quebec. Watching him straightening a cow's tail to see its set, sometimes twitting the farmer as well with a significant twist of his wrist, it was clear he enjoyed his work. Whole families were present, dressed in white milking suits and wearing glasses, swallowing their smiles, moving their sensitive-looking nostrils. The father would exhibit the cow he considered his best, his wife the second-best, and so on down to their youngest child. But after a rigorous inspection, the Canadian judge might choose the five-year-old girl's cow over the others, to her papa's astonishment, and give the blue ribbon to her.

As at a ball park, you can eat supremely badly if you

want to: cold hot dogs from East St. Louis and dirty buns. Instead, I went to the Eureka Grange to have sweet corn and warm blueberry muffins. The girlie shows lay low during the afternoon, but the carnival rides whirled round and round. A pinto pony, furry, chipper and haughty, with a mane so thick in front of its eyes that it could hardly see, was raffled off. A boy with high-set cheeks won and for the rest of the fair rode around the grounds, seated straight up like a trooper; he was the winner that the pony needed. I went to Floral Hall to check the vegetables: limpid translucent onions and shiny green peppers, speckly cauliflowers, bagged brown potatoes, fat green tomatoes, along with understated boxes of eggs. There were lovely summer vegetables like beets, chicory and butternut squashes tagged with prize ribbons and heaped together in a kitchen pan as if for supper, and chocolate cakes, canned venison, and maple candy, and soap cakes carved, and afghans, woolen mittens, and rugs woven from baling twine. Also, inevitably, the utility company was pulling its oar with an exhibit; a service club had a tableau advocating motherhood; and among the motor vehicles in the commercial section I was brought up short by a tombstone display.

At the grandstand Don D., the emcee, an indoor-looking man in a cowpoke suit, was trying to lead the crowd in "The Marine's Hymn," with maybe less response than he'd expected—his notions about Vermont were hawkish. Happy Dave, the clown, performing first as Happy Davis, made up in sad-face, talked to his hat, miming explanatory squibs, and had some trouble with his trampoline—

said a mock prayer. He tugged off a series of vests and, finally, a bra, and got two legs in one leg of his baggy dungarees before at last stripping down to a striped gym suit and doing somersaults high in the air while puffing a cigar. Later on, without the bulbous nose, he appeared as Dave Hanson, driving a "1913 Rolls Rotten" which spurted firecrackers, seemed to catch fire, and ultimately threw him in one grand explosion right through the roof. He wore a flat hat and overalls with ruby writing on them and was awfully weary of that carful of slapstick stuff when he came off the track. He's the tough clown, banging through his routines, pepper-talking like a movie newspaperman, machinegunning his words; he is a law-and-order buff, a bitter guy, an honorary member of the Pottstown, Pa., police force, with a strong yen to join full time. He talks of car smashups, and the effect a shotgun blast has on its victim. When you look closely, even his makeup breaks down to rat-tat points under the eyes.

The booking agent reminisced about when Ginger Rogers broke into show business. He himself got started with an act in which, using his fingers, he projected shadow figures on the wall. The clown was talking about the flattening impact of .45-caliber gunfire. The emcee left the stage after bullying the audience with his latest singalong ("The Battle Hymn of the Republic"), making them clap two or three times. He is a sallow lady-killer with pockets underneath his eyes. The strange thing about him is his incongruous voice, all mellifluence and volume. When the clown kidded him about the quality of his humor, he said he wasn't going to expend his best stuff on a crowd like this one.

Guy Gossing had driven to the slaughterhouse in Lyndonville for beef hearts for his cats. Now it was night. The shadows were even more fancifully vivid than the lights—long glamorous amber shadows. The tigers, smelling like ouzo-and-straw, lay on their backs, propping their legs against the bars, their paunches showing, and Gossing woke them up before the act to start them scrapping and roaring. "Allah! Rajah! Bengal!" Mrs. Gossing, a Chinese-faced Belgian housewife, shrieked the names, too, to remind them that they were outnumbered. They roared like motorcycles and lunged and slunk, a fine youthful passel of tigers. It's a good fighting act when Gossing chooses to exert himself. He's a journeyman trainer, a fellow tired of it now but who knows all the jumps and moves, whether or not he ever was able to do the stoutest feats himself. Like any aging professional tired of his work and touring the hinterlands, he's ready to be lackluster if there is no occasion to be more than that, but by hopping quickly to stay off his bad leg, chasing and punching the cats, escalating each spark of resistance on their part, milking every chance for furor, hefting the heavy stools and pretending to fight his way along the bars, he can recapture his old flair. Still, there's a lot of wasted rigamarole with them on their stools, sitting up, or posing in a row on their hind legs leaning against a horizontal pole. He forces one up on top of a ball and has her foot it along a metal track; then has the eight of them roll over and over on the ground in pairs, to wind up lined up close, alert and gorgeous in an orange mass, with all heads turned toward him. It isn't really very much, and to add action and enthusiasm, he makes the tigers move around, and jogs, and shifts the furniture, and whips the air, evincing modest ferocity. His wife, sluggish but shrill—she's the eyes in back of his head—yells any tiger's name who seems to be stirring. Gossing, wearing a short-sleeved shirt, looks like a sunburned Congo mercenary, and unless you have no sympathy for aging athletes, you cheer him on.

Billiard balls seem to enjoy themselves. Painted brightly, they seem to revel in the zigzag sociability of the table, crowding each other, then flying apart. Birds flock in, flock out like flying sparks, and water spiders run away and run together in ticktocking compatibility, and the Brownian motion of crowds is similar. All of us meandered at the fair, averting collisions as carelessly as if it were part of the mechanism by which we walked. We strolled with many turns and stops, paying little attention to our neighbors but with no object in mind so fixed that it couldn't be abandoned if the path was blocked. Our whimsy was our freedom.

The carnival, operating with almost equal intricacy, had the same aura about it of participation in a grand design. The Octopus—six angular arms with buckets on the ends—reeled in a circle round and round, each bucket revolving on its own axis. The Round-up, a centripetal device, started flat, like a potter's wheel, and then stood up on edge, with the riders pressed hard against the rim. The Scrambler was a thicket of buckets mixing and jibing at great speed. There were Bumper-cars; a carousel with a small but effective organ—tin-tin, tub-tub —and bleached but convulsive horses; a Tilt-a-whirl, which was a rattling dizzy ride supervised by a broken-nosed movie star from Texas; and my favorite, the Tip Top, a Humpty-Dumpty-like creation which bounced on cushions and blasts of air while playing goofy wheezy nursery music as it turned. The mechanical activity—big Allis-Chalmers engines pistoning under a subtler, wider roil—gave the carnival some of the sweeping majesty of a steamship which makes shuttle crossings and doesn't register its significance by where it's going so much as by what's going on within its hub of lights. The roaring rides, the string of pitch games and shooting galleries with feathery prizes, the local Legionnaires offering their versions of craps and roulette, all amounted to a vast riverboat that was traveling slowly through town. Sometimes the machines ran the men and sometimes the men enjoyed their dominion over the machines, but though the announcer for the hell drivers apologized to the crowd many times for the fact that they weren't astronauts and seemed dejected on account of the Moonshot, nobody who worked in the carnival felt in the least eclipsed by this event.

Freak shows are a vanishing item of Americana, however. The Phineas T. Barnum "gallery of weirdos" was "sculpturistic and pictorial," according to the spiel, meaning that the spectator would have to make do with plaster models and photographs. You could see "Miss Betty Lou Williams, born to go through life with her baby sister growing out of her stomach, and Zip the Pinhead, Glommo the Human Garbage Can, Grace McDaniels the Mule-faced Girl, too ugly to go to school, and Little Frieda Pushnik, the Living Torso." Freak-show faces are ordinary, homely faces which have been brought to a tragic apotheosis—there may be a usefulness in seeing them, in other words. But freak shows are disappearing from carnivals because the naïveté that gawked at Grace McDaniels is now surfeited with war and medical science and the old commonplace, neighborly appeals to one's half-smirking sense of mercy and of sadism. We who have stayed far away from Vietnam for these past years are nevertheless shellshocked; we are survivors. P. T. Barnum, like Noah Webster, is now in the public domain, so anything may be offered under the cover of his name. These photographs, not wrenched or tragic but simply blurred, represented the one kind of gyp Barnum didn't impose on the public. He gave people a laugh or a lesson, but never *nothing* for their money.

Ox pulling is another fading game. Oxen crossed the country, logged, dragged freight wagons for a century, and plowed the plains, yet you see them at only a few fairs. Judging from the Orleans contests, ox pulling is in its final amateurish throes as a sporting event and might be better accepted as dead. It *is* a start to see those ornamental antique-looking ox yokes actually worn instead of fastened over somebody's door; it's like seeing a bald eagle close up. The animals are docile, bland, smooth-skinned; they seldom seem to act, only react. Except for their color they look like water buffaloes, and have big horns and empty dangling scrotums. Blocks of cement, each weighing a thousand pounds, are lifted by fork-lift onto a sort of metal toboggan, called the boat, which the competing teams drag as far as they can. A measurement is recorded and then a tractor with a winch pulls the boat back again. But the men were rusty at handling the oxen and the oxen seemed to have been hastily trained, as though as a weekend hobby; either the drivers were clumsily embarrassed with them or else angrily agitated and cruel. An oxlike old fellow in green overalls with vicious-looking X suspenders and glinting eyeglasses bashed the noses of his team incessantly with the butt of his whip with all his strength regardless of whether or not they pulled with a will. Maneuvering them was so difficult, apparently, that I was glad when the contest was over, glad that tractors had been invented. The brutes, who had been munching grass before the action started, stood bushed and bewildered, twisting in their yokes like collared boys.

That evening, the pony pull was quite a different prop-osition—brisk, jingly and eventful, like a living Western, and with a partnership between the men and teams. There were many spectators, many young men compet-ing. The dusk, too, lent the scene a romantic flavor, and the ponies' polished harnesses were studded with brass. The ponies responded to the announcer's instructions, taking their places quickly and throwing themselves into the pull. The drivers put their hands on the rumps of the teams and convivially helped them heave. A pony pair weighing a total of 990 pounds pulled 4000 ("forty hundred") pounds of cement for sixteen inches. A team that weighed 1100 pounds pulled the same load twenty-two inches and won. The feat is done with a tremendous jerk applied immediately as the hitch is made, and so, because of the nervousness of the ponies, the moment of making the hitch is like the tension around a starting gate—everybody, the people and the ponies, knowing what is about to happen and anticipating. Whipping is not permitted, whereas the oxen had suffered all the penalties which the world dishes out to the stupid.

On Saturday and Sunday afternoons the full-sized horses pulled—these actual workhorses employed for skidding logs out of the woods. Big Percherons, heavily shod, they were called Dan & Tom, and Duke & Jim, Dick & Spike, Queen & Molly, and other cheerful names like that. The tourney was "Open to the World," meaning to entries from Canada, and it was very busy, with numerous teams waiting, their handlers rubbing them and running around, maybe not as animated or swift a sight as the pony pulling but more intimate and professional and appealing. Again the teams were classed by weight—up to 3000 pounds, 3200 pounds, 3500 pounds, and the free-for-all, which can include any two horses alive. Indeed, the teams can weigh up to two tons, and for a brief inspired instant may pull up to ten tons. Six tons was the most I saw pulled, but I was astonished that such a rockpile could be moved even a foot. "We're trying to keep our kids on the farm, trying to keep them from running to the city," said Payson Davis, the fair's entertainment director, and it seemed that by rights the horse pull ought to help, if anything would. A Dalmatian dashed about, encouraging his master's team; the husky young drivers pitched in, assisting each other, and whooped and smoked and gossiped as twilight fell. I noticed that although the boys in the carnival had wilder hair and cursed a little more often, their faces and those of these loggers and farm hands were not different. The poverty and hard woods life and winter nights beside an iron stove had marked some of the local people similarly.

The oxen and the tigers we had watched were on the path to oblivion—the tigers were striped for extinction just like a doomed building's windows. But this tic-like strolling and seethe of human beings shopping for entertainment—the auto-smash show scheduled hard on the heels of period-piece presentations—were in the current mode.

The hell drivers had driven from Toronto after a late performance to play the Orleans Fair on Sunday, and they slept across the front seats of their crash cars, leaving the doors open for extra space; all morning they were on view, asleep. "Champions, stand by! . . . Signal Six, all champions! . . . Danger takes to the raceway! . . ." Badgering their cars, they drove through flames, did "cross-overs" and hurdled "elevations." Sideburned, rangy young men who looked like unsteady mechanics, they limped along the racetrack in tennis shirts, white pants and boots, and were a masculine equivalent to the girlies, being much admired, much despised.

A girlie is a girl who strips, but where the emphasis formerly was on her procrastinations in going about doing this, now it's a matter of how fast and directly she gets the garments off, since she is racing a hundred girlfriends and bar-and-grill pickups. While she is in the public eye outside the tent, she dances in the old-fashioned filmy robes with bumps and grinds, but when the customers have been segregated inside, away from abstainers and wives and kids, she simply walks through the curtain and proffers her bare body to be licked by those close to the stage for five or ten minutes, until the time is up. Striptease is gone; the girlie is pressing against the barriers of human sacrifice. If someone bites her hard she screams and the exhibition is cut short.

Although Vermont isn't a state where one would go planning to see blue movies, on the other hand, the sort of rural area where night riders can shoot into a house and not be denied community support and the support of the police may not be as conservative in its social customs as it's cracked up to be. The really cunnilingual girlie shows, where "lunch is served"—much stronger spectacles than the skin flicks that city men see—travel between agricultural towns on the back ridges, whether in New England or Tennessee. At the Orleans Fair, the big drawing card with the Catholic Canadians across the border a few miles away was what they could expect to glimpse in these four tents, so having a high attendance at the other programs on the fairgrounds partly depended upon satisfying their expectations. It didn't seem peculiar, in any case: farming people are familiar with nakedness.

Two shows were owned by a fellow named Bob, who also managed the other two for an absentee owner. Bob was a New Yorky barker, fast-talking, factual, hard-shelled but fair. He was stocky, in his forties, and enjoyed confiding to the crowd how tough the life was on the girls, a pair of whom were at his side like two leashed mink, dancing in the heat and cold. "Two hard-working girls. They've been working hard all summer and they're going to work hard all fall." Neither was specifically sexy except for the fact they were up there go-going to the Rolling Stones. One had the face of a British shopgirl and one looked like Andy Warhol. They smiled at Bob's jokes glazedly, staring over the upturned heads. As the night darkened and the Midway crowd grew thick and bold, mostly they worked inside, only reappearing to assure the fellows in the ticket line that Casa Kahlua was a live show, and to catch a breath of air and shake the spittle off themselves.

Next door, at Puss 'n Boots, a black-haired boy from Boston rasped into a microphone, "Red-hot ramble, long and strong; they strip to please and not to tease," with a grimace of real distaste, as if he were pulling a cross-cut saw. He had a coed winker beside him, with curly hair down to her shoulders, a heart-shaped face, a sweetheart smile—a tireless flirter, straight from the ivied halls, she said. She was the beauty of the fairgrounds and loved the exposure, the gazing, pushing guys; she picked out individuals to play to outside, ducking through the curtains with coaxing glances to strip for the spendthrifts inside. She had the flushed look of a college girl—stoned, loving the evening, yet about to cry. Matched with her was a lethargic fat blond substitute flown in the day before, who was an experienced stage caryatid but wholly a neophyte at this carny grab bag. She had her little daughter with her and her husband—a Simple Simon type—and was being hurt at nearly every performance because, sulky, joyless, she made only the required moves. "Too many hands! Handle with care!" yelled the big balding ticket-taker, like a bookkeeper gone wrong. "Be nice!" she said, watching everybody apprehensively; but the men, who had been awed by the pretty coed, moved to make up for their restraint with her. "Will you be nice?" she asked each guy. He would promise, but then he'd cup her thighs like a melon and bite.

The Dancing Dollies—a small china doll with compressed face and a trim, giddy short-haired redhead—exercised diligently like majorettes. The redhead seemed sorrowful and abandoned, and looked like girls I knew. The barker was a sailorly beefy native of Maine. "Showtime! Alley oop!" he cried. He had a rug merchant competing with him for lung power (rugs of the Yellowstone and the Last Supper), as well as the traditional hammer-and-bell—three swings for a quarter, and a nickel cigar if you managed to ring the bell. The Green Hornets, motorcyclists, were at it, stirred up by the sight of the girls; the old man who ran the concession bent humbly next to their brawn.

Inside the girl tents, the vulnerable, androgynous bodies were like a shower room: flesh-colored, breadboard backs and dabs of pubic hair. A Southern heavyweight from

Selma spieled for the French Quarter, chuckling his words like dirty jokes until the farmers' smiles changed to pie-eating grins. He had the assistance of a yellow-haired belle called Penny, a hot mama who waddled. In the tent, she caught hold of a codger and polished his pate with her fat boobs and rubbed his glasses on her pussy. "Be nice. Be like you aren't," she told the customers, making them clap like seals. The early birds had been determined middle-class persons, embarrassed to be there, ashamed but curious, standing with their arms crossed, hoping none of their friends would spot them and ripe for bullying. Later, the Johns climbed the tent pole; a roll of chicken wire was laid along the sidewall to prevent sneak-ins, gang rapes and such events. The loggers of French Canada were fighting to get in the entrance and the girls scarcely needed to show themselves outside on the platform, or when they did they simply sat resting with their legs crossed. Like politicians who no longer listen to dinner speeches but who know when to smile, they kept track of when they were supposed to appear robed and when they should be in the nude.

This Penny knew the motions and was unflagging as a man, leaving the people puffing. If she hadn't coached her relief girl, whose name was Susie Wong, they probably would have ripped Susie apart in retaliation. Susie was a dumb-eyes with small mishandled breasts, a hanging plume of hair, an inaudibly piping voice, and was a girl who looked undressed no matter how much she had on because she kept her mouth moistened and open. She had a boyish, sexual, scrawny body, a slim cat face, and somehow represented the entire southern hemisphere, being vaguely Indonesian and vaguely mulatto. But when somebody cradled Susie with any comprehension, she did what Penny did; she got a deep grip on his head of hair with both hands, so that if he bit her he would be scalped—or lose his ears, if he was bald.

A steer named Bar-B-Que was raffled under a quarter moon. Wednesday had been perfect weather; on Thursday high humidity and a hot sun cut attendance until sundown; the third day was a dry scorcher; the fourth day there were showers; and by the fifth day, Sunday, people were tired, though the weather cleared and cooled. A livestock cavalcade, another display of the march from birth to death, was held; also a parade of milk coolers and snowmobiles. The trotting horses raced, their gait oddly manlike, an unnatural-looking, pumping step corresponding to heel-and-toe. It made them seem six-legged, crablike, although their bodies still gracefully waved like satin ribbons around the track. But I was only raggedly interested in these events by now. Caressing women loosens and softens us for caressing children later on or it's soon wearisome, as in a girlie show, and lately I was thinking that even the supposedly Bedouin austerity of being alone in crowds might not be strengthening or Bedouin at all—merely lonesome—maybe I was getting old.

I talked with Nancy and Leigh Heisinger, the Sensational Leighs. He's a practical, physical young man from

Tallahassee, and his wife is timidly pretty, especially in costume, with girlish pigtails—not really a show person, more like a child bride. He has a fluty voice and struck me as light-headed and rather dumb, but he does "walk in space," romping in the air, a spinning, running, rhythmic spectacle, as much as fifty feet high. The Loop Swing, as he calls it, is like two blades of a windmill, each end having a hoop attached where Heisinger and his wife walk as the blades turn so that they balance one another and regulate the rotations, propelling themselves. She's not as good, and when he hangs a weight on the opposing spoke and performs on his own, he rollicks in the air, with music in his motions, outdoing himself.

Mrs. Smoky Gilmore looks like a woman in a comic strip: the widow woman down the block who cuts an eccentric figure, stomping around, good-humoredly muttering to herself. She wears mud boots and baggy pants and has hair like tarred, unraveled rope, but she's her husband's partner; she works in a centrally located peanut booth where she can watch the action and what's going on and who is who. Smoky stays in their trailer, available for consultation. He sits near the doorway, leaning heavily on his elbows. He is an unshaven Irishy man of middle age with a great stomach but sturdy legs. He has a year-round lumbering business in Maine and runs the carnival from May to October. The logging is a better life but the carnival is "a challenge among men," he says —other men are always trying to take it away from him or pinch his profit margin. "You're either cut out for it or you're not." I made several attempts to see him before he was free. Either he would have a visitor or he'd be on the telephone to Seattle for a replacement part or would be "wrapping money" with his back to me—"Gotta lot of money to wrap." It's not as rough a business now in terms of whom you hire (many a mother's pretty son is going native just for the summer), but getting any help at all is harder; he must quintuple the old salaries. Also, to take an example, he paid $10,000 in rent to set up at the Lobster Festival in Rockland, Maine, for a skimpy three days, and one day's rain hurt him badly. He has fourteen county fairs to play this year, but although everybody wants a carnival for old time's sake, they want it to be extra clean—no "controlled" joints, "bucket" joints or "swing" joints, where the operator decides who wins, and which, along with the rides, should be the backbone of a carnival's profits. "There's only so many dart-balloons and duck-ponds that you can put in."

Smoky started with a balloon joint thirty years ago and gradually amassed a show. Just in the minutes I was with him, a woman customer came to report that the Ferris-wheel driver was drunk (untrue) and that the cotter on one of the seats had wiggled loose and two kids had almost fallen out. Then Penny, the mama from the French Quarter, ran up with her big barker to report a fight; a troublemaker had hit them both. A detective appeared too. And Mr. Conley stopped by, asking for Smoky's check for the week's rent. Smoky didn't want to pay it yet in case he needed bargaining power later on. Smiling, he said his wife had to co-sign and that she was busy on the Midway. Conley, lanky-looking, was stumped. He seemed uneasy at my presence too, as if afraid I might be going to pillory him the way he thought the *Life* reporter had done. Smoky chatted away indicating that I was welcome to stay as long as Conley did. In fact, though, it was during these interludes when Conley was trying to deal with the show-business folk that I liked him best. He was outclassed and kind of a hillbilly, and yet he seemed more tolerant of them than some of the other local men. His pride at the fair's whirlyburl was likable, but then you'd see him over in the parking lot with a bunch of tough young country boys, a snicker on his mouth.

On the last night the broad grounds were illuminated with islets of light; a band played high-pitched hectoring music, the trombones fluff-fluff-fluffing underneath. The Cyclonians practiced their lifts; they were off to Sherbrooke, Quebec, the next day. The vendors caught the excitement of winding up: "Hamburgers with stinky onions! Hamburgers with stinky onions!" *"Roll it, roll it, roll it!"* the Ringling Bros. straw bosses used to yell on nights when there was a teardown. Everybody's worth was measured by how fast he did his job. Now each individual package of a stage show packs up separately, some waiting till the morning to leave, others, like Happy Davis, who is impatient, pulling away immediately.

Guy Gossing's tigers, lying in their row of boxes thirstily, watched Gossing's German shepherd drink. He watered them and limped about barefoot, doing housekeeping chores. He was sweating and drinking Pepsi after the vicissitudes of the last performance. His father owned a circus in Europe, and now he has to drive himself between obscure fairgrounds. Speaking a weighty, accented, staccato speech, sniffing because of the pain that his broken hand caused him, he said it was easier for the animals than for him. He said he'd worked with leopards, whose small faces are difficult to read, but had come to America with a cheery gang of lions, then sold them and bought these tigers. Mrs. Gossing was sneezing from the Vermont combination of cold midnights and August days. The tigers, filling up their boxes—huge painted-pasteboard faces—had galvanized themselves, with Gossing's help, into a headlong sendoff show, as if to make this exit memorable. Gossing had jerked and jumped in the essential gestures like an old boxer, conveying a sense, above all, of the labor involved in earning a living. After dismantling the act cage and cleaning up, he finished watering Rajah, who was the biggest, and touched noses with him.

I too used to finish my work at night by giving water to a tiger called Rajah and touching noses with him (how many tigers have performed under that stilted name?), so I felt nostalgic, driving away. I was relieved that the week of crowds was over and that the next month would be a quiet one for me. But I still love crowds, just as I still love tigers, and keep going back at convenient occasions to feel the breath of each: neither taste withers away with age. Since we're all brothers to the tiger, we will probably find some kind of substitute for him when he's extinct. And since we're all mob-lovers as well as Bedouins, we will continue to mix delight and despair equally, churning in churning crowds.

THE
COURAGE OF
TURTLES

Turtles are a kind of bird with the governor turned low. With the same attitude of removal, they cock a glance at what is going on, as if they need only to fly away. Until recently they were also a case of virtue rewarded, at least in the town where I grew up, because, being humble creatures, there were plenty of them. Even when we still had a few bobcats in the woods the local snapping turtles, growing up to forty pounds, were the largest carnivores. You would see them through the amber water, as big as greeny wash basins at the bottom of the pond, until they faded into the inscrutable mud as if they hadn't existed at all.

When I was ten I went to Dr. Green's Pond, a two-acre pond across the road. When I was twelve I walked a mile or so to Taggart's Pond, which was lusher, had big water snakes and a waterfall; and shortly after that I was bicycling way up to the adventuresome vastness of Mud Pond, a lake-sized body of water in the reservoir system of a Connecticut city, possessed of cat-backed little islands and empty shacks and a forest of pines and hardwoods along the shore. Otters, foxes and mink left their prints on the bank; there were pike and perch. As I got older, the estates and forgotten back lots in town were parceled out and sold for nice prices, yet, though the woods had shrunk, it seemed that fewer people walked in the woods. The new residents didn't know how to find them. Eventually, exploring, they did find them, and it required some ingenuity and doubling around on my part to go for eight miles without meeting someone. I was grown by now, I lived in New York, and that's what I wanted on the occasional weekends when I came out.

Since Mud Pond contained drinking water I had felt confident nothing untoward would happen there. For a long while the developers stayed away, until the drought of the mid-1960s. This event, squeezing the edges in, convinced the local water company that the pond really wasn't a necessity as a catch basin, however; so they bulldozed a hole in the earthen dam, bulldozed the banks to fill in the bottom, and landscaped the flow of water that remained to wind like an English brook and provide a domestic view for the houses which were planned. Most of the painted turtles of Mud Pond, who had been inaccessible as they sunned on their rocks, wound up in boxes in boys' closets within a matter of days. Their footsteps in the dry leaves gave them away as they wandered forlornly. The snappers and the little musk turtles, neither of whom leave the water except once a year to lay their eggs, dug into the drying mud for another siege of hot weather, which they were accustomed to doing whenever the pond got low. But this time it was low for good; the mud baked over them and slowly entombed them. As for the ducks, I couldn't stroll in the woods and not feel guilty, because they were crouched beside every stagnant pothole, or were slinking between the bushes with their heads tucked into their shoulders so that I wouldn't see them. If they decided I had, they beat their way up through the screen of trees, striking their wings dangerously, and wheeled about with that headlong, magnificent velocity to locate another poor puddle.

I used to catch possums and black snakes as well as turtles, and I kept dogs and goats. Some summers I worked in a menagerie with the big personalities of the animal kingdom, like elephants and rhinoceroses. I was twenty before these enthusiasms began to wane, and it was then that I picked turtles as the particular animal I wanted to keep in touch with. I was allergic to fur, for one thing, and turtles need minimal care and not much in the way of quarters. They're personable beasts. They see the same colors we do and they seem to see just as well, as one discovers in trying to sneak up on them. In the laboratory they unravel the twists of a maze with the hot-blooded rapidity of a mammal. Though they can't run as fast as a rat, they improve on their errors just as quickly, pausing at each crossroads to look left and right. And they rock rhythmically in place, as we often do, although they are hatched from eggs, not the womb. (A common explanation psychologists give for our pleasure in rocking quietly is that it recapitulates our mother's heartbeat *in utero*.)

Snakes, by contrast, are dryly silent and priapic. They are smooth movers, legalistic, unblinking, and they afford the humor which the humorless do. But they make challenging captives; sometimes they don't eat for months on a point of order—if the light isn't right, for instance. Alligators are sticklers too. They're like war-horses, or German shepherds, and with their bar-shaped, vertical pupils adding emphasis, they have the *idée fixe* of eating, eating, even when they choose to refuse all food and stubbornly die. They delight in tossing a salamander up towards the sky and grabbing him in their long mouths as he comes down. They're so eager that they get the jitters, and they're too much of a proposition for a casual aquarium like mine. Frogs are depressingly defenseless: that moist, extensive back, with the bones almost sticking through. Hold a frog and you're holding its skeleton. Frogs' tasty legs are the staff of life to many animals— herons, raccoons, ribbon snakes—though they themselves are hard to feed. It's not an enviable role to be the staff of life, and after frogs you descend down the evolutionary ladder a big step to fish.

Turtles cough, burp, whistle, grunt and hiss, and produce social judgments. They put their heads together amicably enough, but then one drives the other back with the suddenness of two dogs who have been convers-

ing in tones too low for an onlooker to hear. They pee
in fear when they're first caught, but exercise both pluck
and optimism in trying to escape, walking for hundreds
of yards within the confines of their pen, carrying the
weight of that cumbersome box on legs which are cruelly
positioned for walking. They don't feel that the contest
is unfair; they keep plugging, rolling like sailorly souls
—a bobbing, infirm gait, a brave, sea-legged momentum
—stopping occasionally to study the lay of the land. For
me, anyway, they manage to contain the rest of the animal
world. They can stretch out their necks like a giraffe, or
loom underwater like an apocryphal hippo. They browse
on lettuce thrown on the water like a cow moose which
is partly submerged. They have a penguin's alertness,
combined with a build like a Brontosaurus when they
rise up on tiptoe. Then they hunch and ponderously lunge
like a grizzly going forward.

Baby turtles in a turtle bowl are a puzzle in geometrics.
They're as decorative as pansy petals, but they are also
self-directed building blocks, propping themselves on one
another in different arrangements, before upending the
tower. The timid individuals turn fearless, or vice versa.
If one gets a bit arrogant he will push the others off the
rock and afterwards climb down into the water and cling
to the back of one of those he has bullied, tickling him
with his hind feet until he bucks like a bronco. On the
other hand, when this same milder-mannered fellow isn't
exerting himself, he will stare right into the face of the
sun for hours. What could be more lionlike? And he's at
home in or out of the water and does lots of metaphysical

tilting. He sinks and rises, with an infinity of levels to choose from; or, elongating himself, he climbs out on the land again to perambulate, sits boxed in his box, and finally slides back in the water, submerging into dreams.

I have five of these babies in a kidney-shaped bowl. The hatchling, who is a painted turtle, is not as large as the top joint of my thumb. He eats chicken gladly. Other foods he will attempt to eat but not with sufficient perseverance to succeed because he's so little. The yellow-bellied terrapin is probably a yearling, and he eats salad voraciously, but no meat, fish or fowl. The Cumberland terrapin won't touch salad or chicken but eats fish and all of the meats except for bacon. The little snapper, with a black crenelated shell, feasts on any kind of meat, but rejects greens and fish. The fifth of the turtles is African. I acquired him only recently and don't know him well. A mottled brown, he unnerves the green turtles, dragging their food off to his lairs. He doesn't seem to want to be green—he bites the algae off his shell, hanging meanwhile at daring, steep, head-first angles.

The snapper was a Ferdinand until I provided him with deeper water. Now he snaps at my pencil with his downturned and fearsome mouth, his swollen face like a napalm victim's. The Cumberland has an elliptical red mark on the side of his green-and-yellow head. He is benign by nature and ought to be as elegant as his scientific name (*Pseudemys scripta elegans*), except he has contracted a disease of the air bladder which has permanently inflated it; he floats high in the water at an undignified slant and can't go under. There may have been internal bleeding, too, because his carapace is stained along its ridge. Unfortunately, like flowers, baby turtles often die. Their mouths fill up with a white fungus and their lungs with pneumonia. Their organs clog up from the rust in the water, or diet troubles, and, like a dying man's, their eyes and heads become too prominent. Toward the end, the edge of the shell becomes flabby as felt and folds around them like a shroud.

While they live they're like puppies. Although they're vivacious, they would be a bore to be with all the time, so I also have an adult wood turtle about six inches long. Her shell is the equal of any seashell for sculpturing, even a Cellini shell; it's like an old, dusty, richly engraved medallion dug out of a hillside. Her legs are salmon-orange bordered with black and protected by canted, heroic scales. Her plastron—the bottom shell—is splotched like a margay cat's coat, with black ocelli on a yellow background. It is convex to make room for the female organs inside, whereas a male's would be concave to help him fit tightly on top of her. Altogether, she exhibits every camouflage color on her limbs and shells. She has a turtleneck neck, a tail like an elephant's, wise old pachydermous hind legs and the face of a turkey—except that when I carry her she gazes at the passing ground with a hawk's eyes and mouth. Her feet fit to the fingers of my hand, one to each one, and she rides looking down. She can walk on the floor in perfect silence, but usually she lets her shell knock portentously, like a footstep, so that she resembles some grand, concise, slow-moving id. But if an earthworm is presented, she jerks

117

swiftly ahead, poises above it and strikes like a mongoose, consuming it with wild vigor. Yet she will climb on my lap to eat bread or boiled eggs.

If put into a creek, she swims like a cutter, nosing forward to intercept a strange turtle and smell him. She drifts with the current to go downstream, maneuvering behind a rock when she wants to take stock, or sinking to the nether levels, while bubbles float up. Getting out, choosing her path, she will proceed a distance and dig into a pile of humus, thrusting herself to the coolest layer at the bottom. The hole closes over her until it's as small as a mouse's hole. She's not as aquatic as a musk turtle, not quite as terrestrial as the box turtles in the same woods, but because of her versatility she's marvelous, she's everywhere. And though she breathes the way we breathe, with scarcely perceptible movements of her chest, sometimes instead she pumps her throat ruminatively, like a pipe smoker sucking and puffing. She waits and blinks, pumping her throat, turning her head, then sets off like a loping tiger in slow motion, hurdling the jungly lumber, the pea vine and twigs. She estimates angles so well that when she rides over the rocks, sliding down a drop-off with her rugged front legs extended, she has the grace of a rodeo mare.

But she's well off to be with me rather than at Mud Pond. The other turtles have fled—those that aren't baked into the bottom. Creeping up the brooks to sad, constricted marshes, burdened as they are with that box on their backs, they're walking into a setup where all their enemies move thirty times faster than they. It's like the nightmare most of us have whimpered through, where we are weighted down disastrously while trying to flee; fleeing our home ground, we try to run.

I've seen turtles in still worse straits. On Broadway, in New York, there is a penny arcade which used to sell baby terrapins that were scrawled with bon mots in enamel paint, such as KISS ME BABY. The manager turned out to be a wholesaler as well, and once I asked him whether he had any larger turtles to sell. He took me upstairs to a loft room devoted to the turtle business. There were desks for the paper work and a series of racks that held shallow tin bins atop one another, each with several hundred babies crawling around in it. He was a smudgy-complexioned, serious fellow and he did have a few adult terrapins, but I was going to school and wasn't actually planning to buy; I'd only wanted to see them. They were aquatic turtles, but here they went without water, presumably for weeks, lurching about in those dry bins like handicapped citizens, living on gumption. An easel where the artist worked stood in the middle of the floor. She had a palette and a clip attachment for fastening the babies in place. She wore a smock and a beret, and was homely, short and eccentric-looking, with funny black hair, like some of the ladies who show their paintings in Washington Square in May. She had a cold, she was smoking, and her hand wasn't very steady, although she worked quickly enough. The smile that she produced for me would have looked giddy if she had been happier, or drunk. Of course the turtles' doom was sealed when she painted them, because their bodies inside would continue to grow but their shells would not. Gradually, invisibly, they would be crushed. Around us their bellies—two thousand belly shells—rubbed on the bins with a mournful, momentous hiss.

Somehow there were so many of them I didn't rescue one. Years later, however, I was walking on First Avenue when I noticed a basket of living turtles in front of a fish store. They were as dry as a heap of old bones in the sun; nevertheless, they were creeping over one another gimpily, doing their best to escape. I looked and was touched to discover that they appeared to be wood turtles, my favorites, so I bought one. In my apartment I looked closer and realized that in fact this was a diamond-back terrapin, which was bad news. Diamondbacks are tidewater turtles from brackish estuaries, and I had no sea water to keep him in. He spent his days thumping interminably against the baseboards, pushing for an opening through the wall. He drank thirstily but would not eat and had none of the hearty, accepting qualities of wood turtles. He was morose, paler in color, sleeker and more Oriental in the carved ridges and rings that formed his shell. Though I felt sorry for him, finally I found his unrelenting presence exasperating. I carried him, strug-glinging in a paper bag, across town to the Morton Street Pier on the Hudson. It was August but gray and windy. He was very surprised when I tossed him in; for the first time in our association, I think, he was afraid. He looked afraid as he bobbed about on top of the water, looking up at me from ten feet below. Though we were both accustomed to his resistance and rigidity, seeing him still pitiful, I recognized that I must have done the wrong thing. At least the river was salty, but it was also bottomless; the waves were too rough for him, and the tide was coming in, bumping him against the pilings underneath the pier. Too late, I realized that he wouldn't be able to swim to a peaceful inlet in New Jersey, even if he could figure out which way to swim. But since, short of diving in after him, there was nothing I could do, I walked away.

CITY RAT

Delightedly, I used to cross
Park Avenue wearing an undershirt on my way to digs far
to the south and east. I could remember waiting, as a boy
of eight, on almost the same street corner for the St.
Bernard's school bus in a proper tweed blazer, striped tie
and shiny shoes, and so this gulf between costumes
seemed sweet. Sweaty, bare-shouldered, strolling the summer streets, I felt my class or creed unidentifiable, which
very much pleased me. Physically I was in my prime, I
liked to jog, and, long and loose like a runner, though still
smooth-faced, I felt as if I were a thousand miles and a
whole world away from that small boy. I'd sit around on
door stoops after a walk of eighty blocks or so, up from the
Battery or down from Yankee Stadium, and watch the
world go by. If I'd been an out-of-towner, awed by the
city, these walks would have been ideal for adjusting.
Wherever I ran out of steam, I'd sit, keeping an eye
peeled, and try to pretend that this was now my territory
and I must figure it out quickly. It should be remembered

that fifteen years ago violence in New York City was fairly well contained within a framework of teenage gangs attacking other gangs, not wayfarers; Negro bitterness bore down mainly on other Negroes, and though sometimes the Mafia in Brooklyn dumped a body on Avenue D, the Lower East Side itself and other such areas were quite peaceful.

I was in the theater district once, sitting on a stoop, enjoying the stream of life, when a brisk, well-preserved man with custom-fitted pants, a cane and good coloring halted in front of me. "Young man," he said abruptly, "are you trying to break into the theater?" Aware that it was a funny question, he raised his eyebrows while he waited, as if I'd been the one who'd asked. I was holding my knees and looking up at him. He tapped my feet with the point of his cane as though he were buying me and I was supposed to stand.

I was too nervous to answer. Superciliously he stared at me. "You'd better come along. There are a great many young men trying to get into the theater. I'm in the theater." He tapped me again. I still didn't trust myself to speak, and he glanced at my Army boots, laughed and said, "Are you a paratrooper? Come now, last chance, young man. Fame and fortune. There are a great many of you and one of me. What's going to set you apart?"

My embarrassed silence made him uncomfortable, as well as the possibility that somebody might recognize him standing there in this peculiar conversation. As he left, he called back, "Good luck, little friend, whoever you are." But I grinned more confidently at him as he got farther off, because a couple of months before I'd had my picture in *Time* as a blazing new author; perhaps he never had. That was the second fillip to wandering in my undershirt along Fifth or Park Avenue: the fact that on other days I'd be wearing a snaky gray flannel suit, slipping through the crowds in the skyscraper district, and shooting up high in a building for a swank lunch. I wasn't really masquerading as a carpenter; on the contrary, I'd made no choices yet— I was enjoying being free.

Banging around on a motor scooter down the length of Manhattan by way of the waterfront, I'd unwind in the evening after writing all day. New York was compartmentalized; Harlem was in Harlem, and on Delancey Street there were live ducks for sale, and in a shop with big windows, shoemakers cutting soles for shoes. I looked at coming attractions under the various movie marquees and watched the traffic on the stairs to a second-floor whorehouse (sailors coming down and a cop going up). Since I was both bashful and lonely, I would leave notes on the bulletin boards of some of the coffeehouses— "Typist wanted"—then wait by the telephone. The girls were under no illusions about what I was up to when they called, except that they usually did want some work out of the arrangement as well, and, unfairly enough, that's what I was reluctant to give. I kept my manuscripts in the refrigerator as a precaution against fire and was a nut about safeguarding them. Inevitably, then, the sort of girl who'd phone me blind and invite me over for a screw on the strength of a note I'd left in a coffeehouse was not a girl I'd trust my typing to.

One girl had a beachboy crouching naked on the floor painting her bathtub red when I arrived; the rest of the apartment was a deep black. Another, on Houston Street, immediately embraced me with her head swathed in bandages from the blows that her husband had bestowed the night before. Pulling the bookcases over, he'd strewn the books around, broken all the china and announced he was leaving. Nothing had been picked up since. The baby, only a year old, cried desperately in the playpen, and though his mother naturally hoped I would be able to step right into the father's role and comfort him, I wasn't that skillful. A window was broken, so it was cold. She took me to the bedroom, moaning, "Hit me! Hit me!" When things there didn't work out she led me downstairs to a kind of commune, introduced me around and announced to the members that I was impotent.

Still, I was busy, once sleeping with three different women in as many days, and covering the city better than most news reporters, it seemed to me, recognizing innumerable street nooks and faces which epitomized New York for me. Perhaps the air was rather sooty, but it didn't cause headaches or give people bleeding throats. Now I sometimes spit blood in the morning and feel raw sulfur in my gullet from breathing the air; in midtown or around Canal Street I breathe through my teeth like a survivalist who specializes in outlasting Black Lung. This morning when I went out to buy milk for breakfast I saw a clump of police cars and a yellow car which had slid out of the traffic and come to rest against the curb, empty except for a gray-looking dead man in his thirties slumped sideways against the wheel. I stood rubbernecking next to the delicatessen owner. One night last year I'd stood in a crowd and watched most of the building that houses his store burn to a shell, all of us—he wasn't there—as silent and spellbound as if we were witnessing public copulation. Though he is not a friendly man, I like his Greek bluntness and at the time I'd felt guilty to be watching as a mere spectacle what was a catastrophe for him. But here he was, rubbernecking at this fellow's death just like me, only less solemnly; he chuckled, shaking his head. I kept a straight face and felt a pang, but while I crossed the street with the groceries and rode up in the elevator the incident entirely slipped my mind; I didn't even mention it when I got home.

Such imperviousness is a result of changes in the city as well as in me. If I have lost my bloom, so has the city, more drastically. Among the beggars who approach me, almost weekly I see a mugger who is clearly screwing up his nerve to do more than just *ask* for money. I have the New Yorker's quick-hunch posture for broken-field maneuvering, and he swerves away. A minute later, with pounding feet, there he goes, clutching a purse, with a young woman in forlorn pursuit. Recently, riding in a bus, I saw a policeman with his gun drawn and his free hand stretched out tiptoe hastily after a suspect through a crowd and make the nab as the bus pulled away. It's not any single event, it's the cumulative number of them—shouted arguments, funerals, playground contretemps, drivers leaning on their horns, adults in tears, bums falling down and hitting their heads, young men in triumph over a business

126

deal—that one sees in the course of a midday walk which veneers one with callousness.

We each work out a system of living in the city. With music, for instance. I put trumpet voluntaries on the phonograph in the morning, organ fugues after supper, and whale songs or wolf howls in the silence at night. I go to a Village bar which is like a club, with the same faces in it day after day, although as a hangout it does acquire a tannic-acid taste if you go too often because most of the people are divorced or on that road. The newspapermen see it as belonging to them; hungry poets and movie novelists view it as a literary saloon; the seamen, photographers, carpenters, folk singers, young real-estate impresarios, political lawyers, old union organizers and Lincoln Brigade veterans all individually believe it's theirs.

I'm tired of Washington Square, Tompkins Square Park, Abingdon Square, even Central Park (I lived next to it for several years and found it to be ground as overused as the banks of the Ganges are). And the last time my wife and I picnicked in Van Cortlandt Park, which is more countrified, we needed to cut at top speed through the woods to escape two men who were stalking us. Space is important to me, and each of these public resting spots has its own character and defines a particular period for me. In the early sixties I was in Washington Square, watching, among other things, the early stirrings of Negro belligerence, still indirect. It seemed to take the form of their ballplaying, sometimes one man alone, throwing a rubber ball as high as he could and catching it on the second or third bounce. They were lanky, like men just out of the

Army or prison, and when they played catch they loped all over the park, taking possession everywhere. Already they had secret handshakes and contemptuous expressions, and this gobbling up the whole park with their legs and lofting a rubber ball into the stratosphere bespoke the blocked energy, the screened anger that would soon explode. The explosion is past; new developments are brewing in these parks, but I am fatigued with watching.

The Chinese laundryman we go to is mean of heart and keeps his children home from school to iron for him while he loafs. The two girls next to us are sleeping with the super, and sit in triumph while their apartment is painted, as a consequence. Perhaps he sleeps well, but I'm almost sleepless from fighting with my wife. And there are explosions going off nightly down in the street. I have no idea what they are; years ago I would have thought just firecrackers. New York is a city of the old and young, and looking out the window, I sometimes see old people fall. One man has cancer of the mouth. When he feels well he sits outside the barber shop or in the park, not looking up, withdrawn into his memories, but seeming tranquil there; certainly nobody enjoys the sunshine more. But the next day when you walk past he is sitting quietly hemorrhaging into his handkerchief, looking at it fearfully, then boosting himself off the bench to go back to the nursing home.

In the apartment on the other side of us are two young men who entertain a lot, and one day somebody leaned out their window with a rifle equipped with a spotting scope, searching the courtyard and the street. I assumed it was a toy, but in any case I simply pulled down the blinds; one can't react to everything. We'd had a stink in the corridor the week before that gradually grew stronger. It was a really hideous smell, subterraneanly terrifying, and we and some of the neighbors began to wonder whether somebody might not have died. It was pervasive, hard to isolate, and we were all city procrastinators—with so many emergencies, so many lonely people, why get involved? At last, however, where our consciences had failed, our noses got the better of us and we called the cops. It turned out to be a decomposing chicken which someone had defrosted before a trip and forgotten about. A month or so later the same putrid smell invaded our floor all over again. Holding our noses, we complained left and right, trying to ignore it. Even so, again the police had to be called. This time they found a young woman dead of an overdose of heroin, with her headband wrapped around her arm as a tourniquet and her cat still alive, having managed to subsist on her body fluids.

Year round, I keep my air conditioner on, its steady hum submerging the street sounds. But one of the neighbors upstairs, finding this noise, too, unnerving, has lent me a white-sound machine, an instrument which, like a sort of aural sun lamp, manufactures a sense of neutrality and well-being. Right now neutrality seems to be the first condition of peace; these devices have become commonplace. People are seeking to disengage, get out of town, or at least stay indoors and regale themselves with surfy sounds. The question everybody is asking is, Where does one live? New York is the action scene; one won't feel the kinesis of the 1970s in a Sicilian fishing village, and very few people are really quite ready to write all that off. Maybe the best of both worlds is to be a New Yorker outside New York. Anyway, I'm at my best as a traveler, and looking back when I am elderly, I may be fondest of some of my memories of hauling a suitcase along, grinning, questioning strangers, breathing the smoke of their wood fires, supported, although I was far from home, by the knowledge of where I'd come from. Arriving in Alaska, straight from New York, one feels tough as a badger, quick as a wolf. We New Yorkers see more death and violence than most soldiers do, grow a thick chitin on our backs, grimace like a rat and learn to do a disappearing act. Long ago we outgrew the need to be blow-hards about our masculinity; we leave that to the Alaskans and Texans, who have more time for it. We think and talk faster, we've seen and know more, and when my friends in Vermont (who are much wiser folk than Alaskans) kid me every fall because I clear out before the first heavy snow, I smile and don't tell them that they no longer know what being tough is.

Setting out from home for the landmark of the Empire State Building, I arrive underneath it as a countryman might reach a nearby bluff, and push on to the lions at the public library, and St. Patrick's, and the fountain in front of the Plaza. Or in fifteen minutes I can take my two-year-old daughter to the Museum of Natural History, where, after waving good-by to the subway train, she strides inside, taking possession of the stuffed gorillas, antelopes, spiny anteaters, modeled Indian villages and birds and fish—the pre-twentieth-century world cooked down to some of its essentials. Six or seven puppet shows and several children's plays are being presented in the city this afternoon, and there are ships to watch, four full-scale zoos, and until recently goats, monkeys, chickens and ten horses were quartered on an eccentric half-acre a few blocks from our building. Just the city's lighted skyscrapers and bridges alone will be with my daughter forever if her first memories are like mine—she lies on her back looking upward out the window when we ride uptown in a taxi at night, with the lights opals and moons.

But is it worth the blood in the throat? Even when we go out on a pier to watch the big ships, what comes blowing in is smudgy smoke instead of a clean whiff of the sea. For me it's as disquieting as if we had to drink right out of the Hudson; our lungs must be as calloused as the soles of our feet. Is it worth seeing a dead man before breakfast and forgetting him by the time one sits down to one's orange juice? Sometimes when I'm changing records at night I hear shrieks from the street, sounds that the phonograph ordinarily drowns out. My old boyhood dreams of playing counterspy have declined in real life to washing perfume off my face once in a blue moon when, meeting an old girlfriend in a bar, I get smooched, but I still have a trotting bounce to my walk, like a middle-aged coyote who lopes along avoiding the cougars and hedgehogs, though still feeling quite capable of snapping up rabbits and fawns. Lightness and strength in the legs is important to me; like the closed face, it's almost a must for the city. There's not a week when I don't think of leaving for good, living in a *house*, living in the West, perhaps, or a smaller town. I will never lose my New Yorker's grimace, New Yorker's squint and New Yorker's speed, but can't I live with them somewhere else?

HEART'S
DESIRE

Of all the poignant ways to earn a living, one that seems most affecting in this well-clothed age is when somebody undresses and tries to win fame and fortune by presenting to us his body. The "strong back," mocked by the brainy for centuries and now by the machine, is an endangered animal. As for prizefighting—two people bashing each other for our delectation—it's almost too barefaced to be believed. So is the whole carry-over, the outrageous labor relations, the predatory eating—three-pound sirloin steaks—the tax men crouching in the wings, and the stars floating in a balloon in the comic strips to signify a knock-out—that not merely symbolic death, but a near approach, like sniffing too much glue.

In the American Dream one socks one's way to success, and here is a man who is doing just that, bloodying the loser, puffing up his face, leaving him for dead. Fight fans congregate in the arcades under the arena before entering, eyeing each other for sudden shifts of fortune (ups and

133

downs are what fighting is all about), and watching the retired boxers, now rather chapfallen, and the columnists, the gamblers, the tanned well-heeled fellows with their women who like to rub shoulders with the fight crowd three or four times a year. Right alongside the fat ticket holders with rings on their pinkies who've made some sort of K.O. in the world are harried scalpers, who dodge among them, barely eluding arrest, and maybe part of the best of it for some of these prosperous guys in the good seats is knowing that, however much in earnest the victor is, the entire production is a joke on him. He's taken the injunction literally. He's too dumb to know that one can't actually *sock* one's way to success—that isn't how it's done—and so his shambling victory dance in the ring, when he thinks he is "champion of the world," is the dance of a dunce. Even during his moment of victory he's a loser as well; he's getting nowhere, a champion only in Harlem, if anywhere. From the vantage point of the spectator, it's heads I win and tails you lose.

But there are also plenty of likable boxing fans, especially, as with other sports, those who resemble hobbyists. Hobbyists are men who allow a few chinks in their city armor to show, gathering together for the sake of their enthusiasm and revealing, whether diffidently or in raucous tones, something of what they really live for. One hears a combo of them blowing Dixieland down in a cellar, sees them with cameras in Inwood Park, hears about "frog and toad freaks" from a pet-store owner, reads news of medallion collectors deep in the *Times,* and of the volunteers who varnish each new acquisition at the South

Street Seaport. Some cycle, or sing hymns or just explore New York as a hobby—knowing about the chocolate and coffee stores on Christopher Street, the bums who fry slabs of pork over a blaze in a barrel on Gansevoort after the wholesale butchers there close up.

Fifteen years ago boxing fans were like that. They'd go to Stillman's Gym to watch Isaac Logart or Joey Giardello work out—pay fifty cents, chat with the trainers, nod to the fighter himself. These private excursions were necessary for a fan who wished to go far with the sport because it was so corrupt that several of the best fighters were never seen outside a gym—at least not till their sharpness was gone and they wouldn't derail anybody the smart money was in league with. Such wastage might be impossible today because there's less talent around, but the best fighter I ever saw was a light heavyweight named Harold Johnson. Though he was finally permitted to try for the championship in 1961 and won, by then fifteen years had passed since he'd started fighting, and seven years since he'd last fought someone of championship caliber, and he was past his prime. I managed to watch him during the middle 1950's by going to South Philadelphia and finding a certain empty flat over a vacant store in a sunny slum square where this superb dynamo was sparring. He was laughing because of his own speed and strength, even though only three or four of us were witness to what a panther he was. Archie Moore wouldn't fight Johnson for fear of losing the title; the other contenders wouldn't sign with him lest he knock them out of contention; the up-and-comers were

135

avoiding him because he would blight their careers—so that long years of waiting were in the offing. Yet he was at such a peak that he couldn't help laughing.

The gym was also the place to be in the case of dizzy youngsters who were being overmatched and trained up for slaughter. Sugar Hart, another Philadelphia fighter, a welterweight as slim and vain as a girl, was such a one. Just as the isolation of Philadelphia may have helped to smother Johnson's career, so it favored building Hart up. Nobody saw him, but they heard that in Philly he was looking very good. He chalked up knockouts and got on TV, until everybody was willing to fight him—the comers because his name would look fine on a list of victories, and the better contenders because he represented a pay-day they needn't fear. So, very soon, overmatched, he got into some fast company, got smashed and smashed again, till the fanciness, the eagerness, the confidence and the vanity were crushed. But in the gym, among friends, this hadn't happened as yet. Here, for the interested fan, was talent and youth, assurance and innocence, quick feet, stylish hands.

Boxing is a waning sport, not turning silver-plated as so many sports have. There would be no dearth of fans if there were more excellence, but what hope can there be that in the America which we foresee people will trouble themselves to fight for money that can be had much more easily? Fewer fighters mean fewer gyms, and fewer fans in them. The best left in New York is the Gramercy Gym, "Home of Champions," on 14th Street a few doors from

Luchow's, among the diamond buyers and chow-mein places, next to a discount store called Straight from the Crate. Floyd Patterson trained here and later Jose Torres, during the years that their manager, Cus D'Amato, operated it. Yellow, black and red posters paper the walls, announcing historical events starring such luminaries as Frankie Ryff, Sonny Liston, Buster Mathis—fights at the Roseland Ballroom in Taunton, Mass., the Jersey City Armory, the Alexandria Roller Rink, and Sunnyside and Madison Square Gardens.

The Gramercy Gym is two flights up some littered, lightless stairs that look like a muggers' paradise, though undoubtedly they are the safest stairs in New York. Inside, two dozen bodies are chopping up and down, self-clocked, each fellow cottoned in his dreams. Some are skipping rope, turbaned in towels, wrapped in robes in order to sweat. These are white-looking figures, whereas the men who are about to spar have on dark headguards that close grimly around the face like an executioner's hood. There are floor-length mirrors and mattresses for exercising and rubdowns, and two speedbags banging like drums, and three heavy bags swinging even between the rounds with the momentum of more than a decade of punches. The bell is loud, the fighters jerk like eating and walking birds, hissing through their teeth as they punch, their feet sneakering the floor with shuffly sounds. They wear red shoelaces in white shoes, and peanut-colored gloves, or if they're Irish they're in green. They are learning to move their feet to the left and right, to move in and out, punching over, then under an opponent's guard, and other repetitive skills

without which a man in the ring becomes a man of straw.
The speedbags teach head-punching, the heavy bags teach
body work, and one bag pinned to the wall has both a
head and torso diagrammed, complete with numbers, so
that the trainer can shout out what punches his fighter
should throw. "Bounce, bounce!" the trainers yell.

There are mongooses and poleaxes, men who hog the
floor with an aggressive stance, men whose heavy arms
flip out of a clinch like a thick tunafish. The room is L-
shaped with a rickety ring set in the L, and so crowded
that one might infer that the sport is thriving, though most
of the young fighters speak Spanish now. Chu-Chu
Malave, a promising welterweight of twenty-one with
hard fists and a 15–3 record, has girl-length hair that he
ties in a rubber band when he is fighting; and he trains in
a shirt with Bach's head on it. He is an acting student,
lives in the East Village, and seems touching and young.
Another boy wears an "Alaska Hiway" shirt and lizard-
green shoes. He sucks in a mouthful of water and spurts it
out grandly. Everybody is trying to sock his way upwards
through life, but they are divided between those who
prefer to fight while moving forward and those who like
to fight as they move back. Naturally, the arena match-
makers will try to pair a man from group A with one from
group B.

In the ring the spittle flies when the punches connect
and the real rumbles start. Gym fighters sometimes don't
look quite as good under the klieg lights, and sometimes
are never given much chance to fight anywhere else—the
"animals" down in Philadelphia, who are left to rot in

their gyms and fight their hearts out where nobody can see them, are still joked about—so everybody likes to look good at least here.

The Gramercy Gym's king is Carlos Ortiz, a blocky lightweight who has been fighting professionally for seventeen years. He was the champ in 1962–65 and 1965–68, retiring the next year, but in 1971 began a comeback. He has fought four or five tune-up appearances in the same number of months, and the word is that although he may have lost his legs, he has not lost his punch. He sports a red headguard, baggy blue sweatpants and an NMU shirt, has a nose that looks bobbed because of all the violence wreaked upon it, and fights as watchfully as a lathe operator bending to a machine. It is perhaps this attentiveness that's so overwhelming. But with the youngsters he is gentle, pulling every punch even as he shovels their resistance aside and swarms over them. (I thought of the legendary way wolf cubs take on their lupine form, licked into shape by the tongues of their mothers.) Then he leaves for the day with a gorgeous redhead with a million curls.

It's a career that's naked to the world—just the simple matter of wins versus losses, the vitality or lack of it observed exactly by a horde of thousands. And there is no disguising the cruelty of the losses; they've watched the man nearly get killed, jeering and pitying him, shaking their heads with a chuckle. Only a series of savage beatings awaits the fighter as he approaches his middle years, the doctors sardonically stitching his eyelids. Maybe this is what makes these personalities so unassuming when you sit down with them. I was eavesdropping on the interviews done by Vic Ziegel, the *New York Post's* boxing specialist, and watching the managers handle their fighters, wiping a hand across the face of a black man to find out how much he was sweating, then slapping him lightly like a horse if it seemed not enough. When this happened, the kids who hadn't yet proved themselves withdrew into a private smile, the dreams of glory someday, when they might cut a swath. Floyd Patterson's simon-pure teenaged face looked out from the wall above this inscription: "Congratulations to America's greatest boxing expert" (unnamed). "Your prediction of my success is a great encouragement to me. I shall try to keep your record perfect."

Walter Seeley is a roofer and a featherweight who commutes every day after work from Long Island to train. He has a victim's gutsy tired face, a bear-it grin, and has suffered only one loss in thirty fights. A career assessment of him would say that not only aren't the fans very much interested in his weight division (the featherweight limit is 126 pounds), but there are very few fighters competing in the same class outside the Far East.

Bobby Cassidy is a left-handed middleweight, a bar owner and marathon runner who also comes in all the way from Long Island. He's had fifty-four fights in eight years, losing just twelve, has had good management and was ranked tenth in his class. His nose, however, looks double-parked, his eyes are recessed, and he bleeds easily. Being left-handed probably helped him early in his career because other young fighters were baffled by that, and he has good fists and good underneath shots, but is not much for strategy. He is black-haired, fun-loving, yet oddly quixotic, and impressed me as a lovely man riding along on a battered wide smile that might carry him through almost anything.

Dan McAloon has milk-white legs, an amused, mustached face, squaring into a beard, and teaches phys ed at a private school. Sometimes he brings his wife and baby to the gym to watch him train. By last year, at twenty-eight, he'd worked up a string of nice showings, including two at Madison Square Garden that earned him a bout with Emile Griffith. Griffith, who is the last of three marvelous Cuban fighters (he was Isaac Logart's protégé, as Logart was Kid Gavilan's), was welterweight champion for a number of years, and gave him a boxing lesson, beating him painfully. Then another former welter champ, Billy Backus, outpointed him badly and humblingly at Syracuse. But he has offers from Italy and the West Coast.

Benny Huertas has been an up-and-down fighter since 1964. Recently he'd accumulated a string of wins, then was knocked out in the first round. Shook up by that, he lost twice more and is only now springing back, fighting well in France. He is another heedful lightweight, weaving, protecting his face like a purse.

Tom Kocan is a dishwasher, a heavyweight with a thin face but an unsettling right hand. Lonely-looking in a lonely sport, he fights best late in a bout when exhausted and loose.

Smoky Roy Edmonds at twenty-four is soft-spoken,

hopeful, endearing. He runs on the horse path in Central Park every morning, fueled by his aspirations. He was sidetracked by two automobile accidents last year but is waiting now for his manager, who is a guard at Sing Sing, to finally arrange for him to appear in Madison Square Garden in a preliminary for the first time.

The gym is a period piece, as authentic as rope, and these people bring it alive. For their pains, their long months of training, they are paid $150 for fighting four rounds at the Garden, and $50 or $75 at the lesser show-places where most bouts take place. For a six-rounder the fee jumps to $500—$100 or $150 elsewhere—an increase due more to the punishing competition accompanying the jump than the number of rounds. At Sunnyside Garden in Queens, a famous old club where all boxers fight eventually, the men in the main event get about $1000 apiece, as an advance against 10 percent of the gate. The manager takes one-third, and since even wrestling outdraws boxing today, the prices have not changed in twenty years. One night I went to see Bobby Cassidy battle an awkward, stubby rock of a barroom brawler named Gil Diaz, whose middle-aged legs soon gave out and who even before then hadn't dared take the chance of sitting down between rounds. Eight hundred and ninety-five people had paid $4,950 at the Sunnyside box office. The promoter barely broke even.

Beforehand, Vic Ziegel and I ate supper with Cassidy's manager, Paddy Flood, and his previous manager too, an antique dealer named Al Braverman, both of them enthusiasts and former fighters. A scout from Madison Square Garden was there, and the *Daily News* man was expected as well. As the sport sinks, these hands gather around and retell the myths, the bad-guy stories: how the best time to pay off your fighter after a fight is as you walk away from the arena in the dark of the night. You count his share of the money into his hand, and exhausted, cut, beaten up anyway, and what with the bad light, he doesn't know what he is getting. They all seemed like decent men, however, exhilarated like kids as fight time approached—this stuff was for the sake of the mystique. Braverman talked about "the chills" he'd gotten during the great sequences of a fight last week, though he's been watching prizefights for forty years. Paddy Flood, Ziegel and I had driven out from Manhattan with an off-duty cop, a friend of Flood's who beat the stoplights and drove up on the sidewalk and made U-turns and used every other trick to twist through the usual jams. On First Avenue we saw a man with a chimpanzee in his car and hooted at him. We saw Johnny Carson, ferretlike in a red sweater, dodging on foot between the stalled cars. The cop began telling celebrity stories, and we yelled out the window at Carson, "Hey, Johnny. Hey, Johnny," until he turned. Then, happy as clams, we hollered at him, "FUCK YOU, JOHNNY CARSON!"

Cassidy won by a technical knockout in the fourth round. I got the impression that the other fighter had been accepted as a match for him on the assumption that Cassidy would be able to dispose of him around this midpoint. Cassidy sat panting, smiling and toweling his face in the dressing room while we questioned him, adhering to the tradition that one seldom speaks to the loser. Smoky Roy Edmonds had won his preliminary bout by a knockout too, and he and the fellow he'd beaten were placed knee to knee in another dingy, narrow room as we listened to him softly voice his heart's desire about where he wanted to go from here. It wasn't so different from casually congratulating any man who has had some success, except that the smiles directed by the spectators to the loser were rather as if a good joke had been played on him, instead of his having just died in effigy.

That's it, I suppose. Lose in boxing and you are a joke; win and sooner or later you are a joke also. It's a kind of extravagant burlesque of the course of anybody's career, even of life itself. The fighter who fights too long looks into the mirror one day and realizes that his face has gradually been transformed by the pounding into a skull.

TIGER
BRIGHT

1

Ringling Bros. and Barnum & Bailey circus still tours America, and all the divorced mothers and fathers are glad because it gives them some place to take the kids. The notices that it gets are uniformly friendly and noddly, not like sharp sportswriting or theater criticism, and afterwards the press agent sends out a letter of thanks to everybody concerned. But last year, after seven good weeks in New York City and two in Boston, the circus left for points west with some of its same old impudent alacrity. Zacchini, the cannonball, was fired from his X-15 with a tremendous boom, so that smoke filled the back passageways, and, even before the smoke thinned, twenty elephants, chained in pairs, went rushing past, with that middle-aged, big-footed push to their gait, down the ramp to the street, to the circus train, at least fifty horses hard after them, even before all the patrons were out of their seats. There is no sentiment about how a circus leaves town; it shakes off the dust of your burg just as readily as it quits Kanakee.

I worked in the circus for a few months about twenty

years ago and have followed its fortunes with a fond, mournful eye ever since from the distance of the civilian world—the world that with such a flourish is left behind. The circus has nationhood, but there has been the question whether it will survive. The Depression, then the Hartford circus fire of 1944, in which a hundred and sixty-eight people died, precipitated bankruptcies and changes of management, and after recovering from these crises the more mundane problems of budget in a swept-wing economy caused the Big Show to forswear tenting in 1956 and resolve to play only arena engagements indoors. Whereas the old circus used to need three trains, leaving at intervals, in order to travel, now that the acres of canvas and poles, the seats, cookhouse, generator wagons, box offices, sideshow and much of what was the menagerie have been dispensed with, one train is enough. The money saved is more than matched by the loss of so much buoyant tradition and color, but the change may have been necessary in a day when workmen are paid $70 a week instead of $14, as they were in my time, and the youngest dancing girl gets $140, and the greenest clown $165.

Still, the customers keep coming, and in 1967 the heirs and successors of the Ringling family sold Ringling Bros. and Barnum & Bailey for eight million dollars to two pop-music magnates and a former mayor of Houston, who soon got it listed over-the-counter as a growth stock. Their first act of reorganization was to split the show into two separate circuses which can play simultaneously in different cities, the ultimate plan being to expand to four units, all operating at the same time. Only one of the four would have to be staged new each year, with new acts from Europe and new choreography. This one would appear in New York and Los Angeles and so on, while the others hedgehopped, just as road companies in the theater do, carrying the presentations of previous years to smaller cities. Expenses have been pared so skillfully that the main cost of fielding additional units has become the buying and converting of Pullman cars as the railroads abandon them. Apparently a torrent of children fills all available arenas and halls, and more are being built, so that if there really are going to be four Ringling Bros. and Barnum & Baileys, with twelve rings to fill, the only hitch may turn out to be whether there is enough circus artistry left in the world to display in them. Already, with two shows going, the cream has been spread rather thin.

I spent a week with the Madison Square Garden edition of the show, then another week down in Birmingham, Alabama, with the version that was playing there, remembering all the time the grinding fatigue of the life, yet feeling an extraordinary yearning to be with it again. In Birmingham I sat next to an old acquaintance who had once worked in the menagerie taking care of the pygmy hippo and who felt the same way. His home is ninety miles north, near the Georgia border. He needs a cane nowadays and is feeling poorly, his eyes are going bad on him, he has no teeth and is stout in a petrified way, though he was wearing pants so wide that as stout as he was, they must have been hand-me-downs. He said he hadn't worked in a circus since I had known him—"It takes a mighty good man to work on a circus and travel and all"—but that for the sake of his memories he hitchhiked down every year when the show was in Birmingham. (Yet *I* remembered him as a man tormented continually, frequently raped, prison-style, his arms twisted behind his back, nearly twisted off.)

Before the performance we watched the propman lug the elephant tubs and the chimp- and lion-act furniture, the rigging boys stunt in the rigging, the clowns' hypertense terrier snort around the clowns' goose as it ate, the Roman-nosed, wooden-looking horses, and the browsing camels, all joints and humps. Then the performance began as if irrevocably, like a giant aroused—old blondes somehow mustering up a dazzle to their faces, a brave workaday walk turning into a glamorous strut. Squally, heavy-beat music was played for the elephants, songs from *My Fair Lady* for the trick dogs; the trainer's whip was a swagger stick. A *March of the Olympiads* fanfare announced the trapezists, and sweet-swaying ice-skating music accompanied their clocked twists. I recognized a few of the old hands, twisty and lame, among the roughnecks backstage. They didn't look strong these days, but they were probably very strong. A circus travels and never stops: this is the point, and it is addictive. The mud, the heat, the privation, the gypsy allegiances and easy good-bys, the chaotic glory and whirl, all mix together and fix a man into the troupe, and as long as he's traveling he need never stop and take stock; his situation is fluid, in a sense his life is ahead of him; things may look up. Even if he's not young, the ashes of his past are well behind him and he's in new country this week, next week, and forever on.

But there's more to it than that. Twice daily the organization builds to its performances, which are created to convey amazement and glee. Formerly a circus hand might go through the year and practically never see a performance because so much was going on outside the big top. Band music accompanied his chores, but he lived with the herds of horses and a horde of wild characters in the satellite wagons and tents. Now that the performance is all there is, he's with the performers, most of whom really light up and come to life when the show gets under way; and it's contagious. Though they may look as wilted and crumpled and sad over breakfast as civilian folk, every evening their faces spread into the same beaming lines that the children wear, and receiving the cheers of thousands, are lifted beyond the expressions of wonder and childhood to the graceful wide grin of a conquering king. Over the years, their mouths enlarge and their faces grow ever more malleable. A man who has just staked his life on his physical skill isn't modest. He stands in the platinum-colored spotlight used only for danger and princes, and casts his head back, throws his arms wide, his body undulating sensuously as the ovation bathes him, and listens to the crowd rejoice that he is alive.

Women performers aren't quite so dramatic. Rogana is a flawless-bodied tall personage who grips the hilt of one sword in her mouth and balances another by its point from the point of the first, with a tray and six glasses balancing on the second sword's hilt. Meanwhile she climbs a swaying ladder and straddles the top, swinging eerily, poising the swords nearly perpendicularly. After this and other feats, she accepts the applause with reserve, withholding some of herself and looking, despite her long legs and black hair, like Babe Didrikson Zaharias; her face is unfortunately masculine, which may be the trouble. "La Toria," who in fact is Vicky Unus—her father stood on one finger in performances for many years—is another slightly sad athlete. Except for her muscular arms she is slimmer but gawkier and shorter than Rogana, and like an exotic, she paints her eyelids white with streaks of black, though she seems timid and at a loss with men. (Rogana is married to a ringmaster.) Vicky Unus does a brave series of vertical arm twists, fifty-two of them for matinées and seventy-two in the evening, while hanging by one hand from a rope above the center ring. The act, an American invention, is plaintive and arduous, although she looks like a young girl swimming as her legs wrench her body around and around in a sort of scissors kick. She's a small girl built like a big one—rawboned, with a swinging walk, a sharp nose, a gaunt masklike face, but terribly human and touching and feminine because of that jerk her legs make. She tapes her wrist where the rope cuts in, wearing Band Aids under the tape and sometimes a cape. In a way, her stunt and her father's before her seem somewhat the same, perhaps because it is such a short distance from what is compelling to what is compulsive, and they both have managed to stay on the side of the angels in this regard. The great Lilian Leitzel did twice as many twists, varying the number according to mood, suffering more torment from the wounds in her wrist, and, full of fire, eventually fell to her death.

Most performers are Europeans from one or another of a dwindling number of circus families. America has not produced many headliners: just some daredevil types and high-wire men, several great clowns and a few bravura animal trainers of the Clyde Beatty kind. Without circus parents to steer them, kids here were going to school when they should have been learning to tumble and flip, so that daredevil stunts and clowning were the only crafts they were still eligible for by the time they left home. Now even the trainers are German and most of the notable clowns have died or retired. Ringling Bros. has started a school for clowns, and scouts seeking young performers who have been painstakingly schooled in the physical arts are going all the way to the Eastern-bloc countries, where the lag of a decade or two has preserved an old-style dedication to the crafts of the past (also they're cheaper to hire). The Silagis, who are Bulgarian teeter-board tumblers, and the Czechoslovakian Poldis are examples. The youngest Poldi somersaults thirty feet into the air from an aluminum swing, a very shy man who locks his heels when he takes his bow so that his legs won't wobble and looks straight out from under his brows at a dot in the audience, as he's been taught to.

The best acts are hard to write about because they are consummate cameos, long-practiced, that an imprecise process like writing cannot reproduce. Furthermore, in this milieu all words are considered venal by the insiders—if not hyperbole, then frankly bilge. Inaccuracies puff every newspaper piece, people hardly know the difference between a straight man and a strong man anymore, and especially now, after the circus has endured years of decline, the truly incomparable feats are often not recognized for what they are. The excellence of Tito Gaona on the flying trapeze is not like that seen in a competitive sport, for instance; it is perfection. His triple, done blindfolded, is done in the single tick of a clock. He elaborates on what can be done, and leaps, finally, to the net, springs unexpectedly high to land sitting up in the catcher's swing, does a lazy man's dive, bounces to grab the trapeze again, does a sailor's dive, a dead man's dive, and a duck dive, toying with his body's limberness. When at last he touches the ground, he keeps right on bouncing, as if the very ground had spring. He gets a shrill, steely ovation, and Antoinette Concello, now in her sixties, who was the greatest woman trapezist and who stands below at every performance—a tiny, quick-looking woman with eyes alluringly deepened and darkened and a long, sly, survivor's face—smiles at him. He reaches exuberantly toward the crowd for his cheers. He has a huge chest and a broad pre-Columbian face.

There are other young men who may carry the show for the next few years: Emanuel Zacchini (the cannonball), Elvin Bale on the single trapeze, and Gunther Gebel-Williams, who constitutes a circus all by himself and is a Nureyev of show business, a man geared for great fame. It's a question whether he will achieve it—what with the circus's low estate in the world—but in Imperial Rome the crowd's accolade for him would have lapped over the rim of the Colosseum like a tidal wave; he would have been installed in public office. He makes marble steps out of his elephants' trunks and ascends and descends. Obviously if he could afford to have fifty elephants he could lead them all, ride into the jungle, as in some fantasy, and live with them there in his sleek gold boots and open red tunic. With his large mouth, large teeth, young-Satan's grin, and a big cross on his chest that bobs as he runs, he seems almost perpetually elated. His first wife, Jeanette, like a deposed queen, and his second wife, Sigrid, direct high-school horses in adjoining rings, and he stands on the ring curbing just between, ready to dart into the thicket of hooves and plumes to enforce their rule.

When he is waiting his turn, Elvin Bale looks like a cockney sharpster with a beaklike nose and pasted hair but once in the air he swings on the single trapeze with absorption and even a kind of onrushing joy. He swings higher and higher, as a child would wish to, pulling, reaching for extra height; he has no implements to encumber his act, just his arms and legs. Then, when he is swinging as high as he can go, he delicately lets himself slide backwards head-down, only halting his fall with his bent heels. He varies these heel catches in every possible way, catching the bar on his thighs in the most dangerous dives, letting the force of the swing hold him there, before slipping farther down as the arc of the trapeze peaks and reverses itself. He squints anxiously for an instant as he hangs by his heels, until, finding that he's secure, he spreads his arms, marking the finish of the feat. He pulls himself up and lolls, gazing into the expanse of the crowd, swinging and grinning. His body, which had been red with tension, turns golden in the spotlights.

In the New York edition of the show, the first half displayed mostly the arts, the second half the thrills, and Zacchini and a girl named Marcia who masqueraded as his wife—his real wife was recuperating from a broken neck—closed the performance. Zacchini, like many thrill men, is no more daredevil in manner than an astronaut and is not a promising subject for an interview; he appears to be a quite ordinary bloke except when alone during his bout in space. He is flat-faced, built like a running back, and looks petted and plump like a mama's boy until the trapeze act, when he begins guying himself up to risk his life. His wife, neatly dressed in a suit, pushes her wheelchair to a good vantage point, and he gives her his wedding ring to hold. Watching Tito Gaona work but wincing and covering his ears when the clowns' firecrackers go off, he chins himself on the bleacher piping, stretching his back and neck, stretching even his mouth; briefly his stolid face contorts into the visage of a man fighting for life.

The cannon is a giant slingshot contoured to fit inside a rocket which emits lots of noise. He and Marcia load themselves into the muzzle. His father, Zacchini Senior, who limps from having once broken *his* neck, stage-manages the buildup and sound effects and watches as they are shot out, separated by an interval of less than a second, soaring so high that they seem to pause in the air —Zacchini's trajectory slightly higher—before following long, logical parabolas down onto a net, landing carefully on their backs, as trapeze flyers do. Always they keep as straight as possible during the flight; they don't ball up. Unlike most performers, their job is *not* to turn somersaults, because any activity in the air might turn them off course.

Before the event, the band stops playing, forebodingly, and Zacchini Senior calls out their names in the voice of Abraham standing over his son. A terrifying siren wails, and there is a thunderous explosion and the astounding sight of two bodies propelled half the length of the hippodrome. As they recover themselves and roll out of the net, the band strikes up, the performers who have been watching breathe easier and smile, the crowd is rejuvenated, and since the circus's purpose is to evoke emotions like this, it seems altogether a fitting end. Zacchini walks toward the cheers with his arms raised high, his head back, as dazed as a man reborn from the grave, his face in a kind of ecstasy, and moving as if he were swimming in cream. In a day of casual death everywhere, we are rejoicing *he lives! he lives!*

Elvin Bale, a subtle man, structures his feat, entering it intelligently, whereas Zacchini, brave and plump, following in his father's footsteps, is just shot off, then rises and runs forward to meet the crowd's jubilation—radiant, reborn. Tito Gaona doesn't risk his life comparably on the flying trapeze, but he sprouts wings on his heels, bounding practically into the crowd to take their cheers. Flying is special, classical, the *haut monde*, though sociable at the same time, going from hand to hand. On the street near Madison Square Garden, raggedly dressed, Tito looks like one of the Spanish-speaking men who push racks of clothes through the garment center, but as soon as he recognizes me he straightens like a man who knows he's considered to be the greatest trapezist in history.

2

It would be more fun to announce the existence of all this talent if the announcement would cause a stir. Instead, the circus remains a private passion for children and loyal fans; among sophisticates it occupies a niche similar to that of primitive art. Even more than the theater or sports, however, it is a way of life. The clowns are odd loners, the roustabouts are sometimes headed for prison or fiery ends, the performers are clannish; yet they all team up with a collection of candy butchers, nightclub girls, homeless Negroes and Germans and cowboys and Indians, and put on a permanent itinerant show.

The elephants and the horses are citizens too, and one mark of the circus man is that he can deal with this jumbled constituency. Gebel-Williams, who in Europe directed his own show, is remarkable for his impartiality. He guides his elephants with his voice and hands, touching and steering them, waving some to circle the track clockwise and others counterclockwise. He also touches the people he's talking to, intent and good-humored like a young general who fights alongside his troops. He's remarkable for being ebullient whether in the ring or backstage, taking the crowd's admiration in stride and seeming, as far as an outsider can tell, to live in a state of direct gaiety. He seems not to have the death wish, so his act is not a conquest of that.

Evy Althoff's tiger is nearly as big as the stallion it rides. Like most big tigers, it's a slumbering, deliberate-mannered beast. Evy wears a silver dress with a snaky motif, combs her yellow hair high, and makes abrupt, idiosyncratic, female movements in giving directions, as if she were guiding a lover, although in fact the tiger was trained by Gunther. She doesn't hurry the two animals but fits herself into their sense of time. Both she and the horse serve mainly as stand-ins while the tiger, well schooled but bored, with a peculiarly humpy run which resembles a wolverine's, leaps through an oily flame, picks its way on and off the deadpan horse, and lies down and rolls on request. The story goes that the first several horses died of heart failure while they were being trained, and even this valorous Appaloosa used to be so drenched with sweat after a session that its color changed from roan to gray. Being placed in the cage was bad enough but was nothing compared with *carrying* the tiger—that momentous pounce when the grisly creature landed on its back, sickening the instincts of a million years.

Evy is the same height and type as Sigrid, Gunther's second wife, except that her face is more compact, less enlightening. Sigrid is pert, freckled and communicative, whereas Jeanette, who is Gunther's stepsister as well as his ex-wife, looks like a smoldering ribald beauty. She's a blonde too, with a mocking mouth, chubby nose, large sidelong eyes, a fleshier body and more of a head of hair.

While the band plays *Carmen*, she rides on a black Friesian stallion, which is accoutered in silver and muscled like a war-horse but glossy and curly in the tail and mane.

Gunther has a rounded, big, forward nose, too sensual to fit a clown, white-blond hair that his ears tuck into, flat cheeks, a mobile face—a cloven-hoofed, urchinish, inspired look—and a swaying, slim walk of quick persistence. His eyes are usually wide open, especially at any sign of trouble; smiling, he dodges into a tangle of animals. He wears brief-skirted gladiatorial costumes and does tight turns in Roman riding; when he needs a whip somebody throws him one as he is passing, and he twitches it, so that it clicks rather than cracks. He's not a mystic, not even a specialist, because he meets people just as easily as wildlife; he likes money, golf, cars, rock music, airplanes. The money is here in America, he says; performances are faster-paced and more sumptuous than in Europe, the audiences are younger, and though he has not become a celebrity, the traveling is hectic and he is still busy learning English. It's curious that he isn't more famous—being at thirty-five the world's leading circus star, the best animal trainer alive. It is not as if we manage without heroes nowadays or that our heroes are noticeably above the level of *The Jungle Book*. Perhaps his position resembles that of an Indian scout and negotiator in the years after most people had lost interest in Indians and considered them virtually extinct.

He was born Gunther Gebel, far from the aristocracy of tightly knit German circus families, in a Silesian city called Schweidnitz in disputed territory which was transferred after World War II to Poland. When he was eleven his mother and he fled from the approaching Russians toward the Western armies—his father was not in evidence—and finally reached Cologne, where they lived on CARE parcels and Hershey bars until she got a position as a seamstress with the Circus Williams, a large, war-devastated show which was headquartered there. Though she didn't stay with the show, Mr. Williams, the impresario, a splendid stunt man in his own right, wound up adopting the boy. Gunther, keen as the orphan Dick Whittington, learned how to juggle and dance on a wire, flip like a tumbler, ride liberty horses and swing from a trapeze. At first he spoke a primitive, comedian's dialect of German because of the border region he came from, but he had coordination and presence and soon could do anything. He had a way with animals in particular, so Mr. Williams encouraged his involvement with them: it was a rarer gift. When he grew expert with horses he began training lions, and when he felt easy with lions he worked with elephants, and then on to tigers.

In talking with Gebel-Williams, I suggested the loneliness of his position in those years might have something to do with his extraordinary responsiveness to animals, but he disagreed. Indeed, there is nothing misshapen or compensatory about his skill with them; it is more an extension of his talent with people. He is charismatic and graceful rather than driven, not even very ambitious professionally. He is inexhaustible and delights in his work, but his talent exceeds his ambition. This might seem to be his weakness if he were set beside the few greats of the past; his strength would be his joy and versatility.

In the postwar havoc Gunther's schooling was hit-or-miss, enabling him to avoid the conventional engineering career he thinks he might have headed for under better circumstances. After five years had passed, his foster father was killed in a chariot race during a performance in London. The next year Williams' only natural son was also killed. Gunther, now seventeen, found himself running a show which traveled all over the Continent and employed more than fifty people. The widow managed business matters and there were family retainers, but Gunther went without sleep, learned to holler orders, hid his uncertainty, and supervised the teardowns, the overnight trips, the struggle to put up the tent the next morning. He was a centerpiece in the performance also, appearing repeatedly, and he married his classy stepsister. Later he encountered Sigrid, who, like him, was not born of the circus elite but was simply a Berliner who came to watch and sat close enough in the crowd. He was like a fish thrown into water; it was the world he had been meant for.

Gebel-Williams is one of the primary trainers, of course, able to prepare an act from its raw beginnings, maybe passing it on to another performer later while he trains a new group of animals. As long as discipline is maintained, the original bunch will keep on doing the chores they have been taught, and if casualties occur the fellow can insert a yearling or two, which will pick up the cues and gradually reach some understanding of what is expected; their quirks can even be exploited to enhance the act.

Generally the group deteriorates to a patchwork, but there is a market for it. Royalties are paid by the secondary trainer to the first trainer or to the impresario who employed him and who still may own the animals he worked with. There may be additional owners, as other animals are acquired along the way, or there may be a succession of trainers, many of whom quit for work that is less dangerous and wearying, feeling that they too are somehow penned in with the cats, a sense akin to what jailers feel. Gunther himself, though he is not punitive with them, says that when he finishes a performance now he closes a door mentally on the tigers and doesn't think about them again; this in contrast to his relations with the elephants, who are uncaged and smarter and with whom he continues to chum.

In America, cat acts are divided between those in which a good deal of fighting goes on—"fighting acts"—and the so-called wrestling acts, where a degree of friendship prevails. The trainer may actually rassle around as if the beasts were sumo wrestlers instead of big cats, stumbling under their enormous weight, demeaning both himself and them. Some movie serials used to feature people who dressed up like Flash Gordon and staggered across the set with four-hundred-pound pets they'd raised from cubs; after a seesaw contest they'd "strangle" the dears. Old World trainers like the Hagenbecks, Alfred Court and Damoo Dohtre worked equally closely with their animals but employed many more at once, and with refinement— no child's play or muscle stuff. They were likely to mix in smaller cats, such as leopards, or bears and wolves; the more of a stew of forces, the more complications. Mabel Stark was of that genre. At the end of her life she still appeared in her Jungle Land amusement park in the round cage, at least for the Sunday show, receiving her tigers one by one because one arm hung dead, the other could only be raised as high as her waist, and she could no longer move on her feet except at a wobble. She communed with them, exhibiting them softly and nobly. The fighting showmen, Terrell Jacobs ("the Lion King") and Clyde Beatty, who toured the country through storms of roars, were not really less knowledgeable about the animals they presented, but their style was to cast them as killers, emphasizing the courage and grace of the man, not the beast. Though probably a number of cats rather enjoyed their company, the tumult of scrapping created confusion and quick changes of mood. Make-believe adversaries could turn into real ones if the fun went sour, and with thirty or forty big cats in one cage, the trainer's first job was to head off trouble between the creatures themselves; a whole bankroll could go in one battle royal.

Charly Baumann, another Ringling Bros. trainer, using tigers owned in part by a woman in Germany, gives a smooth, soft-touch performance, although without the fond intensity of some fellows, who wind up lying down at peace with their cats. He wears an expression like that of a martyr already smelling the flames. (It is not the tigers that distress him, however; practically the only time he seems happy is when he is helping the clowns throw balloons to the crowd.) His trademark is one tiger which does nothing at all during the friendly bustle of hoop-jumping and pussy-roll-over-and-sit-up-and-beg that the rest engage in. Working with his back to her, eventually he gets too close, as if by accident, and she clasps his shoulders with awkward paws, and licks his neck vigorously and rubs her lips hard on his head (cats love rubbing their lips). This wins applause, but you can tell Baumann doesn't entirely like it by the way he neatens up afterwards. Sometimes she holds him there longer than he wishes; yet he can't be too rough in extricating himself because he is at her mercy and will be so again during the next show. Clutching him, she powders her nose on his head.

Gebel-Williams doesn't go in for this kind of thing. *He* does the licking, if any is done, his hands approximating the slow tugging motion of a tiger's tongue till the cat begins to jerk its head to the rhythm. But he doesn't pretend that tigers are living dragons either. A fighting act can be as much a distortion as sumo wrestling, since it caters to the image of tigerish tigers and ferocious lions that we cherish from childhood. No animal could go through life leading such an existence of smoke and fire without burning out.

Ringling Bros. has hired still a fourth cat trainer—Wolfgang Holzmair from Germany. Appearing on the same bill with Gunther in Birmingham, he furnished an ideal foil for him, not least because he was very good. The two of them sat for each other as health insurance, the one off-duty just outside the door of the cage holding a club while the other performed. Gunther has his own cage hands from the Circus Williams for this if necessary, but

Holzmair—like Baumann and Evy in New York City—
would have been on his own if he had fallen under a
pileup and been mauled.

Holzmair looks like a cut-down Kirk Douglas, with the
same challenging chin. He is as heavy as Gunther is light,
and works three-quarters naked, wearing slave armlets and
leather kilts, an ironic curl to his mouth. He is square-
chested, big-backed, a rough playmate, and has the appearance of sleepy fury in the cage, a Wehrmacht con-
tentiousness, so that when he puts on his tux after his act
he looks like a bouncer relaxing. But his work is his job,
not a daydream, and so he's a little amused by it and does
not seem to suffer, as some trainers do (even the mild-
mannered Baumann), from the incongruity of striding out
of a cage full of lions where he has been braving death and
exercising his formidable will, to lay down the whips, the
dominance, the belligerence, and defer to the performance
director, step around the children in the entryway, side-
step the ballet girls and their husbands, avoid offending
police and arena officials, and speak civilly in the dressing
room. Some trainers can't. They go off in a corner, shout
at the walls and whale about with their whips for half an
hour, as if in a decompression chamber.

Lions are different from tigers, more repetitive and pre-
dictable. They operate as a gang without many independent characters, so that the trainer, keying himself into the
swirl of the group, has fewer variables to keep track of. If
he stumbles the whole cage may come down on him at
once, but if he keeps on his feet and stays with the script,
his flanks and over-the-shoulder area are more secure than

if he were working with tigers. Certain lions are the ministers of war, some are followers, and still others—usually including the males—are noncombatants; the trainer's task is to make the best use of each. But even the ruggedest Amazon develops settled reactions to what the trainer is doing; he can almost depend upon her. In most cases he could work up a lion-lamb Androcles act if he wished, instead of the earthslide-of-roars routine, because for months he has carefully aggravated the warriors. If a lioness is in love with him, so much the better; it will put passion into her raging.

But lions roar too well for their own good and, colored a straightforward, soldierly khaki, are too stalwart-looking to bedeck with hugs. Roaring like motorcyclists, they charge as straight as a white circus horse goes round and round. They're prosaic good citizens and infantry, loyal to friends, martial toward foes. They're like bread and butter, and Gebel-Williams, who learned his fundamentals on them as a boy, finds them a bore. To sit beside him while Holzmair works is like sitting next to a bullfighter watching another fighter whose sensationalized style and whose bulls he abhors.

The fact is that lions and tigers are flesh and blood, not myths, and they can be stopped when they charge by the simple expedient of poking a strong oak stick in their path. If they can't get past that they can't reach the man, and their paws are not faster than his hands, especially when he has a whip. However, tigers also require delicacy. They spit up their food, and will balk and brood. Solitaries by temperament, they seldom defend one another against an attack. Being somewhat faster, a tiger can usually kill a lion of the same weight, though he may take a moment to chew past the mane, but in a brouhaha involving a dozen of each the result will be several dead tigers, as the lions proceed in a pack from one to the next, while the surviving tigers quietly observe. Only the trainer weeps at the result, because tigers, who are so nervous that they are reluctant to breed, will cost him ten times as much to replace as lions would. Lions are pragmatists; tigers are creatures of emotion and mood. Their camouflage of crazy cross-hatched stripes—a knitwork on the head, thick on the back and growing practically mad down on the hips and pant legs—are symbolic of this. Sometimes the spaces between the stripes even have eyes. Tigers are the proverbial hundred flowers. There are no leaders for the trainer to watch; any one of them will stick out a paw and the earth may become his sky.

In Birmingham, Holzmair's lions entered snarling, abused by the cage hands, whirling in a sand-colored blur: there were so many of them that not until the third show could I count accurately. They were long-striding and masculine-looking like the hounds of hell, magnificent as they loped, roaring like pianos being rolled on a hollow floor. There were seventeen: so much barracks furor and collective noise that they spent the remainder of the day asleep to recover their poise. Lions are generous in using their vocal cords and are most impressive when they are weaving concertedly around a space that gives them room to dash and jump. Holzmair kept them moving, letting the sight sink in, then arranged them on pedestals around the cage by fives, so that the geography of conflict was clear-cut for him. There were five lionesses who never ceased to rev and roar, providing a foundation of dramatic rage for the act as a whole; these were the savage ones, his enemies. Five other, vaulting lionesses did the strenuous chores, leaping through flames and so on, claxoning like engines only if asked to. They were more businesslike and less self-assured, not such ideologues. Stamping his boots, wielding two whips, he could stampede them into wild climaxes if he chose to. There were also five modest cats who were of little use except to add bulk to the act. They beefed up the admirable milling swirl with which he be-gan—the one natural display of lions presented as them-selves, like a powerful sandstorm. Once posted on their stools, they didn't move, just pulled in their heads to sullen, intractable humps under the lash. Holzmair kept his back turned to them most of the time, as well as to two tame young cats he never roughed up because they figured in a brief exhibition of wrestling and trust towards the end, when he demonstrated that he knew the sweet-ness-and-light technique as well as the coercive stuff. He tried thrusting his head into the mouth of one, but the opening as yet was too small for the task; the lion gagged as if it were being doped, and he had to work at the mouth as if he were hollowing a melon. The other lion he carried across his shoulders; along with handling the fiery hoop, this was apparently his least favorite interlude. The youngster itself didn't like the procedure either, and grim-aced but didn't dare quarrel when Holzmair caught hold of its throat. Like Baumann with his pet tiger, he could hardly control these two, having never dared beat them, and resorted to tidbits to make them move.

With the motorized brigade Holzmair was in command, persuading the toughest of them to charge while he held the flaming hoop, and not only to leap through it but also through a circle he formed clasping the whip above his head. Whereas Gunther's nakedness, expensively costumed, was sexy, his, clothed like a slave's, set off sadistic reverberations and emphasized the violence of the act—we were supposed to imagine him torn. Yet he was more ferocious than the lions, in fact; they watched him pass with frank apprehension, just as the rest of us might anticipate trouble from a loose lion. His every motion increased the racket; the snarls were a demon's snore. Ears back, faces flat, sweating from their mouths and streaming urine, the lionesses turned themselves into tunnels to roar. Twisting their heads to bellow from new angles, they thudded down off their stools and charged, as big as titans—but so was he. This was man's earliest image of wild beasts and how to undo them; this was how ancient lion tamers sneered and strode. An actor, a primitive, Holzmair carried one stiff prod and one long-distance lash, and most spectacular of all, as a finale he pushed the swarm of them into an ulcerous turmoil and then stood straddling the cage's outlet when the gate opened so that in exiting they had to dash through his legs.

Tigers would fly off the handle if hectored so. Not being creatures of habit, and without the communal bond, they don't weather bullying. Like other cats, they are not

168

overly bright. The reason a house cat cannot be trained to do many things is not only its "independence," it just isn't as smart as a dog. Cats are supremely equipped physically and have a simplified, well-defined personality that enhances their bodies' efficiency. The great cats, too, are miracles of physicality, a special version of the life-force continuous since the Oligocene; and Gebel-Williams from boyhood gravitated to an interpretive role, not putting them down but drawing them out.

Every part of his act is a refinement of the usual manner in which tigers are presented. When they take their places on the pyramid of pedestals to show off their coats, each tiger does not head for the closest perch, but goes roundabout to the farthest, so that the crowd sees an extravagant moil. While some roll over and over on the ground, others leapfrog over them in a simulation of the way a litter plays; and when they vault between springboards, Gunther varies this familiar maneuver by stationing a tiger in the middle and having the rest alternately bound over it, dart under it and dodge around in front— a playful effect that seems almost voluntary, in which no imitative momentum is set up. He encourages a male to waltz to the band music—a matter of boxing with him in a comradely fashion—using the butt of his whip. Horses and elephants are often forced to dance by disciplinary means, but tigers cannot be handled so easily because if they become fearful or fly into a fury they move faster and faster. He coaxes hard enthusiastic swipes out of one cat, then moves to the largest tiger, which lunges up on its hind legs, topping him by a couple of feet, and roars and

lashes at a stick he lifts, jumping awkwardly but awe-
somely toward him as he backs up. Since the tiger looms
grand as a dinosaur, roars like an inferno and is not laid
low as a result, the sight is not offensive as is sometimes
the case when trainers stage heroic scenes.

Gunther's tigers are mostly males, because a male,
though surly and slow, is bigger—*"more tiger,"* as he says,
measuring with his arms. They smell like rye bread
smeared with Roquefort cheese. He chants and sings like
Glenn Gould as he works with them, swinging back and
forth, drawing murmuring rumbles and air-blast roars.
Tigers growl softly but roar far more explosively than lions
do. He spreads his arms wide so the animals have both of
them to keep track of, as well as watching his face; it's
like having two assistants in the ring. He holds his whips
in one hand, butt and lash reversed, and pets tiger chins
with the other, grinning like a lapsed angel, a satyr—it's
a lean V face, the flat planes cut for mischief and glee, or
a big-eyed lemur's, a tree-dweller's face. Singing and chat-
tering, he composes their ladylike lunges into a fluttering
of stripes, touching his forehead with his fingers in a
Hindu salute to acknowledge applause, and kneels the-
atrically while the tigers sit. Throwing sawdust on their
turds so that he won't slip, he pitches his whip like a
jokester, his crucifix bouncing on his bare chest, his eyes
big and round, organizing them into a jungle trot. They
look bulky as bulls, but when he bats them they rise into
a pussy pose, paws up. "Ziva!" he calls, running to one,
mimicking the twitch of her white cheeks and black
mouth, and stroking her rump. "Hubblebay!" he says, and

they all revolve. The band accelerates into a keynote of victory.

Maybe the loveliest moment is when Gunther simply has them walk: not a feat many trainers would consider exciting or could even achieve by the adversary technique. Two leave their pedestals and promenade as they might alongside a water hole. He induces another pair to join them—but counterposed—the two pairs passing in the center of the cage. Then he gets the other four to join in, crisscrossing as in Chinese checkers before lining up in formation like the spokes of a wheel. Round and round they slink, keeping abreast, looking up at him, delaying behind the band to exercise their claws (tigers never "march").

Bidding this group good-by, he welcomes a middle-aged, equable tiger, redder than most, and fluffing and scratching it, introduces two elephants, an African with tusks and an Indian one without. The Indian voices its aversion in squeals, the African is indifferent to the tiger, having perhaps inherited no feelings about it one way or the other. The tiger springs to the howdah that each of them carries, down to the ground and up again, then leaps between them, back and forth, finally mounting a platform near the roof of the cage, and jumps again onto the African's back. Gunther directs all this choreography only by words, sitting at his ease on the ring curbing and watching. The elephants and tiger mount three pedestals and rotate quietly as he talks to them; he tugs on the African's tusks and feeds it a loaf of Italian bread. The band plays traditional Spartan brass, the tiger mounts the African

171

elephant again, and so does Gunther, his face in a Pan-like grin. He sits on the tiger, and leaning over, tugs its tufted chin, rubs its eyes and lips, and has it roar elegantly into his face. Then he and the tiger drop down to the ground, the elephants leave the cage, and he fondles the cat, tickling its black lips and its orange rump. Then he sits lightly astride its hips and rides it across the stage at a lumbering gallop, a sight not often seen.

Combining the elephants with the tiger is an exploit no rival trainer has managed to duplicate in the six years since Gunther first did it. He himself gave up trying at one point. Unlike horses, elephants are much too powerful to hold still, and the Indian elephant went crazy with fear. Gunther says he probably could train anything, "even mice—only you yourself must a little change." The limitations of a tiger act make it come to seem static and stylized as a Noh play; yet he dislikes training other animals. Bears hold their swinging heads inscrutably low, and have tiny eyes and a locking dentition. If he put lions into his act there would be fights, a challenge which doesn't interest him. Nor does he want to try riding a moose or training hyenas or tapirs. Like a gifted young man at a standstill stage, he seems not to have any plans for what he will do with his abilities, only for what he may do with the money he earns. He has a few scars, for which he blames himself. "You get very close to play, but one time it is not possible." He wears a red robe that says "Animal Trainer," and aimless and ebullient, drives his Toronado around town, honking at friends.

The elephants please him. He has one wise female who

runs from a distance and tromps accurately on the teeter-board on which he's poised, flinging him into a somersault to land on her back. "Hup-hup!" he yells, sliding down by way of her trunk and front legs. The *Colonel Bogey March* switches to *Elephant Boogie,* and all twenty elephants rush out in a line for the final parade, clutching each other's tails with their trunks. Gunther runs and runs, directing the herd with his hands and voice, sorting them into different rings as they fly by. They curl their trunks in, wave their ears and perform practically on their own while he talks and talks, directing them. His wife, Sigrid, swings on a rope held by two elephants while the others gnomishly do a jig. When Gunther shouts over the waterfall of applause they all heave themselves up on their hind legs, like whales of the earth, each one balancing herself with her front feet on her neighbor's rear.

The band slides from minor to major key for the finale; the trombones fluff-fluff, the trumpets blow like blue sky, the elephants stomp like mahogany. Shy-seeming skittering people turn into troupers as the lights hit them. All of the stars come out to recapitulate the evening. Alert showgirls ride by on gray horses, and guys in drag wear flapping shoes that extend out like dachshunds in front of them. Tumblers turn cartwheels relentlessly, and aerialists scramble up ladders, their spangled costumes glittering off the ceiling. And they're all smiling because it's the night of the teardown and they're leaving your town.

KNIGHTS AND SQUIRES:
FOR LOVE OF
THE TUGS

The greatest sightseeing jaunt in New York City is to cross Brooklyn Bridge on the footway, which is raised above the vehicular traffic, a relic of the day when pedestrians were thought to be gentlemen and had at least equal footing with horses and buggies. The bridge is constructed of beautiful sandstone pillars, gothically arched, and cables which cross one another as in a fish net but which are engineered into gigantic parallel harps. "I love you, Hart Crane!" somebody has written up there, and it is kingly, it's like skywalking, with the architecture of a couple of centuries crammed into the enclave of downtown Manhattan, and the harbor out past Governor's Island glinting like platinum when the sun is right. If you like beaches, maybe the pleasantest beach within the city is South Beach on Staten Island, bordering the Narrows. Take the ferry—the floating hatbox—and a No. 2 bus. The small-town reliefs and relaxants of Staten Island are finally disappearing and we have in their place Verrazano Bridge, with a long, low, regal trajectory, as splendid and cool as mathematics is.

But by early summer I, for one, become something of a menace to myself. Spring fever isn't the word for it; I want to get to the country. Impatiently, I don't bother looking for cars when I cross the street, my favorite parks hardly hold me, and while these great bridges, triumphs of tension and engineering, and the real pitch pipes of a maritime city, boost me out of the banging streets for a minute, they make me squint because they perform a balancing act I can't perform—that kinetic balancing. Eventually, what I do is to call up the Moran tugboat company and ask to go out on one of their boats for the day. They're Irish believers in brotherhood, and year after year they benignly agree.

Moran, which is an old paternal firm closely involved in New York harbor politics, has been pressed by its competition lately and its personnel no longer effuse quite the confident air of a local navy. But compared to the other freeholders of the life of the city, the tugs have kept a remarkable independence. A Huck Finn type wouldn't feel any more crowded on board now than in the days before the invention of radios when the boats sold water and chandlers' stores and waited outside the Narrows to bargain with every ship's captain as to what he would pay to be escorted in. ("Big storm comin'!") When you watch from the shore, the boatmen pop in and out of hatches and cause visual tricks in moving around. If they walk forward they accentuate the rush of the tug and look to be wearing Bunyan boots, whereas, going aft, they are a study in conflicting motions, striding so fast yet apparently standing still. And when you see a tug steam down the North River against the backdrop of the Palisades—it's a wide Adirondack river smelling of fir forests and mountain streams poured together (among other things)—the rustic tug coasts down like a square trader's raft, painted rough colors and draped with those pelty hemp fenders that look as brown and chop-edged and sloppy and wild as so many beaver furs or big bear-skins.

Moran boats are barn-red with black stacks exhibiting a prominent white M. They deal with most of the ocean-going ships and do a good part of the other work of the harbor as well—pushing the garbage, fuel and traprock barges, sand scows, lighters, dredges, coal buckets. Moran operates towboats down the Atlantic seaboard to New Orleans, Bermuda and Puerto Rico, and in the Erie Canal; here in New York they have twenty to thirty boats working. Each one is a corporation, to limit lawsuit liability, and each is crewed by three men for a shift, besides a cook. Some are round-the-clock boats and some are "day boats," which go out in the morning and come in at night, with long but varied hours according to the work scheduled. For a twelve-hour day a captain's base pay is around $75 and a deckhand's perhaps $50. A captain who handles shipping, however, is also a docking pilot, earning a separate fee for each ship that he docks. The fee is determined by the ship's length ($10 per 100 feet) and goes into a pool with all the fees other docking pilots in the harbor have earned, to be divvied up at the end of the month like the spoils of a World Series team. Though there are half and quarter shares, experienced pilots may make $40,000 a year. "I don't even let myself think about it," says the public relations man.

Ten years ago I was reading the *Journal American* in tugboat galleys, and five years ago the *Daily Mirror*, and recently I went to the Battery again and was led aboard the *Teresa Moran*, a new, 4290-horsepower, round-the-clock boat which had just changed crews, as it does every other day. Captain Biagi was to pilot the *United States* from its slip in the North River at noon. Earlier in the morning, according to the log, the *Teresa* had docked the *Raeffaello* and sailed the tanker *Stolt Falcon*. Biagi's back hurt because he'd been raking fertilizer into his lawn the day before; he's peppy, talkative, competent, clever, and lives in East Brunswick, New Jersey. His co-captain, also licensed as a pilot, was Ray Carella. Carella, who started on the Erie Canal at sixteen as a deckhand, now lives in East Meadow, Long Island, but is a gaunter, less assured, somber man. Throughout the day the two of them shared the piloting jobs so that both would stand well in the pool. The deckhands were Ture Eklund, a soft-spoken, civilized fellow who lives in Westchester County and builds model boats, and Walter Anglim, a raw-boned, rugged American sort. The two engineers were Tom Rasmussen—young, gangly and energetic—and Joe Gallant, a husky, hard-headed old customer; the cook was Candy Coelho, a

177

Portuguese who is a veteran of forty-four years on the tugs, though his tightly smooth face doesn't show it. He and Biagi and Gallant told stories of the Depression.

The assignments came at two-hour intervals instead of an hour apart, as they often do. We made no extended trips to Newark or Constable Hook or into the Kills, didn't get tangled in Newton Creek, Brooklyn, or spend the day locked into Wallabout Bay. The nearest tug to a job usually gets it, so you can spend a whole shift just in the thickets of Red Hook, emptying slip after slip and filling them up again. The railroads have their own tugs, as do the principal oil companies, but the free-lance tugboats handle the freighters and do the hundreds of queer little noncom jobs in the back corners, hauling copper and newsprint, and stopping along the way as a favor to somebody, to tell the *Gunvor Brovig*, for instance, which is anchored off Rosebank, that a Sandy Hook pilot should be getting to her about four o'clock—her radio's off.

The *United States*, though the biggest of ships, is not a particularly memorable proposition among all the tasks that come to a tug. We were helped by the *Esther Moran*, which tied onto the stem: we were at the bow, with Carella in the wheelhouse. Captain Biagi, on the ship's bridge, gave his directions by walkie-talkie, each tug answering with its peep whistle to confirm that the order was understood. Two longshoremen cast the hawsers off, and the ship, its engines reversed, provided its own motive power, while the *Teresa* and *Esther* kept it clear of

178

the pier. Especially at the Manhattan piers, which are finger wharfs, built at right angles to the river, undocking a ship is a great deal simpler than docking it. The ship has been moored bow-in, so the tug which is at the bow only acts as a rudder as the ship backs away. In a kind of a dance, the *Teresa* nudged first one side of the stem, then the other—the stem looming overhead as sharp as a blade. There were acres of black steel plating, rivets in twisting patterns, and the two anchors like a whale's eyes. The ship blasted its whistle to warn any traffic on the river and in no time it had backed into the current, whereupon the two tugs pushed it around ninety degrees to head towards the sea. Compared to the rigamarole of warping a big ship into its slip, this was easy as kicking your shoes off, though we did have to bustle over to the pier once again, and out to the ship, and then back over to the pier again in a comedy routine because a bevy of voyagers had missed the gangplank and some partying visitors on board the ship had gotten drunk and forgotten to leave.

Afterwards Biagi called 17 Battery Place for the next assignment, and we were sent around Lower Manhattan and up the East River to an oil depot at 138th Street in the East Bronx to sail the Liberian tanker *St. Grigorousa*. I went to the engine room with Rasmussen, who wears earmuffs, and examined the twin diesel engines, the steering mechanism, the air compressors, but I couldn't pay much attention, becoming panic-stricken as I was painfully deafened. However, the cabins are comfortable places, and the wheelhouse has high-legged chairs and lots of windows amidst all the radar equipment and compasses. The radio drawled messages to the other tugs in a comradely fashion: "Seventeen to the *Harriet*"; "Seventeen to the *Eugenia*." A brusque rainy wind blew outside, and the ebb tide boiled spray at our bow. Manhattan is variegated, sway-backed and dumpy as you go by, not composed of monolithic glass towers, and the piers are almost all ramshackle; yet in a way the view is encouraging because from the water New York does not have the appearance of a city destroying itself—there is just too much of it. Even the loss of a specific harborside landmark like the razing of the Fulton Fish Market will scarcely be noticeable from out on the water.

A silent back stretch, 138th Street is beyond Hellgate Bridge, off Sunken Meadows and by North Brothers Island, where the planes sweep low every thirty seconds to land at LaGuardia Airport. The *St. Grigorousa,* scruffy, patch-painted, offered no problems, except that our tug in maneuvering got careless and snapped a few pilings on an adjoining dock. The Greeks on the ship watched this little miscalculation with the attention which seamen of different nationalities bestow on each other's blunders. Anglim had had trouble throwing a line up on deck, and that interested them too. They were unwashed, unsmiling, windblown, and they had a nubile-looking young boy aboard.

A bit past Gracie Mansion, while we were accompanying them downriver, Biagi still piloting on the bridge of the ship, we saw the *Marie Moran,* the *Patricia Moran* and the *Esther* pushing against the broad side of a lumber boat, the *Seamar* from Coos Bay, Oregon, which had managed to draw parallel with its pier but was unable to approach closer. This was at Green Street, in Brooklyn. The radio told us to go to its assistance quickly, the captain of the *St. Grigorousa* gave his permission, and in a moment the Greeks had let our line down. Without waiting for Biagi to come off the ship, we swung away, and putting our bow amidships on the *Seamar,* shoved full ahead for what amounted to nearly an hour. Our extra horsepower did stop the drifting, but then no more progress was made, though the four tugs shifted position and pushed as hard as they could. First the outflowing tide had been the villain, but soon it was just a case of the ship being so heavily loaded that her keel was touching the bottom; we were trying to push her into a list sufficient to bring her deck close to the dock where the cranes would be able to unload her. It was a tedious business; the tug captains talked back and forth on the radio and talked to the pilot, who was from the *Patricia.*

Until recently walkie-talkies weren't used from ship to tug. Instead, the pilot signaled a tugboat at the bow of the ship by blowing codes on an ordinary police whistle. One whistle meant half speed ahead; several shorts, full ahead; two shorts, two shorts meant slow. The tug would repeat the message on its peeper, and then the pilot would signal the tugs at the stern with the ship's own deep-throated, significant whistle, which they promptly answered, all in the same code: so the harbor has lost some of the chatter it had.

Finally we left the *Teresa*'s three sisters shouldering

the *Seamar* and headed for Governor's Island to pick up Biagi, who had been deposited on a small barge boat called the *Lester,* as we were told. A German freighter, the *Hilde Mittman,* was traveling beside us as we entered the curve that the East River makes near Delancey Street. At the same time, however, a tug called the *Carol Moran* was coming upriver, as well as a Penn Central Railroad tug which was roped between two unwieldy carfloats. The *Hilde* was outside of us and signaled them both to go outside of her—or, in other words, closer to Brooklyn —but the *Carol* swerved inside instead, between the *Hilde Mittman* and us. The *Hilde* had to veer toward the railroad tug suddenly, and the railroad tug was almost forced into a pier on the Brooklyn side of the river— trying to avoid a collision, she reversed engines and swung dangerously sideways, and the bow lines on one of the carfloats broke. The *Carol* went on, the *Hilde* went on, but we lingered a moment or two to see whether she needed help.

Our next job, not scheduled till six o'clock, was to help a McAllister tug sail the freighter *Fraternity,* registered in Monrovia, from Pier 1 in the Erie Basin. We passed a good many ships in berths on the way: the *Alamahdi,* the *Concordia Lago,* the *Lexa Maersk,* the *Lichtenfels.* A paint-company launch puttered by, towing rafts and scaffolding; also a union launch collecting dues from the barge and the lighter men whom it encountered. The sun had come out, the weather was warming up genially. Tugboats ride very low in the water, with the stubby bow pushing waves that are higher than the decks. It was a lovely, foamy, noisy trip. Standing on the fantail, I had the sense I was aquaplaning, a feeling of victory. "How are you doing—meditating?" asked Eklund.

Erie Basin is a narrow, rectangular, concrete facility with a narrow hole for an entrance which lies in South Brooklyn not far beyond Buttermilk Channel. There were at least six other ships in there, and one of the captains stepped out in his shirtsleeves on the bridge to lean on the railing and watch the work, in case any sideswiping occurred. McAllister tugs are parvenus that have taken a good deal of business away from Moran lately, so some rather elaborate courtesies ensued between the *Helen McAllister* and us. "At your service, Captain." "Surely, Captain." But we squeezed the *Fraternity* out of its slip and through the hole of the basin without difficulty. Eklund, a relaxed man, worked with brief motions, snuggling the thick Dacron line around the horns of the bitt as easily as if he were tightening his belt. He added coils to snub it fast, funneling the tugboat's power through the stretching rope—which makes a sinister sound like a rattlesnake's rattle—or loosening and changing the coils during the lax interludes when the tug, on instructions, floated at dead stop. Since the foredeck of the tug is short, he worked ten feet inboard, watching not the ship but the rope. And when the tug's rumbling engines announced another session of physics, he tossed several more coils on the bitt, watching them writhe and creak and tighten.

The sailors threw down our line. The McAllister man, who had been the pilot, climbed over the rail and down a ladder, leaving the Sandy Hook pilot in charge. It's always a sharply focused instant when a ship separates from the tugs. Water slashed in as the gap opened; the wind seemed to blow harder, no longer blocked by the ship, and it was an ocean wind. For the first time, the ship's screw kicked up a deep, worldly froth, a green wake, and the *Fraternity* pointed away, leaving us where we were.

There are about a hundred and forty-five Sandy Hook pilots, who guide the ships in and out of New York, from the Sea Buoy off Sandy Hook to the Battery or to the vicinity of the pier. They are paid a fee of $10 per foot of draft by the shipping company, so routinely they may make $250 per ship, but out of that they must pay the expenses of their profession—the pilot boat and crew—and they get no additional salary, such as a docking pilot receives from Moran. As often as not, the Sandy Hook pilot, the tugboat pilot and the ship's master spend their half hour together on the ship's bridge exchanging stock-market tips—at least I've often heard a tug captain come down the ladder and say that's what they'd talked about, complaining because the ship's master only knew about foreign stocks.

We were told to wait awhile in the Gowanus Canal for an eight o'clock job. The cook fed us cube steak and beet salad. Years ago, when I was younger and hungrier, part of my pleasure was the feasts on a tugboat. The cooks buy their own food on an allowance of three dollars a day for each crew member, but the money went further then and the meals were baronial. A first course of herring in wine sauce, honeydew melon, shrimp cocktail, pickles and olives, soup and a choice of juices, all of them served simultaneously. A main course of roast beef, roast lamb, fillet of sole, macaroni and cheese and cold cuts, plus corn, squash, peas, lima beans, two salads, two kinds of potatoes. And there would be pies, rice pudding, a cake, ice cream, brownies, date bread, iced and hot drinks, Camembert cheese, and canned and new fruit. "Goes with the meal. Eat up. That's the best meat right next to the bone," the Norwegian cook used to say, bending over and pointing or pouring gravy, crushing an empty milk carton in his other hand.

Anglim and Eklund took the opportunity to hook a hose to the hydrant there in Gowanus and freshen the water tanks. The *Aqua*, an antique Victorian steam-driven boat that peddles water throughout the harbor, waited her turn alongside. Since the Canal is laughably tortuous and is filled with ships, you can get stuck there working all night. But the *Kerry Moran* was heading our way from Bush Terminal, so she was switched to our post and we were asked to move on across the Upper Bay to Pier F in Jersey City, which faces some of the grass-grown, abandoned piers of Lower Manhattan. En route we stopped like responsible citizens to tie up three Lehigh Valley barges that had broken loose from a dock. We saw a large fire in the Houston Street area, and I wrote down more names of ships that we passed: the *Covadonga*, the *Nordfarer*, the *Baie Comeau*, the *Cap Norte*, the *Todos os Santos*, the *Cyril*, an almanac of the world.

The *Baltic Sea* (Goteborg) was our new eight o'clock

ship. Eklund heaved up the throwing line, which has a ball on the end so that it will hang over the ship's rail until it's retrieved. Since the ship was white, he put a white cloth over our bow, where we would rub paint. Up on deck the silent Swedes with their beards and curly blond hair and muted manner looked down at us, though their captain was pacing restlessly. We waited three quarters of an hour while they finished swinging cargo aboard and setting the hatches to rights. Tugboatmen kill these odd bits of time with cards, and tying up all over the harbor, they know little waterfront stores everywhere which can be reached by froghopping over a series of pilings and climbing a fence or two. Then Carella, as pilot, performed a simple and classic softshoe undocking from Pier F "into the stream," as they say, scrambling down to the *Teresa* again while the Swedes watched. The ship had its running lights on, green on the starboard and red on the port, and the uncountable lights of Manhattan were emerging in all their bravado as the dusk darkened. The water churned between ship and tug; the sea breeze struck us as we slid clear of the ship—the mystically warm-and-cold wind of May.

At sunset we took our flag down, still flying snappily. Our nine-thirty job was to bull back to Greenpoint again and help the *Joan Moran* sail the *Ixia,* an English timber boat. The spray plumed like cream at our bow, and the water was like crinkled tinfoil. The lights of the city were like jubilant news. They were flung out so far that what can one say? They're not man-made; they're the work of some several millions of men. The lights in the office buildings are a blunt blind yellow, blaring into the muffling night, but the lights of Stuyvesant Town and the other big centers of home life are like stippled banks of amber, glowing. I sat on the capstan in the stern, and it was like a whole screwy radar screen. It's so dazzling that one's eyes go dead every minute or so, looking. You can't take it in; you look till your eyes go blank, turn them away to the darker water, and then look again at the sweep of it and the shining water, until again your vision wilts and goes dead.

Over the radio Moran headquarters relayed a suggestion from the *Margot* that we catch up with a self-propelled barge that was running past Williamsburg with virtually no lights on and tell her to hang up a few extra lanterns. But when we did so, the barge captain came out of his cabin and screamed that the regulations had changed and that his dim arrangements were satisfactory. Our captains didn't believe this, so there was some billingsgate of a kind, but since the *Teresa* is not the Coast Guard, we soon went on. Barge captains are the fallen men of the harbor, old drinkers with sorrowful decades at sea behind them, whom you always take care to address as "Captain" every sentence or two.

We roused the mate of the *Ixia* by shining a spotlight along the portholes, then used it to read the draft of the ship for the Sandy Hook pilot so that he would know what he ought to charge. In the spotlight a leaping reindeer on the smokestack came alive, and the smoke, bowel-gray, bulged out of the stack, vaulting and rolling. You don't see so much smoke ashore nowadays. Sometimes I used to go to 13th Street and Avenue D expressly to watch the smoke from the Con Ed stacks jump, flatten, and jump again.

The *Ixia's* hawsers, cast off, hit the water with the smack of rifle reports. Though she is a trim short ship, the slip was narrow, with the heel of another ship just off our stern. The tide was turning, as well; the *Joan's* skipper, acting as pilot, negotiated cautiously. At last, when the ship had been eased out enough, she could start to use her own screw, booting herself briskly out into the stream. We pushed hard on her stern and the *Joan* threw another 4000 horses the opposite way at her bow in order to face her around. The British seamen looked over the rail and let our line down. Their loudspeaker crackled orders to them; and the wind seemed to hit us from the North Sea.

The Moran dispatcher told us to head downriver while he figured out what else to have us do. Finally he said we would have a one-o'clock job—that we should go to Stapleton, Staten Island, and wait for the *Atlantic Saga,* a container ship, which, along with the *Kerry,* we were going to accompany to Port Elizabeth, New Jersey, and dock.

But I shouldn't say "we" any more, because I was dropped off on South Street along the way. Captain Biagi had told me a number of stories that he said I shouldn't print, but now he said that his grandfather had gone on an expedition into the Andes— ". . . one of the first men that ever went into there. And they got lost in the snow. Only two men of the bunch ever came out, you know, including him. And, do you know, he was saved by a St. Bernard dog? That damn dog licking his face. So I owe my life to a St. Bernard! What do you think about that?"

I stood on the bow fender and climbed over the rail at Pier 9, East River, waving good-by and shaking hands, worn out, exuberant, and caught a bus home.

Ten years ago the captains I rode with were Irishmen. In the wheelhouse there was an Irish Mafia, and down in the engine room were the Germans and Danes, usually old merchant seamen who knew the world. The captains lived in Queens Village and looked like Ed Sullivan, and since they'd just started to make lots of money, handling their finances rather scared them, perhaps more than their duties did. I remember one deckhand who was Italian and lived on Prince Street in the Lower East Side and played boccie on his days off. He had just won a bet with his bookie at odds of 140 to 1, but the bookie had only paid off at 50 to 1, claiming that more wasn't possible. It was thought to be part of the fellow's backwardness that he accepted treatment like this from a bookie, or still to be betting on the horses at all, instead of on the market, and playing boccie with the old immigrants. Then the Irishmen would look from him up at the trim heathen Japanese sailors on the many Japanese ships that came in and wonder what in the hell was happening to America that they'd let all these Nips sail into the harbor as freely as that. The captain would clamber down off the ship after docking her, and slanting his eyes with his fingers, imitate the Japanese master gabbling, and do a duckwalk.

There are almost no Negroes on the boats yet. As we went down Manhattan from 23rd Street, every light in the office buildings was on—ranks and ladders of lights like a thousand trombones. All Harlem was there; the cleaning women were working. And the whole city stood on end for me, the light pricks of darkest Brooklyn, the whole grandslam convulsive cacophony. Gradually the black *Ixia* outdistanced us, and a floodlit, ethereal freighter entered the river, as white and as glamorous-looking as some far-ranging knight who can go anywhere and do anything except to stand up or lie down unaided.

DOGS,
AND THE TUG
OF LIFE

It used to be that you could tell just about how poor a family was by how many dogs they had. If they had one, they were probably doing all right. It was only American to keep a dog to represent the family's interests in the intrigues of the back alley; not to have a dog at all would be like not acknowledging one's poor relations. Two dogs meant that the couple were dog lovers, with growing children, but still might be members of the middle class. But if a citizen kept three, you could begin to suspect he didn't own much else. Four or five irrefutably marked the household as poor folk, whose yard was also full of broken cars cannibalized for parts. The father worked not much, fancied himself a hunter; the mother's teeth were black. And an old bachelor living in a shack might possibly have even more, but you knew that if one of them, chasing a moth, didn't upset his oil lamp some night and burn him up, he'd fetch up in the poorhouse soon, with the dogs shot. Nobody got poor feeding a bunch of dogs, needless to say, because the more dogs a man had, the less he fed them. Foraging as a pack, they led an existence of their own, but served as evidence that life was awfully lonesome for him and getting out of hand. If a dog really becomes a man's best friend his situation is desperate.

That dogs, low-comedy confederates of small children and ragged bachelors, should have turned into an emblem of having made it to the middle class—like the hibachi, like golf clubs and a second car—seems at the very least incongruous. Puppies which in the country you would have to carry in a box to the church fair to give away are bringing seventy-five dollars apiece in some of the pet stores, although in fact dogs are in such oversupply that one hundred and fifty thousand are running wild in New York City alone.

There is another line of tradition about dogs, however. Show dogs, toy dogs, foxhounds for formal hunts, Doberman guard dogs, bulldogs as ugly as a queen's dwarf. An aristocratic Spanish lady once informed me that when she visits her Andalusian estate each fall the mastiffs rush out and fawn about her but would tear to pieces any of the servants who have accompanied her from Madrid. In Mississippi it was illegal for a slave owner to permit his slaves to have a dog, just as it was to teach them how to read. A "negro dog" was a hound trained by a bounty hunter to ignore the possums, raccoons, hogs and deer in the woods that other dogs were supposed to chase, and trail and tree a runaway. The planters themselves, for whom hunting was a principal recreation, whooped it up when a man unexpectedly became their quarry. They caught each other's slaves and would often sit back and let the dogs do the punishing. Bennet H. Barrow of West Feliciana Parish in Louisiana, a rather moderate and representative plantation owner, recounted in his diary of the 1840s, among several similar incidents, this for November 11, 1845: In "5 minutes had him up & a going, And never in my life did I ever see as excited beings as R & myself, ran ½ miles & caught him dogs soon tore him naked, took him Home Before the other negro(es) at dark & made the dogs give him another over hauling." Only recently in Louisiana I heard what happened to two Negroes who happened to be fishing in a bayou off the Blind River, where four white men with a shotgun felt like fishing alone. One was forced to pretend to be a scampering coon and shinny up a telephone pole and hang there till he fell, while the other impersonated a baying, bounding hound.

Such memories are not easy to shed, particularly since childhood, the time when people can best acquire a comradeship with animals, is also when they are likely to pick up their parents' fears. A friend of mine hunts quail by jeep in Texas with a millionaire who brings along forty bird dogs, which he deploys in eight platoons that spell each other off. Another friend though, will grow apprehensive at a dinner party if the host lets a dog loose in the room. The toothy, mysterious creature lies dreaming on the carpet, its paws pulsing, its eyelids open, the nictitating membranes twitching; how can he be certain it won't suddenly jump up and attack his legs under the table? Among Eastern European Jews, possession of a dog was associated with the hard-drinking *goyishe* peasantry, traditional antagonists, or else with the gentry, and many carried this dislike to the New World. An immigrant fleeing a potato famine or the hunger of Calabria might be no more equipped with the familiar British-German partiality to dogs—a failing which a few rugged decades in a great city's slums would not necessarily mend. The city had urbanized plenty of native farmers' sons as well, and so it came about that what to rural America had been the humblest, most natural amenity—friendship with a dog —has been transmogrified into a piece of the jigsaw of moving to the suburbs: there to cook outdoors, another bit of absurdity to the old countryman, whose toilet was outdoors but who was pleased to be able to cook and eat his meals inside the house.

There are an estimated forty million dogs in the United States (nearly two for every cat). Thirty-seven thousand of them are being destroyed in humane institutions every day, a figure which indicates that many more are in trouble. Dogs are hierarchal beasts, with several million years of submission to the structure of a wolf pack in their breeding. This explains why the Spanish lady's mastiffs can distinguish immediately between the mistress and her retainers, and why it is about as likely that one of the other guests at the dinner party will attack my friend's legs under the table as that the host's dog will, once it has accepted his presence in the room as proper. Dogs need leadership, however; they seek it, and when it's not forthcoming quickly fall into difficulties in a world where they can no longer provide their own.

"Dog" is "God" spelled backwards—one might say, way

backwards. There's "a dog's life," "dog days," "dog-sick," "dog-tired," "dog-cheap," "dog-eared," "doghouse," and "dogs" meaning villains or feet. Whereas a wolf's stamina was measured in part by how long he could go without water, a dog's is becoming a matter of how long he can *hold* his water. He retrieves a rubber ball instead of coursing deer, chases a broom instead of hunting marmots. His is the lowest form of citizenship: that tug of life at the end of the leash is like the tug at the end of a fishing pole, and then one doesn't have to kill it. On stubby, amputated-looking feet he leads his life, which if we glance at it attentively is a kind of cutout of our own, all the more so for being riskier and shorter. Bam! A member of the family is dead on the highway, as we expected he would be, and we just cart him to the dump and look for a new pup.

Simply the notion that he lives on four legs instead of two has come to seem astonishing—like a goat or cow wearing horns on its head. And of course to keep a dog is a way of attempting to bring nature back. The primitive hunter's intimacy, telepathy, with the animals he sought, surprising them at their meals and in their beds, then stripping them of their warm coats to expose a frame so like our own, is all but lost. Sport hunters, especially the older ones, retain a little of it still; and naturalists who have made up their minds not to kill wild animals nevertheless appear to empathize primarily with the predators at first, as a look at the tigers, bears, wolves, mountain lions on the project list of an organization such as the World Wildlife Fund will show. This is as it should be, these creatures having suffered from our brotherly envy before. But in order to really enjoy a dog, one doesn't merely try to train him to be semihuman. The point of it is to open oneself to the possibility of becoming partly a dog (after all, there are plenty of sub- or semi-human beings around whom we don't wish to adopt). One wants to rediscover the commonality of animal and man—to see an animal eat and sleep that hasn't forgotten how to enjoy doing such things—and the directness of its loyalty.

The trouble with the current emphasis on preserving "endangered species" is that, however beneficial to wildlife the campaign works out to be, it makes all animals seem like museum pieces, worth saving for sentimental considerations and as figures of speech (to "shoot a sitting duck"), but as a practical matter already dead and gone. On the contrary, some animals are flourishing. In 1910 half a million deer lived in the United States, in 1960 seven million, in 1970 sixteen million. What has happened is that now that we don't eat them we have lost that close interest.

Wolf behavior prepared dogs remarkably for life with human beings. So complete and complicated was the potential that it was only a logical next step for them to quit their packs in favor of the heady, hopeless task of trying to keep pace with our own community development. The contortions of fawning and obeisance which render group adjustment possible among such otherwise forceful fighters—sometimes humping the inferior members into the shape of hyenas—are what squeezes them past our tantrums, too. Though battling within the pack

196

is mostly accomplished with body checks that do no damage, a subordinate wolf bitch is likely to remain so in awe of the leader that she will cringe and sit on her tail in response to his amorous advances, until his female co-equal has had a chance to notice and dash over and redirect his attention. Altogether, he is kept so busy asserting his dominance that this top-ranked female may not be bred by him, finally, but by the male which occupies the second rung. Being breadwinners, dominant wolves feed first and best, just as we do, so that to eat our scraps and leavings strikes a dog as normal procedure. Nevertheless, a wolf puppy up to eight months old is favored at a kill, and when smaller can extract a meal from any pack member—uncles and aunts as well as parents—by nosing the lips of the adult until it regurgitates a share of what it's had. The care of the litter is so much a communal endeavor that the benign sort of role we expect dogs to play within our own families toward children not biologically theirs comes naturally to them.

For dogs and wolves the tail serves as a semaphore of mood and social code, but dogs carry their tails higher than wolves do, as a rule, which is appropriate, since the excess spirits that used to go into lengthy hunts now have no other outlet than backyard negotiating. In addition to an epistolary anal gland, whose message-carrying function has not yet been defined, the anus itself, or stool when sniffed, conveys how well the animal has been eating— in effect, its income bracket—although most dog foods are sorrily monotonous compared to the hundreds of tastes a wolf encounters, perhaps dozens within the carcass of a single moose. We can speculate on a dog's powers of taste because its olfactory area is proportionately fourteen times larger than a man's, its sense of smell at least a hundred times as keen.

The way in which a dog presents his anus and genitals for inspection indicates the hierarchal position that he aspires to, and other dogs who sniff his genitals are apprised of his sexual condition. From his urine they can undoubtedly distinguish age, build, state of sexual activity and general health, even hours after he's passed by. Male dogs dislike running out of urine, as though an element of potency were involved, and try to save a little; they prefer not to use a scent post again until another dog has urinated there, the first delight and duty of the ritual being to stake out a territory, so that when they are walked hurriedly in the city it is a disappointment to them. The search is also sexual, because bitches in heat post notices about. In the woods a dog will mark his drinking places, and watermark a rabbit's trail after chasing it, as if to notify the next predator that happens by exactly who it was that put such a whiff of fear into the rabbit's scent. Similarly, he squirts the tracks of bobcats and of skunks with an aloof air unlike his brisk and cheery manner of branding another dog's or fox's trail, and if he is in a position to do so, will defecate excitedly on a bear run, leaving behind his best effort, which no doubt he hopes will strike the bear as a bombshell.

The chief complaint people lodge against dogs is their extraordinary stress upon lifting the leg and moving the bowels. Scatology did take up some of the slack for them when they left behind the entertainments of the forest. The forms of territoriality replaced the substance. But apart from that, a special zest for life is characteristic of dogs and wolves—in hunting, eating, relieving themselves, in punctiliously maintaining a home territory, a pecking order and a love life, and educating the resulting pups. They grin and grimace and scrawl graffiti with their piss. A lot of inherent strategy goes into these activities: the way wolves spell each other off, both when hunting and in their governess duties around the den, and often "consult" as a pack with noses together and tails wagging before flying in to make a kill. (Tigers, leopards, house cats base their social relations instead upon what ethologists call "mutual avoidance.") The nose is a dog's main instrument of discovery, corresponding to our eyes, and so it is that he is seldom offended by organic smells, such as putrefaction, and sniffs intently for the details of illness, gum bleeding and diet in his master and his fellows, and for the story told by scats, not closing off the avenue for any reason—just as we rarely shut our eyes against new information, even the tragic or unpleasant kind.

Though dogs don't see as sharply as they smell, trainers usually rely on hand signals to instruct them, and most firsthand communication in a wolf pack also seems to be visual—by the expressions of the face, by body english and the cant of the tail. A dominant wolf squares his mouth, stares at and "rides up" on an inferior, standing with his front legs on its back, or will pretend to stalk it, creeping along, taking its muzzle in his mouth, and performing nearly all of the other discriminatory pranks and practices familiar to anybody who has a dog. In fact, what's funny is to watch a homely mutt as tiny as a shoebox spin through the rigmarole which a whole series of observers in the wilderness have gone to great pains to document for wolves.

Dogs proffer their rear ends to each other in an intimidating fashion, but when they examine the region of the head it is a friendlier gesture, a snuffling between pals. One of them may come across a telltale bone fragment caught in the other's fur, together with a bit of mud to give away the location of bigger bones. On the same impulse, wolves and free-running dogs will sniff a wanderer's toes to find out where he has been roaming. They fondle and propitiate with their mouths also, and lovers groom each other's fur with tongues and teeth adept as hands. A bitch wolf's period in heat includes a week of preliminary behavior and maybe two weeks of receptivity— among animals, exceptionally long. Each actual copulative tie lasts twenty minutes or a half an hour, which again may help to instill affection. Wolves sometimes begin choosing a mate as early as the age of one, almost a year before they are ready to breed. Dogs mature sexually a good deal earlier, and arrive in heat twice a year instead of once—at any season instead of only in midwinter, like a wolf, whose pups' arrival must be scheduled unfailingly for spring. Dogs have not retained much responsibility for raising their young, and the summertime is just as perilous as winter for them because, apart from the whimsy of their owners, who put so many of them to sleep, their nemesis is the automobile. Like scatology, sex helps fill the gulf of what is gone.

The scientist David Mech has pointed out how like the posture of a wolf with a nosehold on a moose (as other wolves attack its hams) are the antics of a puppy playing tug-of-war at the end of a towel. Anybody watching a dog's exuberance as it samples bites of long grass beside a brook, or pounds into a meadow bristling with the odors of woodchucks, snowshoe rabbits, grouse, a doe and buck, field mice up on the seedheads of the weeds, kangaroo mice jumping, chipmunks whistling, weasels and shrews on the hunt, a plunging fox, a porcupine couched in a tree, perhaps can begin to imagine the variety of excitements under the sky that his ancestors relinquished in order to move indoors with us. He'll lie down with a lamb to please us, but as he sniffs its haunches, surely he must remember atavistically that this is where he'd start to munch.

There is poignancy in the predicament of a great many animals: as in the simple observation which students of the California condor have made that this huge, most endangered bird prefers the carrion meat of its old standby, the deer, to all the dead cows, sheep, horses and other substitutes it sees from above, sprawled about. Animals are stylized characters in a kind of old saga—stylized because even the most acute of them have little leeway as they play out their parts. (*Rabbits*, for example, I find terribly affecting, imprisoned in their hop.) And as we drift away from any cognizance of them, we sacrifice some of the intricacy and grandeur of life. Having already lost so much, we are hardly aware of what remains, but to a primitive snatched forward from an earlier existence it might seem as if we had surrendered a richness comparable to all the tapestries of childhood. Since this is a matter of the imagination as well as of animal demographics, no Noah projects, no bionomic discoveries on the few sanctuaries that have been established are going to reverse the swing. The very specialists in the forefront of finding out how animals behave, when one meets them, appear to be no more intrigued than any ordinary Indian was.

But we continue to need—as aborigines did, as children do—a parade of morality tales which are more concise than those that politics, for instance, later provides. So we've had Aesop's and medieval and modern fables about the grasshopper and the ant, the tiger and Little Black Sambo, the wolf and the three pigs, Br'er Rabbit and Br'er Bear, Goldilocks and her three bears, Pooh Bear, Babar and the rhinos, Walt Disney's animals, and assorted humbler scary bats, fat hippos, funny frogs and eager beavers. Children have a passion for clean, universal definitions, and so it is that animals have gone with children's literature as Latin has with religion. Through them they first encountered death, birth, their own maternal feelings, the gap between beauty and cleverness, or speed and good intentions. The animal kingdom boasted the powerful lion, the mothering goose, the watchful owl, the tardy tortoise, Chicken Little, real-life dogs that treasure bones, and mink that grow posh pelts from eating crawfish and mussels.

In the cartoons of two or three decades ago, Mouse doesn't get along with Cat because Cat must catch Mouse or miss his supper. Dog, on the other hand, detests Cat for no such rational reason, only the capricious fact that dogs don't dote on cats. Animal stories are bounded, yet enhanced, by each creature's familiar lineaments, just as a parable about a prince and peasant, a duchess and a milk-maid, a blacksmith and a fisherman, would be. Typecast-ing, like the roll of a metered ode, adds resonance and dignity, summoning up all of the walruses and hedgehogs that went before: the shrewd image of Br'er Rabbit to as-sist his suburban relative Bugs Bunny behind the scenes. But now, in order to present a tale about the contest be-tween two thieving crows and a scarecrow, the storyteller would need to start by explaining that once upon a time crows used to eat a farmer's corn if he didn't defend it with a mock man pinned together from old clothes. Crows are having a hard go of it and may soon receive game-bird protection.

One way childhood is changing, therefore, is that the nonhuman figures—"Wild Things" or puppet monsters— constructed by the best of the new artificers, like Maurice Sendak or the *Sesame Street* writers, are distinctly hu-manoid, ballooned out of faces, torsos met on the subway. The televised character Big Bird does not resemble a bird the way Bugs Bunny remained a rabbit—though already he was less so than Br'er or Peter Rabbit. Big Bird's personality, her confusion, haven't the faintest connection to an ostrich's. Lest she be confused with an ostrich, her voice has been slotted unmistakably toward the prosaic. Dr. Seuss did transitional composites of worldwide fauna, but these new shapes—a beanbag like the *Sesame Street* Grouch or Cookie Monster or Herry Monster, and the floral creations in books—have been conceived practically from scratch by the artist ("in the night kitchen," to use a Sendak phrase), and not transferred from the existing caricatures of nature. In their conversational conflicts they offer him a fresh start, which may be a valuable commodity, whereas if he were dealing with an alligator, it would, while giving him an old-fashioned boost in the traditional manner, at the same time box him in. A chap called Alligator, with that fat snout and tail, cannot squirm free of the solidity of actual alligators. Either it must stay a heavyweight or else play on the sternness of reality by swinging over to impersonate a cream puff and a Ferdinand.

Though animal programs on television are popular, what with the wave of nostalgia and "ecology" in the country, we can generally say about the animal kingdom, "The King is dead, long live the King." Certainly the talent has moved elsewhere. Those bulbous Wild Things and slant-mouthed beanbag puppets derived from the denizens of Broadway—an argumentative night news vendor, a lady on a traffic island—have grasped their own destinies, as characters on the make are likely to. It was inevitable they would. There may be a shakedown to remove the elements that would be too bookish for children's literature in other hands, and another shakedown because these first innovators have been more city-oriented than suburban. New authors will shift the character sources away from Broadway and the subway and the ghetto, but the basic switch has already been accomplished—from the ancient juxtaposition of people, animals, and dreams blending the two, to people and monsters that grow solely out of people by way of dreams.

Which leaves us in the suburbs, with dogs as a last link. Cats are too independent to care, but dogs are in an unenviable position, they hang so much upon our good opinion. We are coming to *have* no opinion; we don't pay enough attention to form an opinion. Though they admire us, are thrilled by us, heroize us, we regard them as a hobby or a status symbol, like a tennis racquet, and substitute leash laws for leadership—expect them not simply to learn English but to grow hands, because their beastly paws seem stranger to us every year. If they try to fondle us with their handyjack mouths, we read it as a bite; and like used cars, they are disposed of when the family relocates, changes its "bag," or in the scurry of divorce. The first reason people kept a dog was to acquire an ally on the hunt, a friend at night. Then it was to maintain an avenue to animality, as our own nearness began to recede. But as we lose our awareness of all animals, dogs are becoming a bridge to nowhere. We can only pity their fate.

THE THRESHOLD
AND THE
JOLT OF PAIN

Like most boys in their teens, I wondered once in a while how I would take torture. Badly, I thought. Later I thought not so badly, as I saw myself under the pressures of danger or emergency, once when a lion cub grabbed my hand in its mouth and I wrestled its lips for half a minute with my free hand. Another summer when I fought forest fires in a crew of Indians in the West, we stood up under intense heat and thirst, watching the flames crackle toward us irresistibly while we waited to see whether the fire lines that we had cut were going to hold. I've climbed over the lip of a high waterfall; I've scratched inside a hippopotamus's capacious jaws; I faced a pistol one day in Wyoming with some degree of fortitude. However, I knew that all this élan would vanish if my sex organs were approached. The initiation to join the Boy Scouts in our town was to have one's balls squeezed, so I never joined. Even to have my knuckle joints ground together in a handshake contest reduces me to quick surrender—something about bone on bone. I steered clear of the BB-gun fights in my neighborhood, and I could be caught in a chase and tied up easily by someone slower who yelled as if he were gaining ground, so I made friends with most of the toughies as a defensive measure.

As a boy I was much given to keeping pets and showering care on them, but I had a sadistic streak as well. In boarding school my roommate got asthma attacks when he was jumped on, and I always backed away laughing when his tormentors poured into the room. There was another nice boy whom I seldom picked on myself, and with sincere horror I watched a game grip the Florentine fancy of our corridor. Divided in teams, we would push him back and forth as a human football from goal to goal. The crush at the center, where he was placed, was tremendous, and though no one remembered, I'd invented the game.

My first love affair was with a Philadelphian, a girl of twenty-seven. That is, she was the first girl I slept with. She was a love in the sense that she loved me; I was close and grateful to her but didn't love her—I'd loved one girl earlier whom I hadn't slept with. She lived in one of those winsome houses that they have down there, with a tiled backyard and three floors, one room to each floor. We wandered along the waterfront and spent Saturdays at the street market, which is the largest and visually the richest street market in the United States. I was not an ogre to her, but I did by stages develop the habit of beating her briefly with my belt or hairbrush before we made love, a practice which I have foregone ever since. It may be indicative of the preoccupations of the 1950s that I worried less about this than about any tendencies I may have had toward being homosexual; but the experience gives me a contempt for pornography of that arch gruesome genre, quite in vogue nowadays as psychological "exploration," where whipping occurs but the flesh recovers its sheen overnight and the whippee doesn't perhaps hang her(him)self, propelling the whipper into the nervous breakdown which he is heading for.

Seeing eventual disaster ahead, I didn't go deeply into this vein of sensation, just as I was shrewd enough as a boy not to be picked on often or to suffer more than a few accidents. Once I ran my hand through an apple crusher, and once I imitated a child's stutter at summer camp, thereby—or so I imagined (remembering what was supposed to happen to you if you crossed your eyes)— picking up the malady at the age of six. Almost my only pangs, then, were this stutter, which still remains in my mouth. It may strike other people as more than a spasm, but to me it's a spasm of pain of a kind which I haven't time for, or time to regard as anything else. It's like someone who has a lesion or twist in his small intestine, which hurts him abruptly and of which he is hardly aware otherwise. The well-grooved wince I make in shaking the words out seems to keep my face pliant and reasonably young.

Somerset Maugham described his bitter discovery when he was a boy that prayer was no help: he woke up next morning still clamped to his adamant stutter. I was more of a pantheist; I kept trusting to the efficacy of sleep itself, or to the lilting lift that caused birds to fly. Also I went to a bunch of speech therapists. At the Ethical Culture School in New York, for example, a woman taught me to stick my right hand in my pocket and, with that hidden hand, to write down over and over the first letter of the word I was stuttering on. This was intended to distract me from stuttering, and it did for a week or two. The trouble was that watching me play pocket pool that way was more unsettling to other people than the ailment it was meant to cure. At a camp in northern Michigan I was trained by a team from the university to speak so slowly that in effect I wasn't speaking at all; I talked with the gradualism of a flower growing—so absurdly tardy a process that my mind unhinged itself from what was going on. In Cambridge, Massachusetts, a young fellow from the University of Iowa—and oh, how *he* stuttered—took the most direct approach. He got me to deliberately imitate myself, which was hard on me since I was already terribly tired of stuttering, and to stare, as well, at the people whom I was talking to in order to find out what their reactions were. I found out, for one thing, that some of my friends and about a fifth of the strangers I met smiled when the difficulty occurred, though they generally turned their heads to the side or wiped their mouths with one hand to hide the smile. Thereafter, life seemed simpler if I avoided looking at anybody, whoever he was, when I was stuttering badly, and I wasn't so edgily on the alert to see if I'd spit inadvertently.

Not that I lacked understanding for the smilers, though, because for many years I too had had the strange impulse, hardly controllable, to smile if somebody bumped his head on a low door lintel or received sad news. The phenomenologists say this is a form of defense. It goes with childhood especially, and I stopped indulging in it one night in Boston when I was in a police patrol wagon. A friend and I had been out for a walk, he was hit by a car, and as he woke from unconsciousness during the ride to the hospital and asked what had happened, I found myself grinning down at him while I answered. A few weeks later I was walking past an apartment building just as a rescue squad carried out a would-be suicide. He was alive, on a stretcher. When our eyes touched he smiled impenetrably, but I didn't smile back.

As a stutterer, I learned not to write notes. You put yourself at someone's mercy more when you write him a note than if you just stand there like a rhinoceros and snort. I could write a *Stutterer's Guide to Europe,* too: the titters in old Vienna, the knowing English remembering their King, the raw scorching baitings I met with in Greece, surrounded sometimes like a muzzled bear. The fourth means of effecting a cure I heard about was based on the fact that stutterers are able to sing without stuttering; hence, the victim should swing one of his arms like a big pendulum and talk in time to this—which again was obviously a worse fate than the impediment. Though I didn't try it, I was sent to a lady voice teacher who laid my hand on her conspicuous chest so that I could "feel her breathe." For just that moment the lessons worked wonderfully; if I wasn't speechless I spoke in a rush.

Stammering (a less obtrusive word I used to prefer)

apparently is not unattractive to women. It's a masculine encumbrance; five times as many men as women suffer from it. I was seldom alone while I was in Europe, and once or twice girls told me by way of a pick-me-up that they'd loved someone "for" his stutter. When I went into my seizures at parties, if a woman didn't step back she stepped forward, whereas the men did neither. The female instinct does not apply nearly so favorably to other afflictions. In our glib age the stutterer has even been considered a kind of contemporary hero, a presumed honest man who is unable to gab with the media people. Beyond the particular appeal of this image, it does seem to suit a writer. Publishers are fastidious types and some whom I've met have sidled away in distress from my flabbering face as soon as they could, but they probably remembered my name if they caught it. The purity image or Billy Budd stuff didn't intrigue them, just the hint of compulsion and complexity. Though I don't greatly go for either picture, in social terms I've thought of my stutter as a sort of miasma behind the Ivy League-looking exterior. People at parties take me for William Buckley until I begin, so I keep my mouth shut and smile prepossessingly just as long as I can.

Being in these vocal handcuffs made me a desperate, devoted writer at twenty. I worked like a dog, choosing each word. I wrote two full-length novels in iambic meter and a firehose style. Three hundred review copies of the second of these were sent out, but I received, I think, only three reviews. This was new pain, a man's career pain, with its attendant stomach trouble and neck and back cramps. A couple of years after that I got divorced from my first wife, and bawled like a half-butchered bull for an hour, rolled up on the floor of my apartment, while the two homosexuals next door listened in silence close to the wall, wondering what they ought to do. It was a purge, but the pain of that experience I remember best was an earlier scene. I'd announced to my wife, whom I loved and still love, my belief that we needed to separate. The next time we talked she crossed the room to my chair, knelt down beside me and asked what was going to become of each of us. That is the most painful splinter in my life, the most painful piece of the past. With variations the ache was prolonged through many fugitive suppers. In fact we still meet, holding hands and laughing at each other's jokes until we feel tears.

Who knows which qualities are godly? Pain probably makes us a bit godly, though, as tender love does. It makes us rue and summarize; it makes us bend and yield up ourselves. Pain is a watchdog medically, telling us when to consult a doctor, and then it's the true-blue dog at the bedside who rivals the relatives for fidelity. Last summer my father died of cancer. We had made peace, pretty much, a few years before. Although he had opposed my desire to be a writer, he ended up trying to write a book too, and he turned over to me at the last an old family history which he'd been hiding, partly because it mentioned a lot of muteness among my ancestors and partly in order to prevent my exploiting the stories. My voice and my liberal opinions grew a little more clarion in the household during the months he was dying. From a selfish standpoint, I suppose I was almost ready for him to die, but I was very earnestly sorry for every stage of rough handling involved in the process and for his own overriding regret that his life was cut off. Having lost our frank fear of death along with our faith in an afterlife, we have all adopted our fear of pain as a feeble alternative. Our regret, too, is magnified. When he was in discomfort I stuttered a great deal, but when he was not, when he was simply reminiscing or watching TV, I stuttered scarcely a bit. Then, as he was actually dying, during our last interview, he turned on the bed and asked me something. My answer was blocked in my mouth and his face went rigid with more pain than mine. He was startled because in the exigencies of dying he had forgotten that my infirmity was still there unhealed. He straightened, shutting his eyes, not wanting to end his life seeing it. Nevertheless, he'd often told me that it was my problems he loved me for rather than for my successes and sleekness. He loved my sister for being waiflike and my mother for being on occasion afraid she was mentally ill.

We were quite hardy while the months passed. Mother and he lay side by side on the bed clasping hands. Because of the pills, until nearly the end he was not suffering pain of the magnitude he had dreaded. The last couple of days there was a tossing, pitching, horrific pain, but the body more than the mind was responding—the body attempting to swallow its tongue. What I remember, therefore, of death's salutation to my father was that it came as a tickler, making his withered body twitch, touching him here and touching him there, wasting his tissues away like white wax, while his head on the headrest above looked down and watched; or he'd shoot an acute glance at me from out of the hunching amalgam of pricks, jactitation and drug-induced torpor. Death tickled him in a gradual crescendo, taking its time, and, with his ironic attorney's mind, he was amused. His two satisfactions were that he was privy to its most intimate preparations, everything just-so and fussy, and that at last the long spiky battling within the family was over and done. The new summer blossomed. In mid-June I saw what is meant by "a widow's tears." They flow in a flood of tremulous vulnerability, so that one thinks they will never stop.

Most severe on the physiologists' scale of pain is that of childbirth. It's also the worst that I've seen. A year had gone by since I'd left the Army and quit visiting my Philadelphia friend. She came to New York, looked me up, discovered me vomiting, thin as a rail because of girl trouble, and moved in with me on the Upper West Side, spooning in food and mothering me. Then, at about the time I perked up, she told me that she had got pregnant by a chap back in Philadelphia.

We drew out our savings and started for San Francisco, that vainglorious, clam-colored city. In her yellow convertible, with my English setter and her cocker spaniel, we drove through the South and through Texas, taking Highway 80 because it was the autumn and cold. I remember that whenever we stopped by the side of the road in Mississippi to let the dogs pee, and I shouted if one of them dawdled, any black woman or man who happened to be close by would turn to see what I wanted, quite naturally, as if I had called. It was a grueling trip. I'd begun vomiting again after my friend told me she was pregnant, and she was suffering mysterious pains in that region between her legs, which no druggist would touch. But we reached Russian Hill and established ourselves in one of the local apartment hotels. For a while during the seven-month wait this living arrangement didn't work out and she moved to a Florence Crittenton Home and I went to the beach, but we ended the period together. At six one morning I drove her up to a whelk-pink hospital on a breezy hill and sat in the labor room for eight hours, watching the blue grid of stretch marks on her anguished stomach: awful pain. She jolted and screamed, sucking gas from a cup, squeezing my hand and falling asleep between the throes. It took me three days to stop shaking, though it was a normal delivery throughout, and she, by the mental safety catch which women have, had blocked off most of the memory by the time she was wheeled to her room asleep. I'm ashamed to say that I'd spanked her a little the night before, not realizing it was the night before; I never spanked her again.

The contract she'd signed obliged my friend to re-linquish the baby girl to the Home for three weeks, after which she could appropriate her completely as her own. I was privileged to keep her breasts flowing during those weeks, a luxury that would have been fitting for Zeus; and, to the astonishment of the Home, as soon as the interval expired we showed up for the child. This was so rare that they wondered whether we were kidnappers. Then we drove East. The baby acquired a stepfather before she was out of her infancy and is now about ten.

So, pain is a packet of chiseling tools. Women in labor make no bones about protesting its severity. Neither does a dying man once he has stopped lingering with the living —thinking of the memories of his behavior which he is leaving his children, for instance. It's when we have no imperative purpose in front of our sufferings that we think about "bearing up"; "bearing up" is converted to serve as a purpose. Pain, love, boredom, and glee, and anticipation or anxiety—these are the pilings we build our lives from. In love we beget more love and in pain we beget more pain. Since we must like it or lump it, we like it. And why not, indeed?

HAILING THE
ELUSORY
MOUNTAIN LION

The swan song sounded by the wilderness grows fainter, ever more constricted, until only sharp ears can catch it at all. It fades to a nearly inaudible level, and yet there never is going to be any one time when we can say right *now* it is gone. Wolves meet their maker in wholesale lots, but coyotes infiltrate eastward, northward, southeastward. Woodland caribou and bighorn sheep are vanishing fast, but moose have expanded their range in some areas.

Mountain lions used to have practically the run of the Western Hemisphere, and they still do occur from Cape Horn to the Big Muddy River at the boundary of the Yukon and on the coasts of both oceans, so that they are the most versatile land mammal in the New World, probably taking in more latitudes than any other four-footed wild creature anywhere. There are perhaps only four to six thousand left in the United States, though there is no place that they didn't once go, eating deer, elk, pikas, porcupines, grasshoppers, and dead fish on the beach.

They were called mountain lions in the Rockies, pumas (originally an Incan word) in the Southwestern states, cougars (a naturalist's corruption of an Amazonian Indian word) in the Northwest, panthers in the traditionalist East—"painters" in dialect-proud New England—or catamounts. The Dutchmen of New Netherland called them tigers, red tigers, deer tigers, and the Spaniards *leones* or *leopardos*. They liked to eat horses—wolves preferred beef and black bears favored pork—but as adversaries of mankind they were overshadowed at first because bears appeared more formidable and wolves in their howling packs were more flamboyant and more damaging financially. Yet this panoply of names is itself quite a tribute, and somehow the legends about "panthers" have lingered longer than bear or wolf tales, helped by the animal's own limber, far-traveling stealth and as a carry-over from the immense mythic force of the great cats of the Old World. Though only Florida among the Eastern states is known for certain to have any left, no wild knot of mountains or swamp is without rumors of panthers; nowadays people delight in these, keeping their eyes peeled. It's wishful, and the wandering, secretive nature of the beast ensures that even Eastern panthers will not soon be certifiably extinct. An informal census among experts in 1963 indicated that an island of twenty-five or more may have survived in the New Brunswick–Maine–Quebec region, and Louisiana may still have a handful, and perhaps eight live isolated in the Black Hills of South Dakota, and the Oklahoma panhandle may have a small colony—all outside the established range in Florida,

218

Texas, and the Far West. As with the blue whale, who will be able to say when they have been eliminated?

"Mexican lion" is another name for mountain lions in the border states—a name that might imply a meager second-best rating there yet ties to the majestic African beasts. Lions are at least twice as big as mountain lions, measuring by weight, though they are nearly the same in length because of the mountain lion's superb long tail. Both animals sometimes pair up affectionately with mates and hunt in tandem, but mountain lions go winding through life in ones or twos, whereas the lion is a harem-keeper, harem-dweller, the males eventually becoming stay-at-homes, heavy figureheads. Lions enjoy the grassy flatlands, forested along the streams, and they stay put, engrossed in communal events—roaring, grunting, growling with a racket like the noise of gears being stripped—unless the game moves on. They sun themselves, preside over the numerous kibbutz young, sneeze from the dust, and bask in dreams, occasionally waking up to issue reverberating, guttural pronouncements which serve notice that they are now awake.

Mountain lions spirit themselves away in saw-toothed canyons and on escarpments instead, and when conversing with their mates they coo like pigeons, sob like women, emit a flat slight shriek, a popping bubbling growl, or mew, or yowl. They growl and suddenly caterwaul into falsetto—the famous scarifying, metallic scream functioning as a kind of hunting cry close up, to terrorize and start the game. They ramble as much as twenty-five miles in a night, maintaining a large loop of territory which they cover every week or two. It's a solitary, busy life, involving a survey of several valleys, many deer herds. Like tigers and leopards, mountain lions are not sociably inclined and don't converse at length with the whole waiting world, but they are even less noisy; they seem to speak most eloquently with their feet. Where a tiger would roar, a mountain lion screams like a castrato. Where a mountain lion hisses, a leopard would snarl like a truck stuck in snow.

Leopards are the best counterpart to mountain lions in physique and in the tenor of their lives. Supple, fierce creatures, skilled at concealment but with great self-assurance and drive, leopards are bolder when facing human beings than the American cats. Basically they are hot-land beasts and not such remarkable travelers individually, though as a race they once inhabited the broad Eurasian land mass all the way from Great Britain to Malaysia, as well as Africa. As late as the 1960s, a few were said to be still holding out on the shore of the Mediterranean at Mount Mycale, Turkey. (During a forest fire twenty years ago a yearling swam the narrow straits to the Greek island Samos and holed up in a cave, where he was duly killed—perhaps the last leopard ever to set foot in Europe on his own.) Leopards are thicker and shorter than adult mountain lions and seem to lead an athlete's indolent, incurious life much of the time, testing their perfected bodies by clawing tree trunks, chewing on old skulls, executing acrobatic leaps, and then rousing themselves to the semiweekly antelope kill. Built with supreme hardness and economy, they make little allowance for man—they don't see him as different. They relish the flesh of his dogs, and they run up a tree when hunted and then sometimes spring down, as heavy as a chunk of iron wrapped in a flag. With stunning, gorgeous coats, their tight, dervish faces carved in a snarl, they head for the hereafter as if it were just one more extra-emphatic leap— as impersonal in death as the crack of the rifle was.

The American leopard, the jaguar, is a powerfully built, serious fellow, who, before white men arrived, wandered as far north as the Carolinas, but his best home is the humid basin of the Amazon. Mountain lions penetrate these ultimate jungles too, but rather thinly, thriving better in the cooler, drier climate of the untenanted pampas and on the mountain slopes. They are blessed with a pleasant but undazzling coat, tan except for a white belly, mouth and throat, and some black behind the ears, on the tip of the tail and at the sides of the nose, and so they are hunted as symbols, not for their fur. The cubs are spotted, leopardlike, much as lion cubs are. If all of the big cats developed from a common ancestry, the mountain lions' specialization has been unpresumptuous—away from bulk and savagery to traveling light. Toward deer, their prey, they may be as ferocious as leopards, but not toward chance acquaintances such as man. They sometimes break their necks, their jaws, their teeth, springing against the necks of quarry they have crept close to—a fate in part resulting from the circumstance that they can't ferret out the weaker individuals in a herd by the device of a long chase, the way wolves do; they have to take the luck of the draw. None of the cats possess enough lung capacity for gruelling runs. They depend upon shock tactics, bursts of speed, sledge-hammer leaps, strong collarbones for hitting power, and shearing dentition, whereas wolves employ all the advantages of time in killing their quarry, as well as the numbers and gaiety of the pack, biting the beast's nose and rump—the technique of a thousand cuts—lapping the bloody snow. Wolves sometimes even have a cheering section of flapping ravens accompanying them, eager to scavenge after the brawl.

It's a risky business for the mountain lion, staking the strength and impact of his neck against the strength of the prey animal's neck. Necessarily, he is concentrated and fierce; yet legends exist that mountain lions have irritably defended men and women lost in the wilderness against marauding jaguars, who are no friends of theirs, and (with a good deal more supporting evidence) that they are susceptible to an odd kind of fascination with human beings. Sometimes they will tentatively seek an association, hanging about a campground or following a hiker out of curiosity, perhaps, circling around and bounding up on a ledge above to watch him pass. This mild modesty has helped preserve them from extinction. If they have been unable to make any adjustments to the advent of man, they haven't suicidally opposed him either, as the buffalo wolves and grizzlies did. In fact, at close quarters they seem bewildered. When treed, they don't breathe a hundred-proof ferocity but puzzle over what to do. They're too light-bodied to bear down on the hunter and kill him easily, even if they should attack—a course they seem to have no inclination for. In this century in the United States only one person, a child of thirteen, has been killed by a mountain lion; that was in 1924. And they're informal animals. Lolling in an informal sprawl on a high limb, they can't seem to summon any Enobarbus-like front of resistance for long. Daring men occasionally climb up and toss lassos about a cat and haul him down, strangling him by pulling from two directions, while the lion, mortified, appalled, never does muster his fighting aplomb. Although he could fight off a pack of wolves, he hasn't worked out a posture to assume toward man and his dogs. Impotently, he stiffens, as the dinosaurs must have when the atmosphere grew cold.

Someday hunting big game may come to be regarded as a form of vandalism, and the remaining big creatures of the wilderness will skulk through restricted reserves wearing radio transmitters and numbered collars, or bearing stripes of dye, as many elephants already do, to aid the busy biologists who track them from the air. Like a vanishing race of trolls, more report and memory than a reality, they will inhabit children's books and nostalgic articles, a special glamour attaching to those, like mountain lions, that are geographically incalculable and may still be sighted away from the preserves. Already we've become enthusiasts. We want game about us—at least at a summer house; it's part of privileged living. There is a precious privacy about seeing wildlife, too. Like meeting a fantastically dressed mute on the road, the fact that no words are exchanged and that *he's* not going to give an account makes the experience light-hearted; it's wholly ours. Besides, if anything out of the ordinary happened, we know we can't expect to be believed, and since it's rather fun to be disbelieved—fishermen know this—the privacy is even more complete. Deer, otter, foxes are messengers from another condition of life, another mentality, and bring us tidings of places where we don't go.

Ten years ago at Vavenby, a sawmill town on the North Thompson River in British Columbia, a frolicsome mountain lion used to appear at dusk every ten days or so in a bluegrass field alongside the river. Deer congregated there, the river was silky and swift, cooling the summer air, and it was a festive spot for a lion to be. She was thought to be a female, and reputedly left tracks around an enormous territory to the north and west—Raft Mountain, Battle Mountain, the Trophy Range, the Murtle River, and Mahood Lake—territory on an upended, pelagic scale, much of it scarcely accessible to a man by trail, where the tiger lilies grew four feet tall. She would materialize in this field among the deer five minutes before dark, as if checking in again, a habit that may have resulted in her death eventually, though for the present the farmer who observed her visits was keeping his mouth shut about it. This was pioneer country; there were people alive who could remember the time when poisoning the carcass of a cow would net a man a pile of dead predators —a family of mountain lions to bounty, maybe half a dozen wolves, and both black bears and grizzlies. The Indians considered lion meat a delicacy, but they had clans which drew their origins at the Creation from ancestral mountain lions, or wolves or bears, so these massacres amazed them. They thought the outright bounty hunters were crazy men.

Even before Columbus, mountain lions were probably not distributed in saturation numbers anywhere, as wolves may have been. Except for the family unit—a female with her half-grown cubs—each lion seems to occupy its own spread of territory, not as a result of fights with intruders but because the young transients share the same instinct for solitude and soon sheer off to find vacant mountains and valleys. A mature lion kills only one deer every week or two, according to a study by Maurice Hornocker in Idaho, and therefore is not really a notable factor in controlling the local deer population. Rather, it keeps watch contentedly as that population grows, sometimes benefitting the herds by scaring them onto new wintering grounds that are not overbrowsed, and by its very presence warding off other lions.

This thin distribution, coupled with the mountain lion's taciturn habits, make sighting one a matter of luck, even for game officials located in likely country. One warden in Colorado I talked to had indeed seen a pair of them fraternizing during the breeding season. He was driving a jeep over an abandoned mining road, and he passed two brown animals sitting peaceably in the grass, their heads close together. For a moment he thought they were coyotes and kept driving, when all of a sudden the picture registered that they were *cougars!* He braked and backed up, but of course they were gone. He was an old-timer, a man who had crawled inside bear dens to pull out the cubs, and knew where to find clusters of buffalo skulls in the recesses of the Rockies where the last bands had hidden; yet this cryptic instant when he was turning his jeep round a curve was the only glimpse—unprovable—that he ever got of a mountain lion.

Such glimpses usually are cryptic. During a summer I spent in Wyoming in my boyhood, I managed to see two coyotes, but both occasions were so fleeting that it required an act of faith on my part afterward to feel sure I had seen them. One of the animals vanished between rolls of ground; the other, in rougher, stonier, wooded country, cast his startled gray face in my direction and simply was gone. Hunching, he swerved for cover, and the brush closed over him. I used to climb to a vantage point above a high basin at twilight and watch the mule deer steal into the meadows to feed. The grass grew higher than their stomachs, the steep forest was close at hand, and they were as small and fragile-looking as filaments at that distance, quite human in coloring, gait and form. It was possible to visualize them as a naked Indian hunting party a hundred years before—or not to believe in their existence at all, either as Indians or deer. Minute, aphid-sized, they stepped so carefully in emerging, hundreds of feet below, that, straining my eyes, I needed to tell myself constantly that they were deer; my imagination, left to its own devices with the dusk settling down, would have made of them a dozen other creatures.

Recently, walking at night on the woods road that passes my house in Vermont, I heard footsteps in the leaves and windfalls. I waited, listening—they sounded too heavy to be anything less than a man, a large deer or a bear. A man wouldn't have been in the woods so late, my dog stood respectfully silent and still, and they did seem to shuffle portentously. Sure enough, after pausing at the edge of the road, a fully grown bear appeared, visible only in dimmest outline, staring in my direction for four or five seconds. The darkness lent a faintly red tinge to his coat; he was well built. Then, turning, he ambled off, almost immediately lost to view, though I heard the noise of his passage, interrupted by several pauses. It was all as concise as a vision, and since I had wanted to see a bear close to my own house, being a person who likes to live in a melting pot, whether in the city or country, and since it was too dark to pick out his tracks, I was grateful when the dog inquisitively urinated along the bear's path, thereby confirming that at least I had witnessed *something*. The dog seemed unsurprised, however, as if the scent were not all that remarkable, and, sure enough, the next week in the car I encountered a yearling bear in daylight two miles downhill, and a cub a month later. My farmer neighbors were politely skeptical of my accounts, having themselves caught sight of only perhaps a couple of bears in all their lives.

So it's with sympathy as well as an awareness of the tricks that enthusiasm and nightfall may play that I have been going to nearby towns seeking out people who have claimed at one time or another to have seen a mountain lion. The experts of the state—game wardens, taxidermists, the most accomplished hunters—emphatically discount the claims, but the believers are unshaken. They include some summer people who were enjoying a drink on the back terrace when the apparition of a great-tailed cat moved out along the fringe of the woods on a deer path;

a boy who was hunting with his .22 years ago near the village dump and saw the animal across a gully and fired blindly, then ran away and brought back a search party, which found a tuft of toast-colored fur; and a state forestry employee, a sober woodsman, who caught the cat in his headlights while driving through Victory Bog in the wildest corner of the Northeast Kingdom. Gordon Hickok, who works for a furniture factory and has shot one or two mountain lions on hunting trips in the West, saw one cross U.S. 5 at a place called Auger Hole near Mount Hor. He tracked it with dogs a short distance, finding a fawn with its head gnawed off. A high-school English teacher reported seeing a mountain lion cross another road, near Runaway Pond, but the hunters who quickly went out decided that the prints were those of a big bobcat, splayed impressively in the mud and snow. Fifteen years ago a watchman in the fire tower on top of Bald Mountain had left grain scattered in the grooves of a flat rock under the tower to feed several deer. One night, looking down just as the dusk turned murky, he saw two slim long-tailed lions creep out of the scrubby border of spruce and inspect the rock, sniffing deer droppings and dried deer saliva. The next night, when he was in his cabin, the dog barked and, looking out the window, again he saw the vague shape of a lion just vanishing.

A dozen loggers and woodsmen told me such stories. In the Adirondacks I've also heard some persuasive avowals —one by an old dog-sled driver and trapper, a French Canadian; another by the owner of a tourist zoo, who was exhibiting a Western cougar. In Vermont perhaps the most eager rumor buffs are some of the farmers. After all, now that packaged semen has replaced the awesome farm bull and so many procedures have been mechanized, who wants to lose *all* the adventure of farming? Until recently the last mountain lion known to have been killed in the Northeast was recorded in 1881 in Barnard, Vermont. However, it has been learned that probably another one was shot from a tree in 1931 in Mundleville, New Brunswick, and still another trapped seven years later in Somerset County in Maine. Bruce S. Wright, director of the Northeastern Wildlife Station (which is operated at the University of New Brunswick with international funding), is convinced that though they are exceedingly rare, mountain lions are still part of the fauna of the region; in fact, he has plaster casts of tracks to prove it, as well as a compilation of hundreds of reported sightings. Some people may have mistaken a golden retriever for a lion, or may have intended to foment a hoax, but all in all the evidence does seem promising. Indeed, after almost twenty years of search and study, Wright himself finally saw one.

The way these sightings crop up in groups has often been pooh-poohed as greenhorn fare or as a sympathetic hysteria among neighbors, but it is just as easily explained by the habit mountain lions have of establishing a territory that they scout through at intervals, visiting an auspicious deer-ridden swamp or remote ledgy mountain. Even at such a site a successful hunt could not be mounted without trained dogs, and if the population of the big cats was extremely sparse, requiring of them long journeys during the mating season, and yet with plenty of deer all over, they might not stay for long. One or two hundred miles is no obstacle to a Western cougar. The cat might inhabit a mountain ridge one year, and then never again.

Fifteen years ago, Francis Perry, who is an ebullient muffin of a man, a farmer all his life in Brownington, Vermont, saw a mountain lion "larger and taller than a collie, and grayish yellow" (he had seen them in circuses). Having set a trap for a woodchuck, he was on his way to visit the spot when he came over a rise and, at a distance of fifty yards, saw the beast engaged in eating the dead woodchuck. It bounded off, but Perry set four light fox traps for it around the woodchuck. Apparently, a night or two later the cat returned and got caught in three of these, but they couldn't hold it; it pulled free, leaving the marks of a struggle. Noel Perry, his brother, remembers how scared Francis looked when he came home from the first episode. Noel himself saw the cat (which may have meant that Brownington Swamp was one of its haunts that summer), once when it crossed a cow pasture on another farm the brothers owned, and once when it fled past his rabbit dogs through underbrush while he was training them—he thought for a second that its big streaking form was one of the dogs. A neighbor, Robert Chase, also saw the animal that year. Then again last summer, for the first time in fifteen years, Noel Perry saw a track as big as a bear's but round like a mountain lion's, and Robert's brother, Larry Chase, saw the actual cat several times one summer evening, playing a chummy hide-and-seek with him in the fields.

Elmer and Elizabeth Ambler are in their forties, populists politically, and have bought a farm in Glover to live the good life, though he is a truck driver in Massachusetts on weekdays and must drive hard in order to be home when he can. He's bald, with large eyebrows, handsome teeth and a low forehead, but altogether a strong-looking, clear, humane face. He is an informational kind of man who will give you the history of various breeds of cattle or a talk about taxation in a slow and musical voice, and both he and his wife, a purposeful, self-sufficient redhead, are fascinated by the possibility that they live in the wilderness. Beavers inhabit the river that flows past their house. The Amblers say that on Black Mountain nearby hunters "disappear" from time to time, and bears frequent the berry patches in their back field—they see them, their visitors see them, people on the road see them, their German shepherds meet them and run back drooling with fright. They've stocked their farm with horned Herefords instead of the polled variety so that the creatures can "defend themselves." Ambler is intrigued by the thought that apart from the danger of bears, someday "a cat" might prey on one of his cows. Last year, looking out the back window, his wife saw through binoculars an animal with a flowing tail and "a cat's gallop" following a line of trees where the deer go, several hundred yards uphill behind the house. Later, Ambler went up on snowshoes and found tracks as big as their shepherds'; the dogs obligingly ran alongside. He saw walking tracks, leaping tracks and deer tracks marked with blood going toward higher ground. He wonders whether the cat will ever attack him. There are plenty of bobcats around, but they both say they know the difference. The splendid, nervous *tail* is what people must have identified in order to claim they have seen a mountain lion.

I, too, cherish the notion that I may have seen a lion. Mine was crouched on an overlook above a grass-grown, steeply pitched wash in the Alberta Rockies—a much more likely setting than anywhere in New England. It was late afternoon on my last day at Maligne Lake, where I had been staying with my father at a national-park chalet. I was twenty; I could walk forever or could climb endlessly in a sanguine scramble, going out every day as far as my legs carried me, swinging around for home before the sun went down. Earlier, in the valley of the Athabasca, I had found several winter-starved or wolf-killed deer, well picked and scattered, and an area with many elk antlers strewn on the ground where the herds had wintered safely, dropping their antlers but not their bones. Here, much higher up, in the bright plenitude of the summer, I had watched two wolves and a stately bull moose in one mountain basin, and had been up on the caribou barrens on the ridge west of the lake and brought back the talons of a hawk I'd found dead on the ground. Whenever I was watching game, a sort of stopwatch in me started running. These were moments of intense importance and intimacy, of new intimations and aptitudes. Time had a jam-packed character, as it does during a mile run.

I was good at moving quietly through the woods and at spotting game, and was appropriately exuberant. The finest, longest day of my stay was the last. Going east, climbing through a luxuriant terrain of up-and-down boulders, brief brilliant glades, sudden potholes fifty feet deep—a forest of moss-hung lodgepole pines and firs and spare, gaunt spruce with the black lower branches broken off— I came upon the remains of a young bear, which had been torn up and shredded. Perhaps wolves had cornered it during some imprudent excursion in the early spring. (Bears often wake up while the snow is still deep, dig themselves out and rummage around in the neighborhood sleepily for a day or two before bedding down again under a fallen tree.) I took the skull along so that I could extract the teeth when I got hold of some tools. Discoveries like this represent a superfluity of wildlife and show how many beasts there are scouting about.

I went higher. The marmots whistled familially; the tall trees wilted to stubs of themselves. A pretty stream led down a defile from a series of openings in front of the ultimate barrier of a vast mountain wall which I had been looking at from a distance each day on my outings. It wasn't too steep to be climbed, but it was a barrier because my energies were not sufficient to scale it and bring me back the same night. Besides, it stretched so majestically, surflike above the lesser ridges, that I liked to think of it as the Continental Divide.

On my left as I went up this wash was an abrupt, grassy slope that enjoyed a southern exposure and was sunny and windblown all winter, which kept it fairly free of snow. The ranger at the lake had told me it served as a wintering ground for a few bighorn sheep and for a band of mountain goats, three of which were in sight. As I approached laboriously, these white, pointy-horned fellows drifted up over a rise, managing to combine their retreat with some nippy good grazing as they went, not to give any pursuer the impression that they had been pushed into flight. I took my time too, climbing to locate the spring in a precipitous cleft of rock where the band did most of its drinking, and finding the shallow, high-ceilinged cave where the goats had sheltered from storms, presumably for generations. The floor was layered with rubbery droppings, tramped down and sprinkled with tufts of shed fur, and the back wall was checkered with footholds where the goats liked to clamber and perch. Here and there was a horn lying loose—a memento for me to add to my collection from an old individual that had died a natural death, secure in the band's winter stronghold. A bold, thriving family of pack rats emerged to observe me. They lived mainly on the nutritives in the droppings, and were used to the goats' tolerance; they seemed astonished when I tossed a stone.

I kept scrabbling along the side of the slope to a section of outcroppings where the going was harder. After perhaps half an hour, crawling around a corner, I found myself faced with a bighorn ram who was taking his ease on several square yards of bare earth between large rocks, a little above the level of my head. Just as surprised as I, he stood up. He must have construed the sounds of my advance to be those of another sheep or goat. His horns had made a complete curl and then some; they were thick, massive and bunched together like a high Roman helmet, and he himself was muscly and military, with a grave-looking nose. A squared-off, middle-aged, trophy-type ram, full of imposing professionalism, he was at the stage of life when rams sometimes stop herding and live as rogues.

He turned and tried a couple of possible exits from the pocket where I had found him, but the ground was badly pitched and would require a reeling gait and loss of dignity. Since we were within a national park and obviously I was unarmed, he simply was not inclined to put himself to so much trouble. He stood fifteen or twenty feet above me, pushing his tongue out through his teeth, shaking his head slightly and dipping it into charging position as I moved closer by a step or two, raising my hand slowly toward him in what I proposed as a friendly greeting. The day had been a banner one since the beginning, so while I recognized immediately that this meeting would be a valued memory, I felt as natural in his company as if he were a friend of mine reincarnated in a shag suit. I saw also that he was going to knock me for a loop, head over heels down the steep slope, if I sidled nearer, because he did not by any means feel as expansive and exuberant at our encounter as I did. That was the chief difference between us. I was talking to him with easy gladness, and beaming; he was not. He was unsettled and on his mettle, waiting for me to move along, the way a bighorn sheep waits for a predator to move on in wildlife movies when each would be evenly matched in a contest of strength and position. Although his warlike nose and high bone helmet, blocky and beautiful as weaponry, kept me from giving in to my sense that we were brothers, I knew I could stand there for a long while. His coat was a down-to-earth brown, edgy with muscle, his head was that of an unsmiling veteran standing to arms, and despite my reluctance to treat him as some sort of boxed-in prize, I might have stayed on for half the afternoon if I hadn't realized that I had other sights to see. It was not a day to dawdle.

I trudged up the wash and continued until, past tree line, the terrain widened and flattened in front of a preliminary ridge that formed an obstacle before the great roaring, silent, surflike mountain wall that I liked to think of as the Continental Divide, although it wasn't. A cirque separated the preliminary ridge from the ultimate divide, which I still hoped to climb to and look over. The opening into this was roomy enough, except for being littered with enormous boulders, and I began trying to make my way across them. Each was boat-sized and rested upon under-boulders; it was like running in place. After tussling with this landscape for an hour or two, I was limp and sweating, pinching my cramped legs. The sun had gone so low that I knew I would be finding my way home by moonlight in any case, and I could see into the cirque, which was big and symmetrical and presented a view of sheer barbarism; everywhere were these cruel boat-sized boulders.

Giving up and descending to the goats' draw again, I had a drink from the stream and bathed before climbing farther downward. The grass was green, sweet-smelling, and I felt safely close to life after that sea of dead boulders. I knew I would never be physically younger or in finer country; even then the wilderness was singing its swan song. I had no other challenges in mind, and though very tired, I liked looking up at the routes where I'd climbed. The trio of goats had not returned, but I could see their wintering cave and the cleft in the rocks where the spring was. Curiously, the bighorn ram had not left; he had only withdrawn upward, shifting away from the outcroppings to an open sweep of space where every avenue of escape was available. He was lying on a carpet of grass and, lonely pirate that he was, had his head turned in my direction.

It was from this same wash that looking up, I spotted the animal I took to be a mountain lion. He was skulking among some outcroppings at a point lower on the mountainside than the ledges where the ram originally had been. A pair of hawks or eagles were swooping at him by turns, as if he were close to a nest. The slant between us was steep, but the light of evening was still more than adequate. I did not really see the wonderful tail—that special medallion—nor was he particularly big for a lion. He was gloriously catlike and slinky, however, and so indifferent to the swooping birds as to seem oblivious of them. There are plenty of creatures he wasn't: he wasn't a marmot, a goat or other grass-eater, a badger, a wolf or coyote or fisher. He *may* have been a big bobcat or a wolverine, although he looked ideally lion-colored. He had a cat's strong collarbone structure for hitting, powerful haunches for vaulting, and the almost mystically small head mountain lions possess, with the gooseberry eyes. Anyway, I believed him to be a mountain lion, and standing quietly I watched him as he inspected in leisurely fashion the ledge that he was on and the one under him

237

savory with every trace of goat—frosty-colored with the white hairs they'd shed. The sight was so dramatic that it seemed to be happening close to me, though in fact he and the hawks or eagles, whatever they were, were miniaturized by distance.

If I'd kept motionless, eventually I could have seen whether he had the proper tail, but such scientific questions had no weight next to my need to essay some kind of communication with him. It had been exactly the same when I'd watched the two wolves playing together a couple of days before. They were above me, absorbed in their game of noses-and-paws. I had recognized that I might never witness such a scene again, yet I couldn't hold myself in. Instead of talking and raising my arm to them, as I had with the ram, I'd shuffled forward impetuously as if to say *Here I am!* Now, with the lion, I tried hard to dampen my impulse and restrained myself as long as I could. Then I stepped toward him, just barely squelching a cry in my throat but lifting my hand—as clumsy as anyone is who is trying to attract attention.

At that, of course, he swerved aside instantly and was gone. Even the two birds vanished. Foolish, triumphant and disappointed, I hiked on down into the lower forests, gargantuanly tangled, another life zone—not one which would exclude a lion but one where he would not be seen. I'd got my second wind and walked lightly and softly, letting the silvery darkness settle around me. The blowdowns were as black as whales; my feet sank in the moss. Clearly this was as crowded a day as I would ever have, and I knew my real problem would not be to make myself believed but rather to make myself understood at all, simply in reporting the story, and that I must at least keep the memory straight for myself. I was so happy that I was unerring in distinguishing the deer trails going my way. The forest's night beauty was supreme in its promise, and I didn't hurry.

THE MOOSE
ON THE WALL

Since it is likely that the last wild animals of large size and dignity that people will see will be stuffed ones, I paid a visit to my neighborhood taxidermist in northern Vermont to learn how he does his work, and what precisely it is: by what means these few crick-necked and powdery phantoms of the great game confluxes of the past will be preserved. The area where I live still has a smattering of black bear, and plenty of deer, some bobcats, and an occasional coyote migrating in from westerly parts. The beaver are beginning to come back, now that nobody traps them, and the groundhogs and skunks and porcupines are flourishing as the farms become summer places, where they aren't shot as varmints. The moose, cougar, wolves and wolverines are long gone, but the humbler animals, meek, elusive, adaptable, are doing all right for the moment—in fact, my friend the taxidermist says that when he was a boy and this was farm country, people would travel for miles just to set eyes on a bear's track, if one was reported. The wildlife left will probably continue to prosper until the seasonal owners break up their properties into smaller and smaller tracts as land values rise.

My friend is a likable man with white hair, a quiet, spacious, mild face well used by his sixty years, a farmer's suspenders, a carpenter's arms, and an acumen in the woods, or a love for the woods, that no doubt exceeds my own, though my bias and his are opposed. We are allies nevertheless, because hunting and nonhunting naturalists when taken together are only a dot in the populace, at least when wildlife conservation is involved. Clean air and water, provision for beaches and lakes and parks—these causes draw a dependable measure of support from good men everywhere, but animals unseen, whose wish is to steer clear of mankind, get less attention. Hunters do fret about them, however, keeping tabs on the toll the winter snows take, and the relentless shrinkage of open land. Hunters miss the moose and mountain lions and pass along rumors that a handful still somehow survive here in the Northeast. Besides, hunters are folk who like to walk half-a-dozen miles before having lunch, to get their feet wet, pant up the ledges and draws, cook over a fire, and perhaps finally haul a load of meat home on their backs; and they take their ration of blood as they find it, in a natural fashion, not transmogrified onto the TV. Hunters are as attentive as the predator animals to the habits of what they are after; and some of them want visible proof on the wall of what

241

they got for their trouble—the taxidermist does this for them. In some ways his work resembles an undertaker's, with the congenial difference that he needn't hurry or pretend to be sad.

In the window of his shop is an old display of two newborn bear cubs, bleached white by the sun, sitting in a tiny boat on a pond. The pond is represented by a sheet of plastic, with realistic-looking trout underneath. There are also some dusty pheasants and ducks, their colors dead now. But the splendor inside is undeniable—deep, virile black hides of bears seized at the prime, just before they would have dug in for a winter's sleep. These are stacked in piles, glossy, blue-black, and there are other mounds of orange and caribou-colored deer hides. Visiting, I was surprised at the number of tools along the workbench: fleshing and cartilage knives, saws and scalpels in rows, pliers, pincers, hammers and mallets, bone snippers and scrapers, curved sewing needles, forceps, punches, drills, picking tools, tweezers, stiff wires. The plywood tables are big enough for him to stretch out a nine-foot skin to dry after it has been soaked in the tanning tub and washed in fresh water. The soaking goes on for six weeks or so—he has sacks of alum, which is the main ingredient in the pickling acid. There is salt in quantity too, for drying the flesh side of the skins when they first arrive, and plaster of Paris, and sacks of a grainy roof-insulation material which is used to thicken the plaster of Paris.

Ideally, the taxidermist is given the skull of the animal along with the hide, if a head job is wanted, not

simply the flat tanned skin. After boiling the skull until
all the meat has fallen away, he rebuilds the original
shape of the head by thumbing plaster into the grooves
and cavities on the skull so that the skin fits over it again
as neatly as before. For deer, whose jaws and teeth are
not to be emphasized, he doesn't need more than the
skull's top plate, where the antlers attach, but a carni-
vore is most realistically mounted when the teeth that
you see are the real teeth, not hoked up from wax in an
oversized jaw. He restructures the underpart of a deer's
face by whittling a small block of cedar or basswood,
though of course he could buy entire preformed heads
made of papier mâché from the wholesalers—heads of
moose, deer, or the numerous and various African antelopes. A ready-made jaguar's wax mouth and paper skull
costs only about $12, for instance; a set of artificial por-
celain teeth is $5.95 for a tiger and $1.95 for a coyote,
because these are higher quality.

He could buy rubber noses by the gross as well, but
usually he moulds the animal's nose out of putty, attaching it to the snout that he shaped from wood or from
plaster of Paris and painting it black. Each ear is a piece
of soft lead bent so that the skin slips onto it alertly. The
eyes are glass; and he has a watchmaker's cabinet of
compartments and drawers filled with fox eyes, owl eyes,
loon eyes, lynx eyes, coon eyes, lion eyes, snake eyes.
Some are veined or show lifelike white corners and carefully differentiate iris and pupil. The catalogue lists
twenty-eight sizes, from a buffalo's down to a humming-
bird's, and there are cheapjack economy grades, eight

pairs for a dollar. He can buy rubber tongues, set into a roll like a wolf's tongue, but unless he is rushed he carves his from wood. He glues the tongue inside the skull, and the lips, gums and roof of the mouth he forms out of wax and then paints them the correct color. Next, he sews and pins the eyelids and cheeks into an appropriate expression and whittles a frame for the neck. He likes to whittle—that basic craft—first using a drawknife, later a delicate spoke-shaver, such as wagon wheels used to be carved with. When only wadding is needed, as for stuffing squirrels and birds, excelsior serves very well, or cotton batting. A bad craftsman would insert the filler as if he were stuffing a cushion, but it's best to wind it tightly first into a credible stance and tie it with thread for permanence. He polishes and lacquers the hooves of the deer and blows with a bellows at the game birds to clean their feathers. Songbirds are wired into a pert pose, wings outspread or beak pointed left; wires bore down through their legs to the varnished perch.

Many droll requests come from customers, surpassing the sort of ideas an undertaker encounters. Some people want blinking lights installed in the eyeholes of the lynx that they've shot. Or they'll put their house thermometer in a deer's leg; they'll want a fat mother porcupine stuffed conventionally but with the fetuses found inside her embalmed in a talcum powder bottle like little rolled-up human babies. A local minister who had served as a missionary in Africa brought back the ears and a foot of an elephant he had shot, and a souvenir strip of leg skin like hard bark. Sometimes a hotel man will buy a pair of bear cubs a farmer has killed and, under the general umbrella of humor, ask that they be preserved in a standing position on their hind legs to hold the ash trays in the lobby. ("Oh, pardon me, little sir, may I use you?")

Understand that I'm making a figurative investigation —the animals native to Vermont which have survived so far are not in danger of quick extinction. The end of subsistence farming has worked to their advantage, and, paradoxically, before the farmers appeared and cleared the land, the Indians of nearby Canada had called this section of New England The Desert because the un-felled timber grew so thick that game was scarce. Still, these modest creatures—flittering does fleeing with a peahen's squawking cry, a pony's hoofbeats, and a car-ousel motion; porcine black bear rooting for mushrooms, rooting for grubs; and all the parade of back-field inhabi-tants, like the varying hares which explode through the ferns and the fire cherry and in winter turn white and nibble ironwood nuts—represent the much bigger ghosts of creatures gone.

Taxidermy, or the notion of saving the scalp, horns and teeth of game, goes along with a fairly advanced stage of settlement. The frontiersmen and homesteaders hunted for meat—it was labor to them, it was feeding the fam-ily; other than furs to dress themselves in, they didn't often keep tokens. The Indians, having evolved a game-oriented religion and culture, were more likely to save an especially superb big skull, but they also killed for use and didn't go in for tricking the animal up as a mannequin. The practice of mounting heads to hang on the wall developed only as the white towns became county seats, long after the first artisans like blacksmiths and carpenters had arrived, when hunters became "sportsmen." Earlier, a fellow might throw a phenomenal skin embodying the memories of real risk and adventure up on the cabin roof to freeze and dry; he might even salt it. By and by the sun would convert the flesh side to a brown board, and it would be tacked in the entryway —that was the taxidermy.

Once in the old gold town of Barkerville, British Columbia, I was talking to a prospector and his wife, both over seventy-five. Their serenity and good cheer were plain; wilderness gardening had obviously agreed with them, so had the solitude, and there was no counting the tonnage of creek sand that they must have panned in a lifetime. But what brought the sense of their achievement home to me as they talked was suddenly to notice two antediluvian grizzly hides hanging in the hallway just behind them: from floor to ceiling, a plush chestnut-brown with darker shades. A basketball player could have enveloped himself in either one with room to spare. Apparently both husband and wife had shot other bears, but had happened to save these. They didn't mention them until I did, and as with every other keepsake they had, didn't stress or boast about the circumstances, just said that the bears had strayed within range on their creek in different years and had seemed to be taking up a settled abode. On a whole host of topics that we touched on, the skins completed what was unsaid.

I'm not against keeping trophies if they define or some-how enlarge the possessor, if they're taken seriously, and if they memorialize the animal world, besieged and war-ranted for an early death as it surely is. Old dirt farm-ers and mild-mannered old taxidermists are outdated too; they will go the way of the wildlife soon. (There is another taxidermist in town, a retired fellow with pouchy cheeks, an upright posture and a face like a squirrel, who keeps his first-prize ribbons from the state fairs of 1911 and 1913 under glass.) This business of my friend's employs three generations. All day outdoorsmen, wearing red shirts or hip boots, drop in and talk, and he and his son and the young boy, scraping the flesh from a black wolf's legs, listen in. They throw sawdust on the floor and handle the beasts that arrive as farmers do their own butchered stock—it lives to live but it lives to be shot. The older man has hunted moose in northern Quebec that put all these little buck deer in the shade, so he's got photographs of the vanished big stuff. When he talks it's always of hunting and game: knolls and ledges to scale, ravines to bypass, and openings which open up as you reach them. Game is like vastly enlivened farm stock; you study it, wish it well, go for the prize.

Along the walls there are shelves of skulls, tagged for insertion into the bear skulls which are being prepared. When the skins are tanned, repairs are made—holes sewn up, bald spots touched over with paint or patched with scraps from another skin. The claws are cleaned, the blemishes concealed, and the obligatory pained-looking snarl, which the animal seldom wore while it was alive, is inscribed on the face. Bear rugs cost the clientele $25 per square foot nowadays, and in a year the shop gets up to seventy of them to work on, though last fall was an unlucky one for hunters because the mast crop was sparse and scattered and a heavy, early snowfall put all the bears in Vermont to bed ahead of time (an estimated thirty-five hundred live in the state). Also, by late November upwards of two hundred deer have been brought in, the floor is heaped high with salted skins, antlers are lying all over the place. Some people want the deer's feet mounted on a plaque under the head and set with an upward poke, to be utilized as a gun rack. The workroom has samples of this arrangement nailed to the walls, and big moose feet, and a great moose head is exhibited, with its pendulous bell, long-suffering ears, and primeval superstructure, bony, leaf-shaped. There's a lovely gray bobcat hanging head down, and a stuffed horned owl, a goshawk, some quail, some black ducks, a Canada goose, a pouter pigeon, two mink, a fox skin, beaver kits, the unfinished head of a coyote with its lips and eyes intricately pinned, and a yearling bear posed standing up, holding a pair of field glasses, as if to help it see better next time.

Snapshots of big men and downed bear, of deer sprawled on the ground and hunters squatting, are tacked on the wall. About fifteen thousand deer a year are killed in Vermont, almost two per square mile, although only one hunter in ten who buys a license is successful in making a kill. The out-of-state hunters do a little bit better statistically, strangely enough, maybe they're at it full time while they're here. Then during the winter perhaps just as many deer starve to death. The deer that we see in the north are still healthy-looking, though there are very few predators left who can prune the herds in a natural fashion, taking the weaker individuals so that the wintering areas are not overgrazed. Bobcats have become scarce because they are hunted year-round, and bobcats aren't really up to the task anyway. Eventually our deer are expected to shrink to the wizened proportions of some of their cousins in southern Vermont or southerly New England, where often the bucks can't even muster the strength to sprout antlers and the fawns that they father are comparably frail—most being shot within the first two or three years of life, in any case. What with the game diminishing in grandeur, the short hunting seasons and complicated regulations, a talented, old-fashioned hunter finds his style crimped. For want of any other game, he exercises himself by hunting coons or the few small surviving predators. One fellow in town, who runs the schoolbuses, a lanky, devoted, preeminent hunter who probably was born too late, goes after bobcats with dogs every weekend all winter, patrolling the snowy deer yards, believing that he is protecting the deer. Bobcats have diminutive chests; they can dash in a burst of speed but soon must get into a tree if the hounds are close, not being equipped for a distance race. A photo shows him with seventeen of the creatures hammered frozen to the side of his house, each with clenched paws and a grimace. He collected the $10 bounty on each, cut off the bobbed tails, and threw the bodies on the town dump.

There is a furred compendium on the tables, a dukedom in furs, not only raccoons and otter and bucks, but skins from the West—grizzly and cougar—as if the supply would never run out. All around the top of the room are fastened dozens of black and white tails—these the whitetail deer tails which they flip up to warn one another when they have cause to bolt, and which they wag vigorously in the fly season, just as a horse does. Almost every evening I watch deer in my field, their coats as red as a red fox. They snort with the sharp sound of a box dropped. Sometimes you only see their tall ears, in a V, the late sunlight shining through pinkly. Originally, a hundred or more years ago, only a moose trail and horse trail wound past where I live. It is exceptionally moosey country, with ponds, mountains, lakes and bogs —country that cries out for moose, in fact. Moose love water. When hard-pressed by wolves, they will spend the whole winter knee-deep in a pond, standing close to where a spring comes in and the water won't freeze; and in the summer, browsing on the bottom, they wade out so far in search of water plants that they finally get in over their heads and push up the tips of their noses every few minutes. The huge bulls, however, are a sight surpassing the vision one had of them, surpassing the mind's inventions. You would think that when they caught sight of themselves reflected on the surface of a smooth lake they would be frightened.

Even the bank in town has the head of a moose fixed to the wall, as a remembrance of the old days. It looks like the head of a horse or a cow poking through the half-door of a stable. And looking at it, I get the benign sense of good existing in the world that I have sometimes when I look at a cow—those big ears thrust forward, and those big eyes, as if we all have at least two ways of communicating with each other in this world: sound and sight. A youngster came into the bank while I was there and stared for a long time at the moose head. After a while he went to the door and tried to go through to the other side so that he could see the rest of the animal. To begin with, they had to tell him it wasn't alive.

MARRIAGE,
FAME, POWER,
SUCCESS

Marriage is taken to be a sign of health even if the marriage is bad just by the fact that the person can sustain its rigors for the sake of appearance and in order to be a good Joe while juggling the other tough aspects of living as well. On the other hand, if a marriage is good, it's life with a blue ribbon around it; there's nothing quite like it, it's Biblically rich, it's riding first-class. This is a month when my marriage is not breaking up, and the days are delicious and pleasant indeed—much kissing, much talking of leaving each other (a subject not mentioned when leaving is really in mind), much seeking new twists for our teasing, each calling the other a monster with teeth clenched in love. No question about it, it's happiness—I carry my child like a mahout on my shoulders for miles. Marriage is the high road, foursquare, a public endorsement, a framework within which a good many things begin to look plausible which otherwise might be dubious indeed.

And success—ah! I remember watching with astonishment my father's confusion as he fumbled to straighten his tie when unexpectedly we met a higher official of his corporation in the dining room at Lake Placid, where we were skiing. Yet some years later, I remember being actually short of breath, and losing control of the muscles of the throat which keep saliva from running down into the windpipe, in the presence of a famous writer. I could hardly breathe; I panted as softly as I could and choked on my spit; my voice changed pitch. The fellow himself might be drunk and miserable, but I was giddy with a sense of spiritual prosperity just being close to him, and this not with one famous author but with several over a decade or more. With wet eyes I followed the celebrated in other fields too—Don Budge, Spencer Tracy—seeing how they reddened with well-being when recognized. It "went to their heads."

Success in my father's realm didn't mean getting in the papers but living well—big lawns, old houses, fine clothes and trips. When he went into the hospital for an operation, he dressed as if for a meeting of the board, that being one way he knew to communicate that he was a man of importance and that any mistake that killed him would cause inquiries. Success also meant clubs: both funny clubs and power-base clubs. There was a luncheon club he belonged to in Paris which had no dues but which required a man to get up on his hind legs once a year and tell a good story. If nobody laughed, his membership was rescinded. Another funny club, in London, was nominally for yachting but mostly existed for its newsletter and its cubbyhole rooms overlooking the Thames. Clubs had their place in *Who's Who,* but some were a serious matter, like the country club where a man played golf and the sailing club where he boated. In the grueling week's schedule these respites, if they didn't perhaps prolong life, certainly made it possible to keep up the pace. Then there was the club down in Washington where one could entertain at lunch and be counted when there on business, and the club or clubs in New York—first just the club of one's college, then a larger circle—which were really a central bastion in the practice of one's profession, almost indispensable.

Being admitted to practice before the Supreme Court, a ceremony within the legal fraternity which had no practical significance for a backstage attorney like my father, was another clublike ritual. One's old law professor, Felix Frankfurter, might nod from the bench. And there were the guest memberships. A friend coming east from San Francisco could enjoy the courtesies of my father's club during his visit, and out there my father would enjoy the conveniences of his. When he was convalescing, still very ill, and couldn't travel more than a handful of blocks, he was living on Park Avenue at 35th Street. His club was on Fifth Avenue, at 54th Street, however, and so it wasn't a question of reciprocal membership in San Francisco then, but at the men's club on Park Avenue at 38th. That favor, done for him by an old friend, seemed a great boon.

When I was in college, hoping to make a splash eventually, somebody suggested that the way to plan for it would be for me to sit home and write the books, which we'd have to assume would be good, and, impersonating me, he would go out night-clubbing and to parties and pat hands with Leonard Lyons and sock Frank Sinatra. Whatever one thought of Hemingway, success as a writer at that time involved being famous like him. Steinbeck, Saroyan, even down to some of the lowly *New Yorker* crew, had satellite images as to how they dealt with their fame. A checkered employment history, a few pals in the underworld, a feeling for animals, kindness to barmen, boldness with friends, marital irregularity, steadfastness in enmity, sacrosanct writing hours and yet quick pick-up-and-go: these were the clues.

Now we have no Hemingways, even in regard to the handling of fame. Nabokov is too wordy and foppish in interviews, Malamud too squirrelly, Cheever and Algren too private and wounded. Mailer has trained up his fame as carefully as a tomato plant, and Bellow is too vulnerable, too much Everyman (once I was with him during a break in rehearsals for one of his plays, and as the beautiful girls in the cast called to him in husky, whispery voices from the door of the delicatessen across the street, it seemed that whether or not he was going to end up going off with one, he was considering doing so with the same guilt and trepidation *I* would have felt).

Mailer does come closest to the role, as he himself used to remind us. For a while, writing little, during the loony period of his life, he seemed like the fellow who had suggested that he could do the night-clubbing if only somebody else would write the books. What especially aroused one's sympathy was his incongruous shortness, like a fireplug, and his crazy, wretched air at parties, most people looking askance at him and giggling cruelly into each other's ears, "There's the madman who stabbed his wife." Well, not all the talent was flung to the winds, and the gap between the man who sits at home writing the books and the man out drumming up printer's ink has shrunk rather than widened, so that his hopes for himself, once seemingly crashed to earth, are still arguable.

With Mailer we have some embodiment of the physical Hemingway concept of fame: the bull-roar voice at a P.E.N. party rocking and silencing the bathtub sailors like a ninth wave; the visiting fireman whom graduate students say they stand next to and surreptitiously match drink for drink to find out what his liquor consumption feels like. William vanden Heuvel edges up to Mailer proffering a paw that's hanging down limp at right angles, like a ritual of submission almost too good to be true, and he is a papa to women, a veritable fertility figure whom my own wife dreamt about when pregnant—he gave her the sound, paternal advice not to get tired, since tiredness in the woman breaks up more marriages than all of the other disenchantments combined. The last glimpse I had of Mailer, he and a slick chick were leaving the Harvard Club on a brisk November evening on their way to eat. He suggested to her, "Let's run," and they did, Mailer doing very creditably—one of those representations of a sprint in which the legs do not step out very far, moving quickly but conserving strength by a very short stride. It was a sprint by which he demonstrated to the girl and himself that he still could run without in any way forcing a test of how fast.

Most Mailer tests are bona fide, but always writing or marital or financial challenges, never physical, and so they are not unlike the tangles that other writers set for themselves. For the old Hemingway physical foolishness and amplitude one must look to a few sideline figures, such as George Plimpton. To be sure, Plimpton has neither the Hemingway physique nor the pugnacity; on the contrary, his commitment is specifically to lose (how sad he would be if he ever won!). But he has staked out for himself challenges of immense physicality, honoring boxers and trapezists far more directly than any of Mailer's protestations do, honoring Hemingway too. Maybe ultimately the man he sets out to do obeisance before is not these temporal champions but the old writing master himself.

Generosity is another Hemingway attribute to fame that one must look to Plimpton for. Probably Hemingway was not very generous at all, no more than Mailer, both being too competitive—nice guys finish last, and all that—generous to women and waiters only. But the physical bulk, the Mosaic beard, the Papa pose, with the passing of time, make us suppose that Hemingway, basking in fame, should have been a generous man. Instead it's the skinny Plimpton who is generous—Plimpton and another New York writer, Pete Hamill, who may be the most generous of all and deserves mention particularly here in connection with Hemingway fame because it is Hamill who, locally, almost alone is maintaining that celebrative function Hemingway valued so much: recording the midnight feasts that he has with movie stars, con artists, revolutionaries, cornermen, the good meals and drinking bouts, the good men who live here in town. Hamill, of course, is proudly provincial, as

Hemingway wasn't, and wouldn't know the first thing to do if invited out into the woods on a fishing trip—wouldn't want to know. But the celebration of the good things that come with success is there.

This sensuous sense of the enjoyment of fame has been scattered and lost. Success for my father was lawns, clubs, trips, a Colonial house and other things that at least were fun to have. But is what writers want so much fun to have? Nowadays they tend to look for investments, to take a block of RCA stock in lieu of an advance, or they are looking at real estate. The clean handling of fame is what's asked for—not too much clowning with Eugene McCarthy, a low profile, a civilized private life well enclaved within the mysteries of the craft. One thinks of the admirably elusive Updike and Roth.

None of my friends who have had movie sales have enjoyed what appeared on the screen, but the big sales of a book itself bring plenty of pleasure. Seeing it displayed, seeing it read—the more readers the better—by the hundreds of thousands in paperback. One wants it on newsstands and in college libraries—this more than fame, like wishing good things for one's children. Just as acting is not really a board and two mummers, but must be vivified by an audience, so writers yearn to reach loads of people and only want to block out the grotesqueries of fan mail, the career calculations, as tainting the dream. I can easily place limits on how much money I'd care to make, how much fame would satiate me if the world were my oyster, but to wonder how many readers I'd like to have . . . None captive, certainly, but millions who opened a book of mine and found something for them—millions! How large would that ideal audience be? Like James Michener's? Johnny Carson's? When the world achieves a population of fifteen billion people, would one want them for an audience, just before they all die? Though we are beginning to sicken of past concepts of growth, artists may never cease longing for a big audience.

Power, now, has that changed? Power has nearly brought the world down around our ears; yet side by side with the revulsion there is love of it still. My Irish friends come back from touring the battlefronts of Londonderry with blood in their eyes—more delight and exultancy than tragedy, really, not like when they flew back from Vietnam. They think it's 1936 and the war in Spain. The Italians embrace the Mafia for their own, and one remembers how every Jewish intellectual who could flag down a cab flew to Israel after the Six-Day War (a lady I knew slept on the desert floor with a tank commander), while here in New York the kids jammed into automobiles and sped through the streets waving Israeli flags and pounding their fists on the doors of the cars, all in the triumph of victory—this after the horrors of World War II.

We have blood in our bones. Power, fame and success, we want them. One's beginnings are humble. Some years ago I sold an idea to *The New Yorker* for twenty-five dollars (a friend wrote it up), and the *Reader's Digest* bought four words out of a book of mine for fifteen dollars. Then three years ago I first heard breathlessness over the phone. A girl called, after I'd published a short story about alligators. "Would you come and talk to our herpetology club?" she asked, her voice trembling.

I go to the *Village Voice* and talk to my friend there,

Ross Wetzsteon. The *Voice* is a child of its times and subject to as many criticisms. Nevertheless it has about it the excitement, the variety and fervor, the many personalities, even the brilliance being nurtured, that one reads of in literary memoirs about *The Nation, New Republic* and so on in their heydays. He and I are old friends and are probably in our busiest years—busy to distraction—and whatever finally comes to us in the way of success, it is great fun.

HOWLING BACK
AT THE WOLVES

Wolves have marvelous legs. The first thing one notices about them is how high they are set on their skinny legs, and the instant, blurred gait these can switch into, bicycling away, carrying them as much as forty miles in a day. With brindled coats in smoky shades, brushy tails, light-filled eyes, intense sharp faces which are more focused than an intelligent dog's but also less various, they are electric on first sighting, bending that bushy head around to look back as they run. In captivity when they are quarreling in a cage, the snarls sound guttural and their jaws chop, but scientists watching pet wolves in the woods speak of their flowing joy, of such a delight in running that they melt into the woods like sunlight, like running water.

The modern study of American wildlife may be said to have begun with Adolph Murie, who, writing about the wolves of Mount McKinley in 1944, realized there was not much point in a scientist's shooting them; so few wolves were left that this would be killing the goose laying the golden eggs. In those days even the biologists dealing with animals which weren't considered varmints mainly just boiled the flesh off their heads to examine the knobs on their skulls, or opened their stomachs to see what they ate. The scrutiny of skulls had resulted in a listing of eighty-six species and subspecies of the grizzly bear, for example (it's now considered that there were a maximum of only two), and twenty-seven specified New World wolves (again, now revised down to two). Murie, in the field and looking at scats, could do a more thorough investigation of diet than the autopsy fellows, who, as it was, knew almost nothing else about the life of wolves.

Murie and Ian McTaggart Cowan in Canada were the best of the bedroll scientists. They could travel with dogs all winter in the snow or camp alone on a gravel bar in a valley for the summer, go about quietly on foot and record everything that they saw. No amount of bush-plane maneuvering and electronic technology can quite replace these methods, by which the totality of a wilderness community can be observed and absorbed. Young scientists such as L. David Mech, who has been the salvation of wolves in Minnesota, which is practically the only place in the lower forty-eight states where they still occur, try to combine the current reliance on radiotelemetry with some of that old bedroll faithfulness to the five senses shared by a man with the animals he is studying.

Big game, like elk and caribou, and big glamorous predators have naturally received first attention, people being as they are, so that much more is known about wolves than about the grasshopper mouse, though the grasshopper mouse is a wolf among mice, trailing, gorging upon small mammals and insects; in fact, with nose pointed skyward, it even "howls." On lists of endangered species you occasionally find little beasts that wouldn't excite much attention on a picnic outing, but despite all the talk about saving the fruits of two billion years' worth of evolution, the funds available go to help those animals that tend to remind us of ourselves—rhinos, whales, falcons—and there aren't many lists of endangered plants.

So it is that the predator specialists are predatory. A hawk man drops out of the sky for a visit; he has radios attached to assorted raptors and albatrosses and swans, and flies around the world to track their migrations. During his chat about perfecting antennas it is obvious that he is full of what in an animal he would call "displaced aggression." The scientist Albert Erickson, who has worked on grizzlies in the north and leopard seals in Antarctica, was known as "Wild Man Erickson" when he studied black bears in Michigan. The Craighead brothers, Frank and John—territorial, secretive and competitive—have been working on a definitive study of grizzlies (which are also territorial, secretive and competitive) for umpteen years, scrapping with the National Park Service at Yellowstone and embargoing many of their own findings in the meantime. Maurice Hornocker, who is now the definitive mountain-lion man and who trained with them, is just as close-mouthed—as close-mouthed as a mountain lion, indeed. Down in Grand Chenier, Louisiana, Ted Joanen, the state's alligator expert, is equally able and reserved. One doesn't understand right away why he happens to be devoting his life to learning more about alligators than anybody else, rather than ibises or chimney swifts or pelicans, until he gets to describing how alligators can catch a swimming deer, pull it under the water, drown it and tear its leg off by spinning like a lathe, and then points to one's own twitching leg.

Wolves *would* be more of a loss to us than some exotic mouse, because they epitomize the American wilderness as no other animal does, and fill both the folklore of childhood and that of the woods—folklore that would wither away if they all were to die, and may do so in any case. We know that the folklore was exaggerated, that generally they don't attack man, which is a relief, but we treasure the stories nonetheless, wanting the woods to be woods. In the contiguous states the gray wolf's range is less than one percent of what it used to be, and that patch of Minnesota wilderness, twelve thousand square miles where they live in much the same density as in primeval times, is greatly enriched by the presence of wolves.

Wisconsin didn't get around to granting its wolves protection until they had become extinct, but Mech got the Minnesota bounty removed and almost single-handedly turned local thinking around, until there is talk of declaring the wolf a "state animal" and establishing a sanctuary for it in the Boundary Waters Canoe Area. Mech is a swift-thinking, urbane, amused man, bald, round-faced, not a bit wolflike in appearance, although he is sharp in his rivalry with other scientists. As an advocate he knows how to generate "spontaneous" nationwide letter-writing campaigns and can gather financial support from the National Geographic Society and the New York Zoological Society,

from Minneapolis industrialists and the federal government. He has a soul-stirring howl, more real than reality,
that triggers the wolves into howling back when he is
afoot trying to locate them, but his ears have begun to dim
from a decade or more of flying all winter in flimsy planes
to spot them against the snow. Sometimes he needs an
assistant along to hear whether a pack at a distance is
answering him.

That wolves do readily answer even bad imitations of
their howl may have a good deal of significance. Observers have noticed the similarities between the intricate life
of a wolf pack and the most primitive grouping of man,
the family-sized band. Often there is a "peripheral wolf,"
for instance, which is tolerated but picked on, and as
though the collective psyche of the pack required a scape-
goat, if the peripheral wolf disappears another pack member may slip down the social ladder and assume the role,
or a stray that otherwise might have been driven off will
be adopted. The strays, or "lone wolves," not being bound
by territorial considerations, range much farther and frequently eat better than pack wolves do, but are always
seeking to enroll themselves.

What seems so uncanny and moving about the experience of howling to wolves, then hearing them answer, may
be the enveloping sense of déjà vu, perhaps partly sub-
liminal, that goes right to one's roots—band replying to
band, each on its own ground, gazing across a few hundred yards of meadow or bog at the same screen of trees.
The listener rises right up on his toes, looking about happily at his human companions.

Wolf pups make a frothy ribbon of sound like fat bubbling, a shiny, witchy, fluttery yapping, while the adults siren less excitably, without those tremulous, flexible yips, although they sometimes do break pitch into a yodel. The senior wolf permits the response, if one is made, introducing it with his own note after a pause—which is sometimes lengthy—before the others join in. Ordinarily pups left alone will not answer unless the adult closest to them does so, as he or she returns to protect them. Wolves howl for only a half-minute or so, though they may respond again and again after a cautious intermission, if no danger is indicated from their having already betrayed their position. Each wolf has a tone, or series of tones, of its own that blends into an iridescent harmony with the others, and people who howl regularly at a wolf rendezvous soon acquire vocal personalities too, as well as a kind of choral sequence in which they join together—cupping their mouths to the shape of a muzzle on cue.

I went out with a student of Mech's, Fred Harrington, who records and voice-prints wolf howls. His wife was along, doing the puppy trills, and so was the trap-line crew, who attach radio-collars to the wolves they catch. We stood at the edge of a cutover jack-pine flat, with a few tall spruces where the wolves were. The sun was setting, the moon was rising, squirrels and birds were chitting close by, and we knew that a radio-collared bear was digging its winter den just over the rise. Howling is not a hunting cry and does not frighten other animals. The wolves howled as if for their own edification, as a pleasurable thing, a popular, general occasion set off by our calls to them, replying to us but not led by our emphasis or interpretation. If they had been actively scouting us they would have kept silent, as they do in the spring when the pups are too young to travel. To us, their chorus sounded isolated, vulnerable, the more so because obviously they were having fun, and we all felt the urge to run toward them; but they didn't share that feeling. A pack needs at least ten square miles for each member, as well as a deer every eighteen days for that individual, or a deer every three days for a pack of six. The figure for moose is one every three days for a pack of fifteen, Mech has calculated. Thus, howling between packs does not serve the function of calling them to confabulate. Instead, it seems to keep them apart, defining rough boundaries for their separate ranges, providing them mutually with a roster of strength, though by howling, mates in a pack do find one another and find solidarity.

In Algonquin Provincial Park in Ontario thousands of people howl with the wolves in the early autumn. Whether or not it is a high point for the wolves, it certainly is for the people. I've gone to one of the favorite locations, where the ground is littered with cigarette butts, and tried, except the day was rainy and the wolves couldn't hear me. Nobody who has had the experience will fail to root for the beasts ever after. Glacier National Park in Montana is next to Canada, like Mech's country, and they may manage to become reestablished there; Yellowstone Park has a small vanguard. In East Texas a few hundred survive, hiding in the coastal marshes. These are red wolves—relic relations of the gray wolf that inhabited the Southeast and lower Mississippi Valley and are probably now doomed, pushed up against the sea, with no reservoir such as the wildlands of Canada provide from which to replenish their numbers.

Apparently a special relationship can exist between men and wolves which is unlike that between men and any of the bears or big cats. One might have to look to the other primates for a link that is closer. It's not just a matter of howling; owls with their hoots and loons with their laughter also interact with wolves. Nor is it limited to the mystery of why dogs, about fifteen thousand years back, which is very recent as such events go, cut themselves away from other wolves by a gradual, at first "voluntary" process to become subservient to human beings as no other domestic creature is, running with man in packs in which *he* calls the tune. Another paradox is that the wolves which remained wolves, though they are large predators that might legitimately regard a man-shaped item as prey, don't seem to look upon him as such; don't even challenge him in the woods in quite the same way that they will accost a trespassing cougar or grizzly.

In the campaign to rescue the wolf from Red Riding-hood status, some scientists, including Mech, have over-done their testimonials as to its liberal behavior, becoming so categorical that they doubt that any North American wolf not rabid has ever attacked a human being. This does violence to scientific method, as well as to the good name of countless frontiersmen who knew more about the habits of wilderness animals than it is possible to learn today. (What these scientists really mean is that none of their Ph. D. candidates doing field work has been attacked by

a wolf so far.) Such propaganda also pigeonholes the wolf
in a disparaging way, as if it were a knee-jerk creature
without any options, like a blowfish or hog-nosed snake.
But the link with man remains. Douglas H. Pimlott, who
is Canada's wolf expert, explores this matter in *The
World of the Wolf*. He mentions behavioral patterns that
are shared by man and wolf, and by indirection might
have come to influence wolves. Both hunt cooperatively in
groups and are nearly unique in that respect; both have
lived in complex bands in which the adults of either sex
care for the young. He mentions the likelihood that there
are subconscious attributes of the human mind that may
affect wolves. After all, the bonds between a man and dog
penetrate far beyond the awe of the one for the other—
are more compulsive, more telepathic than awe—and
cannot be fully explained under the heading of love.
Wolves, like dogs, says Pimlott, are excellent readers of
signs because of their social makeup and their cruising
system of hunting, which does not depend as much on
surprise as the habits of most other predators do: "They
instinctively recognize aggression, fear, and other qualities
of mind which are evidenced in subtle ways by our expressions and actions. . . . In hunting we stalk deliberately,
quietly . . . in winter we move through the woods and
across lakes and streams deliberately, as a wolf does in
traveling over his range, hunting for prey."

These movements indicate to wolves that we are superior predators—superior wolves—and not prey. It
could be added that wolves, like dogs, take a remarkable
delight in submissive ritual, ingratiating themselves, pla-

cating a bigger, more daring beast—this part of their adaptation through the millennia to life in a pack, in which usually only one or two members are really capable of killing the sizable game that will feed many mouths; the rest dance attendance upon them. Of course not only the fellow prowling in the woods is predatory. In the city, when much more driving and successful men emerge on the street for a business lunch, their straight-line strides and manner, "bright-eyed and bushy-tailed," would bowl over any wolf.

THE PROBLEM
OF THE
GOLDEN RULE

Like a good many New Yorkers, I've often wondered whether I was going to be mugged. I've lived in a number of neighborhoods, and being a night walker, have many times changed my course or speeded my stride, eying a formidable-looking figure as he approached. But it's never happened, and I imagine that if it finally does there may actually be a kind of relief, even a species of exhilaration, as I pick myself up—assuming that I am not badly hurt—because a danger anticipated for a long time may come to seem worse than the reality. People who come home and encounter a robber in their apartment who flees are likely to be less shaken up than the householder is who simply steps into a shambles of ransacked bureaus and upended beds: they've seen the fellow; they know he's human. A friend of mine wrestled a burglar for several minutes around the floor of his living room, both of them using the trips and hip throws that they remembered from their teens, until by the time my friend won and phoned the police they were old acquaintances.

I know, too, that to describe the few incidents of violence I've met with in the past makes them sound more grisly than they were in fact. In the army, my platoon was put in the charge of a peculiar sergeant who, mostly for reasons of his own, had us do squat jumps one noontime until we could no longer walk or stand up. Then he strolled among us kicking us to make sure that we weren't faking. It was a hot drill field strewn with packs and stacked rifles and other movie props, and yet the experience was not nearly as bad as one would anticipate if he were told at breakfast what to expect that day. We just followed orders until we couldn't get up and then we lay where we were on the ground until the sergeant was satisfied that we had done what was humanly possible. Even in a true atrocity situation that's all that is ever done: what is humanly possible. Afterwards one becomes unresponsive and fatalistic; terror is no longer a factor.

Next day the sergeant wanted to have it both ways, so he set us into formation and told us what he was going to make us do, and thereupon went off to the latrine to give us a chance to stand at attention and think and stew. Another sergeant promptly walked up and dismissed us, however. We hobbled away in every direction as fast as possible, while the two sergeants met to discuss the issue in the barracks door. They met person-to-person, and we had been punished person-to-person, and the facelessness of the mugger whom one anticipates meeting on Little West 12th Street was never a part of it. This, like our doing whatever was humanly possible, made the experience supportable.

I visualize Armageddon not as a steel-muzzled affair of push-button silos under the earth but as a rusty freighter, flying the Liberian flag, perhaps, which sails inconspicuously up the Hudson past my apartment and goes off. Beyond that I don't see any details—though, as a non sequitur, I expect the tunnels and bridges would fill up with hikers leaving the city before it was too late. A woman I know says she sees Armageddon as getting under the bed. What we do with the insupportable is to turn it to terms we can file and forget. Unfortunately we are able to deal almost as handily with the nuclear bombs that have already gone off as we are with the ones that haven't. If as individual fighting men we had razed Hiroshima, then the horror of its destruction would persist as a legend to our greatgrandchildren because it would have been witnessed and done on the spot—also because of the somber old notion that residing in every man is a spark of divinity, whether the man is an enemy or a friend. This putative spark is central to most religious belief; and right at the root of Western ethics is what is called, under one of its names, the Golden Rule. But spark or no spark, since in practice we cannot react to others with unabashed fellow-feeling, we usually reduce the Golden Rule to a sort of silver rule, doing to them just about what we think they would do to us if they had the opportunity. And this works—has been working—though the new impersonalized technology is challenging its workability, along with another behemoth among changes, which is that today

273

there are too many people. Where there are too many people, we get tired of following even the silver rule, tired of paying that much attention, of noticing whom we are with and who is who. For the agnostic as well, basing his reverence for life on its variety and on a Jeffersonian fascination with the glimmerings of talent in every man, the glut is discouraging. Although we don't ridicule these old ideas, the sentiments that people have for one another in a traffic jam are becoming our sentiments more and more. A groan goes up in any suburb when it's announced that a new complex of housing for two thousand souls is going to be built on Lone Tree Hill. And the vast sigh of impatience which greeted Pope Paul's traditionalist statement of faith in the sanctity of the seed germs of life points to the tone to come. *Life for the living,* people will say: body-counts in war and baby-counts in peace. We grant each union man his $10,500 a year, and then the hell with him. He, for his part, doesn't care if our garbage cans fester with rats when the union goes after $10,900.

Never have people dealt so briskly with strangers as now. Many of us have ceased to see strangers at all; our eyes simply don't register them except as verticals on the sidewalk, and when we must parley with them we find out quickly what they are asking from us, do it—maybe—and that's that. When I was a child I remember how my astonishment evolved as I realized that people often would not do the smallest thing to convenience another person or make him feel easier for the moment. Of course I'd known that *kids* wouldn't, but I had thought that was because they were kids. It was my first comprehension of the deadness of life. Everyone has discovered at some particular point life's deadness, but the galloping sense of deadness which alarms so many people lately, and especially the young, goes way beyond such individual discoveries to dimensions and contexts that have brought revolution to the U.S. Even in the arts the ancient austerities have been deemed insufficient, and we have actors who jump into the audience and do their acting there. When acting seems to fail, they improvise, and finally improvisation isn't enough either, and instead of having an actor play the drug addict, the addict himself must appear onstage and play himself—like the toothpaste tube blown up and hanging on the museum wall: "Look, if nothing else, I'm real." This is the era when students are so busy trying to teach their teachers that they are hard to teach, and when the chip on the shoulder of the man in the street is his "personality"—personality is quarrelsomeness. The revolution, in any case, is overdue, but maybe our best hope is that we remain at least idiosyncratic creatures, absorbed close to home. Dog owners, when they walk their dogs, show nearly as exact an interest in their pets' defecations as they would in their own. The same communing silence steals over their faces, the look of musing solemnity, that usually only the bathroom mirror gets a glimpse of.

The worst public tragedy I've witnessed was in Boston, when from a distance I saw a brick wall fall on a company of firemen. Some, with a great shout, got away, but even the leap that they made while the rest crumpled is blurred as a memory compared to the images of two old men whom I knew very slightly at the time. Mr. Kate wrote cookbooks in the winter and hired out as a cook on a private yacht during the warm months. His other love, besides cooking, was opera, and he lived in a room shaped like a shoebox that cost him eight dollars a week. He served himself candlelit meals on a folding table and concocted all of his recipes on a hotplate set in the sink. By contrast, Mr. Hurth, although a somewhat less cultivated man, was an alumnus of Brown University and lived in a large ground-floor room in the same house. He had ruined himself in a scandal in St. Louis, where he had been a businessman, but that was all I learned. What he'd done next was to come to Boston and throw himself on the old-fashioned, private or "Christian" charity, as it used to be called, of a roommate from college, though thirty years had passed. He was a pleasant subdued man ordinarily, swinging from sweet to vaguely hangdog, but he was a drinker, and so this benefactor no longer asked him to Newton Centre for Thanksgiving because he was likely to break the furniture. When he did, he'd leave his glasses behind by mistake so that he'd have to go back out again for a whole second festival of apologies. Through charitable intercession, Mr. Hurth was on the payroll of the John Hancock Insurance Company, being listed on the books as a claims investigator, though actually (charity compounding charity) his single duty was to work for the United Fund once a year on a loan basis. The campaign was a brief one, but he was a bitter, floundering functionary, faced with his fate if his drinking should snap off his last sticks of presence and respectability.

As I say, next to the memory of two nodding acquaintances the death of some distant firemen is small potatoes. I was reminded of that catastrophe the other night for the first time in years while watching a fire on Third Avenue. Here in the bigger city one is witness to such a cataract of appalling happenings that they pass remembering. I saw a man who had just been burned out of his apartment turned away from a hotel in the neighborhood because he had a little blacking on him, although the shock and fear stood in his eyes. "Sure, there was a fire there, all right," the manager told me with a laugh. "I never take them in, those victims. They're dirty and they're scared to death. They're not worth the nuisance."

He was a modern, casual villain, however, impartial, just the kind who is not memorable. I came upon a much less gratuitous drama a few days afterwards. A child of two or three had been stuck inside one of those all-glass phone booths with a spring door which cannot be opened except by a grown person because of where the handle is placed. The world was passing—this was on the open street—but he was feeling his way around the glass in gathering panic, trying to find an escape route, reaching up and reaching down. Every few seconds he let out a thin, fluting scream so pure in pitch that it was hardly human; it was *pre*-human. You could see him thinking, learning, recording discoveries. He reached for the phone, but that was too high up; he thumped each pane of glass, searching for the door, and pounded on the metal frame, and screamed to find whether screaming would work. He was boxed into his terror, and you could see him grow older by leaps and bounds. I'm just this month a new father, so I was as transfixed as if he were my child. His governess or baby-sitter, baby-walker, or whatever she was, a short shadowy woman such as you might see manning a subway change booth, was standing right next to the glass, apparently feasting her eyes. Whether it was supposed to be a "punishment" or merely a pleasure fest, the child was too frightened by now to notice her.

Maybe our cruelty will save us. At least the cruel do pay attention, and the woman would probably have let him out before the crowd got around to hearing him. She had moved to the door, looking down at him intently as he pushed on the glass. I was seething, partly because I found that some of the woman's sexual excitement had communicated itself to me, which was intolerable, and partly because my cowardice in not interfering was equally outrageous. We've all become reluctant to stop and stick our noses in—a man is run over by a Breakstone cream-cheese truck and we pass quickly by. But cowardice was what it was in this particular event, since even under happy circumstances I stutter and it requires an enormous gearing up of nerve for me to step into a public fracas on the street. I strangle; I can't speak at all and must either use my hands on the stranger or gag and quaver, unable to put two words together. The seams of human nature frighten me in this regard, and the whole confrontation ethic of the sixties, much as I have entered into it on occasion, gives me nightmare visions because I have no conventional means of battling. I see myself as unable to protest in words to the person whose behavior has angered me and so using my hands on him; then just as unable to explain myself to the crowd that gathers, but only shuddering and stuttering; and then in court again enforcedly silent, dependent on the empathy or telepathic capacities of the people who are there to convey my side of the controversy.

Weaving like a nauseous moose, I was working my way toward her, when the woman, with a glance at me, pushed the door of the booth open, reached inside, and pulled the boy to her and walked away. In effect, I was let off, because only an exceptional well-doer would have tracked the woman down from that point on and questioned her about her psyche.

However, there are times one isn't let off, when one's very humanity hangs at issue and perhaps my specific problems with my stutter are an epitome of what each of us meets. Once in northern New England when I was snowshoeing, a hunter started shooting at me, really only to scare me, pinging with his .22 in my immediate vicinity. I was on an open hillside which I'd already realized was too slippery to climb, but as long as I kept scrabbling there in silence on the ice, like an animal in trouble, he was going to keep on pinging. Because a stutterer's every impulse is to stutter softly, unobtrusively, it's twice as hard to shout one's way through a stutter as to wedge through in quiet tones; but from the sheer imperatives of survival I shouted, "I CAN SEE YOU!" I shouted it several times again, although I couldn't see him; he was in the woods. I was insisting and reiterating that I was a human being: if I could get that message across to him he would stop shooting at me. It was even worse than my conception of a courtroom trial because this was one of those rare emergencies when we can't trust to all our faculties to operate together for us—the movements of our hands, our youth or age, our manner and expression— some compensating for the inadequacies of the others. I had to go to bat with my speaking abilities and nothing else. So I shouted to him that I could see him, by which I meant I was a man, and he stopped shooting.

More recently, I was on a tiny Danish island off the coast of Sweden, wandering around some seventeenth-century fortifications and the walled town, now a huddled fishing village. I had sat on the sea wall to watch the cloud action but was distracted by the spectacle below me of a boy mistreating a wild duck. Oddly enough, many times an incident where a person, rather than an animal, is being mauled and manhandled is easier to shrug off. The fact that he's a person complicates the case. As an on-looker you can see, for example, that he has gotten himself drunk and let his guard down, lost his dignity, talked out of turn. But the duck, with its wings clipped, presumably, was only trying to run away. The boy would catch it, pummel it and grip it tightly, trundling it about. Finally I got off my bench and went over and told him falteringly to cut that out. Many Danes speak English, but he was twelve or so and he may not have understood me. Like a mirror of myself, he stared at me without trying to say a word. Then he squeezed the duck again hard in both hands. My bugaboo about trying to explain myself to strangers rose in me, along with my indignation. Instead of looking for a local fellow to translate and take over, I lifted the duck from his arms, and with the sense of right and doom that I have dreaded in foreseeing a confrontation on the street, carried it down the stairs of the sea wall and released it on the beach. The boy ran for help; the duck paddled into the waves; I climbed to the promenade and started walking as deliberately as I could toward the small boat which had brought me to the island.

Uncannily soon, before I'd gone a dozen yards, practically the whole male populace was on the scene. "Hey! Turn around!" they yelled. I took another couple of steps away and then did so. They told me very plainly in English that they were going to throw me over the sea wall. They said the duck had been rescued by the boys of the island—their sons—after it had swum through an oil slick and almost drowned. Now, because of what I'd done, it really *was* about to drown, and when it went under, they would toss me over. This was not spoken in joking tones, and I could see the duck getting heavier in the water; its feathers, though as tidy to the eye as a healthy duck's feathers, had no buoyancy. Meanwhile, I'd fallen into something like what a prizefighter would call a clinch by refusing to acknowledge by any sign that I understood what was being said to me. It is a psychological necessity that when you punish somebody he understand the reason why. Even if he doesn't accept the guilty finding, you must explain to him why you are punishing him or you

281

can't do it. So while they could scarcely contain their frustration, my face displayed bewilderment; I kept pretending to grope to understand. I was doing this instinctively, of course, and as their first impetus to violence passed, I found myself acting out with vehemence how I had seen the boy mistreat the duck. The men, who wanted at the least to take a poke at me, watched doubtfully, but there was a Coast Guardsman, an off-islander, who seemed to be arguing in Danish on my behalf. Another man went down to where the duck was swimming and reached out; the duck perceiving itself to be sinking, had moved cautiously closer to shore. And when the duck was saved I was saved; I only had the island's boys waiting for me in the embrasures of the wall.

Yet this quite comic misadventure, when every dread came real—I couldn't say a single word to save my life—was just as numbing as those ninety-five squat jumps at Fort Dix—only later was it terrifying. And in a way it makes up for the memories I have as a teenager of watching flocks of bats murdered with brooms and frogs tormented—moments when I didn't interfere, but giggled ruefully to keep my popularity and stifle my outcries.

Sociology progresses; the infant mortality rate among Negroes goes down. Nevertheless we know that if the announcement were made that there was going to be a public hanging in Central Park, Sheep Meadow would be crowded with spectators, like Tyburn mall. Sometimes at night my standing lamp shapes itself into an observant phantom figure which takes a position next to my bed. It doesn't threaten me directly, and I stretch out to clutch its throat with careful anger. My final grab bumps the lamp over. This electric phantom is a holdover from my vivid night demons when I was eight or ten. I never saw them outright, thank the Lord, but for years I fell asleep facing the wall to avoid beholding my destruction. I'd "whisper," as I called it, when I went to bed, telling myself an installment of a round-robin story, and when the installment was over I'd wait for the demons, until I fell asleep. Later, just as invariably, I faced the outer room so I could see them come and have warning to fight. Such archaisms in our minds are not an unmixed evil, however, because they link us to humanity and to our history as human beings. My wife says every man she's been familiar with would smell his socks at night before he went to bed: just a whiff—each sock, not only one. I do this too, although the smell has been of no intrinsic interest to me for twenty years. The smell of each sock checks precisely with the other one and smells as vital as pigs do. Maybe it reassures us that we're among the living still. We need to know. In the fifties I also liked the smell of air pollution. I didn't think of it as air pollution then—nobody did—but as the smell of industry and the highways I hitchhiked on, the big-shouldered America I loved.

In 1943 George Orwell said the problem of the times was the decay in the belief in personal immortality. Several French novelists had turned existentialist and several English novelists Catholic (possibly the same reaction), while he himself, like many of the more likable writers, had adopted a hardy humanist's masculine skepticism. Twenty-odd years later, the problem appears only to have grown more piercing, though it is not put into the same terms. You can't have as many people walking around as there are now and still simply see them as chips off the divine lodestone. Nor is the future *1984*: that's too succinct. At first the new nuclear bullying, the new technocracy, made mere survival more the point, because we wanted to be sure of surviving here on earth before we worried about heaven. Lately, instead the talk has been about overpopulation, and city people have started venturing to the outback, buying acreage with all the premonitory fervor of Noah sawing logs. Everyone wants space to breathe; the character of city life has drastically deteriorated, and there's no questioning the statistics, just as there used to be no questioning the odds that eventually a nuclear war was going to penetrate our precautions through that old fontanel of existence: human mix-up.

When we say that enough is enough, that we have enough people on hand now for any good purpose, we mean that the divine spark has become something of a conflagration, besides an embarrassment of riches. We're trying to make a start at sorting the riches, buying Edwardian clothes but also Volkswagens, and settling down to the process of zoning the little land there is. As we also begin to cogitate on how the quality of life can be improved, we may be in for a religious revival, too. It's a natural beginning, and faddism will probably swing that way, and after all, we *are* extraordinary—we're so extraordinary we're everywhere. Next to the new mysticisms, old-fashioned, run-of-the-mill religion is not so hard to swallow. The difficulty will be how we regard individual people, a question which involves not only whether we think we're immortal but whether we think they are. The crowded impatience of suburb-city living doesn't often evoke intimations of other people's immortality, and neither do the hodge-podge leveling procedures of a modern democracy. So much of the vigor of the Victorian church, for instance, grew out of the contrast between its members and the raw, destitute brown masses who covered the rest of the globe. Among an elite, self-congratulatory minority even the greatest of attributes—immortality—seemed plausible.

But maybe I'm being overly sour. We have wiped tigers off the earth and yet our children hear as much about the symbolism of tigers as children did in the old days. And next to the subway station I use there is a newsdealer who was blinded in Orwell's war, the Spanish War, in the mountains behind Motril. He wears the aura of a revolutionary volunteer. He dresses bulkily, as if for weather at the front, and rigs canvas around his hut as neatly as a soldier's tent. Not one of your meek blind men, he's on his feet most of the day, especially in tough weather, pacing, marching, standing tall. He's gray and grim, hard and spare, and doubtless lives surrounded by the companions that he had in the Sierra Nevada. But he's too bluff and energetic to be a museum piece. If you help him cross the street you get the rough edge of his tongue. He searches for the lamppost with his cane like a tennis player swinging backhand, and if he loses his bearings and bumps against something, he jerks abruptly back like a cavalier insulted, looking gaunt and fierce. I pity him, but I take note of him; he counts himself among the living. I buy a paper and go home to my newborn baby, who is as intense and focused (to my eye) as a flight of angels dancing on a pinhead.

I don't believe in a god you can pray to, but I do find I believe in God—I do more than I don't. I believe in glee and in the exuberance I feel with friends and animals and in the fields, and in other emotions besides that. Anyway, as we know, it really isn't necessary to see sparks of a grand divinity in someone else to feel with the old immediacy that he is kin; we can evolve a more sophisticated Golden Rule than that. We will be trying to refine and revivify the qualities of life, and the chief stumbling block is that we must somehow reduce the density of people in our own comings and goings without doing it as we do now, which is by simply not seeing them, by registering them as shadows to dodge by on the street. Without degenerating into callousness, we must develop our ability to switch on and off—something analogous to what we do already with body temperature in a harsh world. Generally we'd button up if we were out walking, but when the Breakstone cream-cheese truck ran over an old man, this would be a time when our ancient instinct for cherishing a stranger would spring to being.

I live in a high-rise apartment and keep a pair of field glasses next to the window to use whenever somebody emerges on one of the rooftops nearby. There are ten or fifteen regulars—old people hanging wash, high school

kids who have come up into the open to talk where they
can be alone. All of them are neighbors to me now, though
on the street I probably would turn away from them—
even the bathing beauties would not be beauties there.
Admittedly I am a bit of a voyeur, as who isn't, but the
population density on the rooftops seems about right. In
fact, I roused myself not long ago to drive some robbers
off a roof across the street by gesticulating sternly. They
waved back as they went down the stairs like people
who've escaped a fall.

FRED KING

ON THE

ALLAGASH

One of the arguments used
by the logging industry in opposing proposals that a few
wilderness areas be set aside is that there is no real wilderness left in the Northeast, anyway, or east of the Mississippi, or in any mountain range in the West that may be
discussed—no tract of forest that hasn't already been
logged, no river drainage that hasn't been dammed. It's
all gone now, say the lumbermen complacently. But it's all
that we have, the conservationists insist, and so the battle
is joined.

On the Allagash watershed in northern Maine, woods
that have been logged over three or four times, a compromise was struck. The lumbermen gave up very little
of their land, and yet the first of the nation's officially
"wild" rivers was brought under state control—conveyed,
in effect, to the canoeists. Because of where it is and
because the acreage involved is small (24,000 acres in
government hands, versus 1.1 million, for example, in the
Boundary Waters Canoe Area of Minnesota), the Allagash

Wilderness Waterway has quickly come under recreational pressure, perhaps representing the managerial dilemmas other areas will soon face. I wanted to see what it was like, and—most unfashionably in this democratic age—hired a guide so that I could use my paddle as a writing table part of the time and, being a novice, not bother with questions of navigation.

Fred King was talking about bush pilots in the motel at Shin Pond, where we met. He said there were old pilots and bold pilots, but he knew of one who was both old and bold. This man would fly out a sick fisherman at night in a little plane with no instruments, by moonlight alone. Fred King keeps track of these things. He's fifty-eight, looks forty-five, has short hair which is bluish gray, round glasses, a boyish doggy grin, a face deeply cut by grinning and a mouth big enough to grin with. It's a pleasing face; his body is straight and quick like a chipmunk's and he has an immediate laugh, provocatively loud, and likes to stop still when on the move and sound off on the matter at hand, then impulsively move forward again, seeming never to walk if he can run. At home in Augusta he keeps a jug of Allagash water to mix with his drinks, and doesn't much like December because of the short days; "I'd sell December awfully cheap." Until he became too controversial for the local talk show, he would go on TV in December, in his red guide's shirt, and kill the long evenings that way.

It's only been in the past ten years that Fred has canoed. His father died when he was young, and though he had started in college with the idea of graduating as an engineer, he quit and went off for two years to the woods, wintering in a cabin he built for himself six days distant by team and wagon from the community of Ashland, Maine. He was trying to trap—this was in the middle of the Depression—but went about it wrong. The right-headed way to learn how to trap would have been to pair up with an older fellow and learn from him, he says. Instead he had a full-time job just surviving, and during the first winter had to reinforce his roof with material hauled on a toboggan from an abandoned shanty several miles away.

He still likes to be by himself. His ideas sound as if they had been worked out in isolation in the woods and perhaps spoken first in a loud voice all alone. He has a tight shipshape cabin on Chemquassabamticook Lake where he goes in midwinter and works on improvements, hauling now with a snowmobile. He's got to break trail for the snowmobile on snowshoes—it's not like the ads—but he loves the rigor of the winter woods, cooks for himself and sleeps fitfully, listening to the radio and waiting for his mouse trap to snap. The mice he feeds to the gorbies—Canada jays—outside.

Fred worked on highway crews and during World War II was a shipyard pipe-fitter in Portland, but has been self-employed ever since. He would buy a piece of land and build a house on it, doing all the work, then "find somebody fool enough to buy." By fifty he tired of that, not so much because it was strenuous as because he wanted to go back to his original vision of himself. Though not an exceptional woodsman, he's taken the trouble to learn some of the historical lore, and particularly to latch onto a few of the vanishing old rivermen and listen and learn from them, trying modestly to carry on some of the traditions in their name. He also has a kind of guffawing admiration of wealth: more successful men who have blasted a steadier ascent in the world he calls "roosters." "Quite a rooster," he'll say of a fellow who wears nifty clothes nowadays, and will boisterously recite a ditty he learned in school:

"Dear Lord, in the battle that goes on through life,
I ask but a field that is fair. . .
A chance that is equal to all in the strife,
And the courage to do and to dare.
And if I should win, let it be by the code,
With my faith and my honor held high,
And if I should lose, let me stand by the road
and cheer as the winner goes by."

Another old chestnut of his is, "So late we get smart, so soon we get old."

The Allagash flows north for ninety-some miles. Its headwaters connect several lakes, and were tampered with in the 1840's by loggers who were competing to float the logs south to the Penobscot and down to Bangor instead of north on the Allagash to Canada by way of the St. John River. The tampering has since been set straight, and now a parking lot has been laid out beside the Great Northern Paper Company's bridge at Chamberlain Lake, a two and a half-hour drive from the nearest town. Fifty-four hundred people were waterborne on the Allagash in

1970, a number that's rising 15 percent a year and is concentrated in the two warmest months, so that the state authorities know that soon they will have to institute a system of advance reservations. The campgrounds, however, are tactfully dispersed, and though logging is going on within four hundred feet of the water, a screen of trees, deceptive but pristine-looking, has been left, like the false fronting of a movie-set street.

We put in at Chamberlain on July 17th in a brisk splashing wind, our old-fashioned cedar canoes contrasting with the light aluminum canoes more modernist types were using—the Sierra Club fellows with their families and dogs who fill up his stage set and offend Fred King's sense of what's wild. The vacationers who employ King like his big tents and good steaks on ice and the canned provisions and sauces he brings, though they're not sure they're roughing it properly. The chic way to travel requires carrying thin packets of freeze-dried food, and not much of it, and feather-light sleeping equipment such as backpacking mountaineers have more reason to want— a line that Fred doesn't swallow at all. In the first place, the men he admires, "Moosetowners" who are now in their eighties, used to earn their living poling thirty-foot bateaux up the Allagash loaded with tons of supplies. The measure of manhood was not roughing it on dehydrated foods but hefting a great big load on a portage and living well. Also, the Maine woodsman usually respected the rich as people who had won their spurs in another world, and did not expect them to prove themselves in the woods with feats of do-it-yourself, but were perfectly willing to

cater to the "sports" a bit for good pay. Fred says the
Sierra Club characters (most of them "lefties"), with
their "tin," "bang-bang" canoes, look like internees as they
stand in a row waiting for reconstituted soup to be ladled
into the tin bowls they hold. Instead of enjoying a meal,
they study their maps as if they were eating them.

We sports in his party probably weren't up to the role.
Sports lately are "pilgrims," he says laughingly, "groping
for something." They believe, as he does too, that even
in its protected status the Allagash River is being altered
irrevocably, and so they have rushed to experience it
before the herds finish it off. But his customers admire the
conservationists and disdain the lumbermen who controlled the region until now, while he admires the lumbermen and has little use for the Johnny-come-lately conservationists. They think that a rainy day on a canoe trip
is a disaster and therefore to be wet and uncomfortable
on a rainy day is natural, whereas he thinks that rain is
natural and that to be wet and uncomfortable on a rainy
day is unnecessary and unnatural.

We had sun, the trees thrashed in the wind and the
surface rippled in shark's-teeth patterns as we went up
the lake, until we turned close to the western shore. There
were mud beaches every quarter-mile. Chamberlain
is an expansive lake, with salmon and togue, and is
potentially dangerous when the wind rises. As we crossed
toward Lock Dam the waves ruffled up to the gunwhale.
King said that a canoeman's basic instrument was his pole,
not his paddle (referring again to the old-timers), so that
this deep-water stuff was an uneasy business for them.

We were using an outboard motor, however. I was a passenger in the bow, his other customers, a Long Island couple, being towed in the second canoe.

The lock tender himself was a summer visitor, a white-haired salesman with an ulcer whose wife wrote children's books. He gave us a couple of minutes of lively water to get us started down the two miles of river that flows into Eagle Lake. Its pitch for a moment looked steep, brimming around us, and we could see varicolored streaks, as lurid as tropical fish, on the rocks underneath us where canoes had scraped. King gave a lesson in snubbing downstream with a pole, the bow being loaded heavily and the steering done by holding the canoe's stern in position, letting the current work on the bow. We saw a muskrat, a loon, and beaver-work in the winding channels, and then emerged on a wide, even prettier lake, the shoreline more indented than Chamberlain's, with moosier swards by the water and a hillier setting, with plenty of leafy hardwoods high up and behind. Terns, ducks, two loons, and an osprey flew over, and we had a fresh breeze at our tail. The loons whinnied in clarinet tones. At Pillsbury Island a boys' camp was in possession, with a great many canoes. We were using the motor all the way, intending to put twenty miles behind us, because in these public playgrounds one must travel out of phase with the particular contingent of enthusiasts who happened to start down the chute the same day, yet not catch up with the parties who set out previously.

We ran into waves tipped with whitecaps, the wind shifting into a headwind, and a navy-blue curtain lowered in front of us. The murky curtain turned purple, the water turned black and the wind hard and strong—the waves coming in gusts, the canoe shipping water—as we met the storm. It was a smothering front, and passing beyond it, we were soaked by a pellety rain, but found some protection in the lee of Farm Island, then in a narrows, where we tied up at Priest's Camp. In the drumbeating rain as, laughing, we threw up our tents, Fred pretended we'd almost drowned to make it more dramatic for us. He said that when he first began guiding he'd been scared he might do something wrong and had gone to an old-timer for advice: "Just take lots of eggs and jam, Fred."

We were sharing the site with a middle-aged Boston couple, the man equipped with muttonchops and a mustache like an English eccentric, and two local Maine fishermen who, trusting in the fact that it was mid-July, had neglected to bring a tent. Fred probably would have lent the Boston people some scraps of canvas, but he left the Maine men to sleep in discomfort under their canoe because they ought to have known better. My own companions were from Oyster Bay, the husband, Jim, once a Marine first lieutenant, now a market-research chieftain, well-heeled, revisiting his memories of sleeping on the ground in the Pacific theater thirty years ago, which he'd promised himself that he never would do again. He had four kids at home, a narrow head, a large jaw and a pouchy face that looked as if he had laughed at his boss's jokes about five thousand times too often, a face that looked as if maybe he had been served up one of his kids at a business lunch once and had gone ahead and eaten it anyway. But he was smoothly bright and intelligent, what is called an omnivorous reader, slept lightly, and was skillful and pleasant and easy with people. His wife, Audrey, whom I liked better, wore a tously blond wig over long black hair that she thought was "too oily," had a touching squint, a good heart and dental trouble. She was soft-natured, vaguely appealing, more loving than loved, a hard struggler; she loyally tramped after her husband in all his nerve-testing undertakings—climbing to fire towers, and so on—and was never allowed to be tired or scared. On Long Island, she said, she ran with him around the high-school track every morning at six o'clock, although she hated it. After twenty-eight years of marriage the word "dear" sounded sad when he said it, but they'd brought along nine days' worth of mixed martinis in plastic bottles, as well as a dose of the anti-Semitism which is sometimes an ingredient of stories around the camp fire. Fred partook too.

Next morning we went to look at a relict tramway which had hauled saw logs in the first years of this century, and a railroad spur used for pulpwood later on, both constructed in order to get the logs from this lake into a different drainage that would carry them south. During the 1920's as many as five thousand men worked here. Beans were cooked all night in holes in the ground; the hogs that went on the table along with the beans were kept on Hog Island. Farm Island was for pasturing the oxen, but half of it was never cleared and is still black spruce. Black spruce and white, and sedges and cattails, cover this industrial blur where "Dynamite" Murphy, the dynamiter, and other famous figures once worked. Now a mother duck was running on the water with flapping wings, teaching her babies to fly. I'm such a child of the times that although half of my ancestors were lumbermen in the West, when talking to a proud lumberman of today I all but blush for him as he recounts his exploits, so King and I didn't always see eye to eye at the railroad site.

We circled the lake, slipping into each estuary and up Soper Brook, then up Snare Brook. Dozens of ducks; fish nests down through the water, scooped in the gravel. A great blue heron flew up. A dragonfly chased by a kingbird got away by dodging close to our bow. The brooks were silty but the wetland grasses were a tender lightgreen. After a half-mile or so the alder growth would close in and beaver cuttings would block the brook, and where we had to stop we'd see moose tracks. When we walked, Fred was quick, and with his small intelligent face looked like a professor afield, though his right arm is beginning to go bad on him—too much holding a chain saw. In the black-fly season he sometimes sews his socks to his pants to protect his ankles, and leaves them on for four or five days, he said.

We admired clusters of magnificent white pine left by the spruce and fir loggers of recent times. The original booty up here was pine. Some trees were a hundred and fifty feet high, seven feet thick at the butt, and wanted for naval masts. Before chopping such a whopper, the loggers would throw a nearby spruce against it, climb to the top of the spruce and so reach the climbable branches of the pine, from which they could see for ten miles across a great spread of spruce forest to other "veins" of pine.

We stayed at Priest's Camp a second evening, enjoying a rainbow. A boys' outing party arrived, and there was a special avidity in the way King and Jim and Audrey watched them set up their camp: *these* boys weren't smoking pot. Rain fell hard most of the night, until a clearing shower came just at dawn. Then trilling loons and King's cry, "Wake up, wake up, up with the buttercups!" I imagined him as the "cookee" around a logging camp in the old days whose light weight kept him from competing in physical feats with some of the men but who bubbled with jokes whenever they broke off work for a meal. He said, though, that he hadn't developed much interest in people until his late forties, having been concerned before then with excavations, machinery and physics.

We always started earlier than anyone else, just as we seized the best campgrounds and pushed past the trippers at every point, but the advantage of this for observing game was lost, either because of the outboard motor or else King's loud anecdotes echoing on the water. At such times, before the sun rose, when for an hour we had the Allagash to ourselves, he exasperated me and I was sorry I'd come with a guide, but of course from his standpoint this silence-on-the-waters was more Sierra Club nonsense. The old-timers moved through frontier America hollering as loud as could be, unless they were hunting—cutting the silence with hoots, dispelling some of the loneliness of the woods and warning the panthers and bears away.

To this day, in parts of Alaska where there are grizzlies a prospector will put a stone in a tin can inside his pack, so that he walks with a constant *clink-clank.* In the passage from Eagle to Churchill lakes we saw mergansers, scaups, herons, gulls, and an osprey again. Baby ducks fled in front of us like fish flipping along the surface to dodge a deep shark, the mother among them flittering strongly to set the example. A logging bridge crossed above us; we saw an otter underneath. The shores displayed "cat spruce" (white spruce), sleek and bristly, beaver houses, cedars and drowned-looking alder-covered beaches leading to a fir point where the Indians used to camp to escape the flies. On Churchill, with the sun a silvery band on the water, we caught up with a swimming cow moose midway across. Her body was invisible; her head was like a blunt boat, the ears the housing, and her hairy neck hump nearly underwater. It was a groping blind-looking head, sightless as a whale's, a feeling and suffering-looking head, the nose so huge and vulnerable that other undiscovered senses might have been contained inside. Two terns were diving on her with creaky cries. Her ears lay back as her big pumping legs hurled her ashore, and she swerved to look at us, first over one shoulder, then over the other.

Churchill is a rangy lake, the shore opening and narrowing, with a mountain skyline. Heron Lake, formerly a holding pen for the logs, leads on to Churchill Depot dam. The ranger there, whose name is Clyde Speed, talked about the moose that he sees, and we toured the outdoor museum of log sleds, water sleds, old bateaux,

Lombard tractors, Watson wagons, and looked into the boarding house, and engine and blacksmith shops, all defunct. Lombard steam log-haulers preceded the internal-combustion engine in the woods for a decade or two around World War I. Each of them could do the work of sixty horses, a blue flame issuing like a blowtorch from the exhaust pipe on a cold night. They were precursors of the tank and farm tractor because they ran on a caterpillar tread. In 1938 Fred King had walked to this spot to explore; he loved its tall tamaracks and big pines and gave us a chance to poke about. In places like this he always announced that he was only a "fake woodsman," and that although occasionally he spoke for some of the old fellows who couldn't go on TV themselves and spout off, if we wanted to meet the real thing we'd have to go farther afield.

The Chase Rips, the one risky spot in ninety-two miles, began here. Fred had been casual in speaking of it, once suggesting that Jim perhaps might want to practice a bit with his pole in Soper Brook, but now as we lugged our craft down below the dam (paying Clyde Speed to truck the duffels around) he began to hum nervously. We watched other voyagers as their canoes first entered the current like the little cars at a carnival being gripped by the cogs of a loop-the-loop.

I had an easy time in Fred's bow. Often he takes old people through these rapids who can give him no help, who are getting their final look at the outdoors. But Jim and Audrey, suddenly realizing they hadn't practiced enough in Soper Brook, were on their own, Jim cautiously trying to get the feel of the pole, hanging himself up against the bank several times. King, who had drifted ahead almost too far to shout, yelled at him to stand up and move more toward the middle of the canoe. "Stand up! You don't fight Joe Louis sitting down. Get on your hind legs!" He'd stripped to the waist. A moosefly bit him, and he laughed and said, "They'll bite a chunk out of you and fly up on a branch and sit there right in front of you eating the chunk."

The river before us fell off, abrupt as the end of a table; all of a sudden it didn't appear to be there. Then, curling up like a hairdo, it fluffed around us, high at the prow, as we slid down into the rapids themselves. The noisy water was popping in points, peaks and tufts, blotting out all other sights and sounds. We could have been surrounded by other canoes and not noticed them. This was the first pitch, full of rocks, several hundred yards long. The second was shorter but "downhilly," the many rips sticking up as if to chum with us, as the water curled and crabbed around. Riffles, bumps, a wild backdrop of trees. Jim was way back in the first pitch still but beginning to grab hold of the river's hand now. "Good boy!" King shouted to him, a regular educator, jittery on his behalf. "We'll make you an honorary Moosetowner. I ain't got the authority, but I can recommend you." Everywhere on the river there was midmorning light and a hiss as of thousands of snakes, the water backing up recalcitrantly into cowls. Jim's canoe came stumbling, angling along like a cub, edging to the bank, but he jumped out at every juncture to wade and push, as a canoeman should. We all took a breather together against some shore rocks to eat raisins and talk.

The third pitch was energetic with knobby rocks sticking up like bad luck itself, every one striped with canoe-belly paint. King has broken canoes here—a rock square-on at 45 degrees will do it, plunging through the bottom. A friend of his tried out a plexiglass design here but gave his bowman heart failure, the rocks skinning by just an inch or two under his feet. A canoe should go where the water goes. "Where's the water?" a canoeman asks himself in the rapids when perplexed. Then, camping alone at supper, all the company he has is the bugs in his cup.

Poling is like snowshoeing and paddling like skiing, and we were able to paddle for a little while. We passed several parties who were "frogging" (walking) their way down the channel, leading their canoes, having become discouraged from tipping over so much. The river was gala with rocks, a hustling hubbub. King's craft snuggled in like an invited guest—but, no, a big jar. We skidded and sidled by the tough spots. Fred said not to try to signal to Jim or he'd misunderstand, and it would distract him. Soon he did tip and swamp, the canoe underwater. "Not too bad being in the river, just lots of water and rocks," Fred said, jumping in too to help hold and right their canoe and recover the gear that was floating downriver. Now that their string of conquests had broken, the two of them fell out again twice in quick succession, but learned to leap when they felt themselves going so that at least the canoe didn't sink. "Once they get wet they'll get wet again." Watching, Fred sang with tension.

After having covered a mile and a half (it seemed much more), we stopped at a place called Big Eddy to dry out and have lunch underneath an old cedar, the water purling like Hiawatha's. When other people passed, we'd hear their piping shouts for a moment, but both the river and the dramatic forest—blue firs and black spruces—made them mirages.

We pushed on, the Allagash partying along, popping with rocks but forty yards wide, leaving plenty of current, till it tipped down steeply again and we slid at the edge of whole thievish mobs of rocks that nattered away, feeling their tug, zipping by Harrow Brook. There were scraps of canoes that had wrecked and washed down, becoming wedged in the rocks; some had been drawn up on the bank where they covered small piles of firewood, because a great many people had crawled ashore and spent time recuperating here. Jim and Audrey fell overboard twice more, though the river wasn't as severe. First he lost his balance; the next time she did. He was strong and uncomplaining but heavy and had lost his confidence, and Fred gradually formed the opinion that he was awkward and that over-education had spoiled him. Fred stopped really rooting for him, though continuing to mutter encouragement—whether or not Jim and his wife were able to hear. Being as safe as a sack of peas in Fred's bow, I felt guilty for having it all so easy and knew that I would have looked worse.

We enjoyed peaceful minutes of drifting too, with the bottom brown mud, just a few round white rocks dotted about, and the banks grassy, cedars leaning over the

303

water, and white-collared birds darting close to our heads. Then for three hundred yards the river would turn feisty, roaring, tergiversating, as busy as rush hour, each rock having its say. We twisted through new rips and rapids, eluding sweepers, seeing the trout jump, and dragonflies in a mating clinch; jays called in the trees. The clouds were lovely, if we took time to glance upward. There were still-water sloughs, and gulls on the mud-banks, and parakeet cries from the bear-jungle. Then a swift chute, dark choppy water, on into a wide, luxurious pool. Buzzing birds in the woods, occasional pines, more shaggy cedar, big pairs of spruce, a heron flying high with folded neck, a gangly flying loon, some green grassy islands. A winter wren sang. Then again the water crawled with ripples, with stream birds flying up, the water slanting alive with bubbles over a gravel bar.

After these last corrugations a wide boggy low-slung valley interrupted the forest, and there were red-winged blackbirds, bitterns, and other signs of slower water. We saw a speck of a bird diving on an eagle or osprey, harassing it for several minutes; hummingbirds and robins do this. The Allagash is thought to be visited by three or four eagles.

The bogs gave way to Umsaskis Lake, which after the rapids seemed placid and big, with bumpy timbered hills all around. We rested our backs, using the outboard. Fred said that in the years following the invention of outboards the Moosetowners kept trying them out and discovering that they could pole upstream faster than a motor could go, so the older men never did bother adopting them.

We'd covered twenty miles, and camped on July 20th in the Thoroughfare leading from Umsaskis into Long Lake. The Oyster Bay couple were telling about their trip down the Colorado River and I was talking about other rivers I'd seen, when I realized that we were making poor Fred jealous; he wanted our attention fixed on the Allagash. They talked about their vacation in Japan too, where Jim wouldn't take his shoes off. "We beat the sons of bitches, so there's no reason why we should take our shoes off."

It was warm and the frogs on the Thoroughfare started croaking at 8 P.M. As I stood listening, the local ranger, making a last swing past, stopped to find out if everything was all right. He said that people in trouble generally just stand on the bank looking out, don't wave or shout. Sometimes he wonders how long they'd stand there if he didn't come over—two days, three days?—before they began to wave and yell.

Fred keeps a jeep at Umsaskis. The next day he drove us forty miles across International Paper Company roads to Chemquassabamticook Lake, where we boated to his cabin. The spot is close to Canada, and during Prohibition a good deal of booze was hauled to Fred's lake, where the canoemen took over and carried it via the waterways to Moosehead Lake and other resorts farther south. We passed some cabins of the era with double-split roofs: cedar shakes overlying a layer of earth, covering an inner roof composed of spruce poles.

Fred's maternal grandfather went to California for the Gold Rush, sold mining timbers there and brought back fifty thousand dollars in gold. Gone now, Fred laughs, with a backward jerk of his head as if he were swinging an ax. His cabin is at what sixty years ago was One Eye Michaud's logging camp; and he's found the "greenhouse" (root cellar), the old beanhole, lined with rocks, with charcoal at the bottom, the outline of the bunkhouse, and that of a trapping cabin which must have predated Michaud. In his own cabin, built of peeled logs that he rolled up on skids to the height of the eaves, he has a hundred-year-old pair of caribou-hide snowshoes, and other antiques; even a scrap from a cedar tree where he cut some life-saving kindling one snowy night when he was caught on the lake by a bitter headwind and had to sit out the storm on the shore. He got under a spruce with the biggest fire he could scrape together and thought of all the things he'd done wrong in his life. Later he came back and cut that particular spruce for his new ridgepole, dragging it home on a sled made from two fenders.

His curtain rods are old setting poles; his clothesline is tied between saplings skinned by the beavers. He had a potato garden to tend, and we went out to see the stump of a virgin pine with the marks of the broad-ax that cut it still visible and a forty-year-old birch tree growing on top. We saw two barred owls calling each other, and a woodpecker drinking down ants on a stump, and moose and deer prints on the sandy beach, among the debris of mussel shells the gulls had dropped. In the winter it's so cold that the wings of the ravens flying overhead seem to squeak like an ungreased hinge. One Eye Michaud is said to have wanted to maintain his reputation as a hard man, and so, out here in winter weather, a four-day walk from the nearest town, he might fire somebody and then, leaning into the kitchen, announce, "Don't give this man any food!" It kept up appearances, and the fellow's knapsack was immediately filled.

Fred used to sneak up here years ago, even building himself a squatter's shack on a ridge of rock maple and yellow birch, since logged. The logging roads now extend everywhere, if one looks down from the air, like tributaries that join the main arteries leading to Canada and the pulp mills. We visited a fire warden named Leslie Caron with a round wrinkled face such as befits a man born in the puckerbrush, who as a boy had carried the mail by dogsled. He said the weather forecasters "must have read last year's almanac," and that he would retire and "be a free nigger" next year. Fred told about catching a six-pound lake trout and taking it up to the watchman in the fire tower on Ross Mountain as a present, assuming he'd catch another on the following day. He didn't, and as soon as the fellow climbed back to his tower, his dog got hold of the fish and ate it. Now the spotting is done by airplanes. Caron in a jeep chases out to where they are circling and tells them where he is in relation to them, because they can't see him through the cover of trees. Then they tell him where the fire is in relation to him.

In the morning the sunrise was golden through the thick trees. A soupy mist covered the lake, which smoked like a hot spring. Two connubial loons floated side by side, then dived together. The water was as dark as blueberry jelly. We drove back to the Allagash and got under way toward Long Lake again. There we encountered some Explorer Scouts, the vanguard of a program which will scatter ten thousand boys every summer through northern Maine; also a private boys' camp, forty-four kids in twenty canoes.

Fred said there are three kinds of bears in Maine: black bears, maybe a few brown bears, and *Jalberts*. Sam Jalbert was born on a rock in the Allagash, and when he was three days old he fell off and has been in the river ever since. He poled upriver so much he grew arms as thick as his neck, and hands as wide as a shovel. He raised a family of ten kids and had to kill a lot of deer out of season to do it. Used to take sports down the Chase Rapids too. Once he stood on his hands in the stern and steered by tipping and balancing his body. The Jalberts helped dig the channels and build the dams, and this twenty miles we were doing today was Jalbert country, where they logged and had their landings. The logs couldn't simply be set on the river ice or they would be lost in the frenzy of spring break-up; they were kept at strategic points along the bank, then rolled in when the river began to relent but before it lowered.

Chemquassabamticook Stream came in from the west through a moosey flat—Fred has poled up there to his lake from the Allagash, taking all day. We saw a swimming beaver and three otter, two of which ran up on the bank like muddy rascals. Here at Harvey Pond is an old farm clearing, once a freight depot during the towboat era, before that a place where people stopped for vegetables as far back as 1820, along the so-called California Road, a wilderness path which headed west. The original Harvey was a squaw man with a long white beard and twelve kids who married and settled here, liking the warmth and bustle after a lonely life.

An osprey and some splendid ducks flew overhead. There was a last dam, with lilies and water weeds and fish jumping. A channel was maintained by the towboaters for the rest of the way to the St. John, and we sought this out where there were rapids. A couple of horses would drag upstream a boat sixty feet long and ten feet wide (One Eye tried one seventy-two feet long). Barrels of pork and beef weighing three hundred pounds were placed in the bow, barrels of flour behind them, and buckets of lard and blueberries alongside the tiny cabin in the stern. Coasting back, the horses got a free ride.

We passed bits of islands covered with driftpiles, saw a doe and a fawn, a sheldrake with seven ducklings, a squirrel swimming the river, its tail like a rudder. A heron flew up and stood for a minute atop a fir tree. The river curved gently in a stretch sweet as honey, softening its watery sounds so that we could hear the white-throated sparrows. After tilting again with a few rocks we entered a dead water which lasted for an hour's paddling, birds warbling all around, the water smooth, black and waxed. Tying the canoes together, we drifted as a raft, eating Fig Newtons, and hearing chain saws. Sweeney Brook, Whittaker Brook and Jalbert Brook joined the current. Fred told the story of a guide on the St. John who used to drift along with a gallon of booze at his side. When he and his sports approached a serious rapids and they shouted across to him from their canoe over the roar of the water to ask how to deal with it, he would raise his tin cup and tell them, "I'll drink to that."

While Fred's "brain was in neutral" we hit some rocks, then met more brief rustling rips, rollicking through the Long Soo Rapids for a mile or so, through lovely still country. Only the water popped, a confabulation of rocks, with sandbars and other complexities and many dead elms and ashes that the ice had girdled in the crush of the spring. Fred sometimes picks fiddlehead ferns for his supper here. Entering Round Pond, we paddled to his favorite campground, and baked some bread, cut up chub for trout bait, and watched the ravens harassing the squirrels. Jim fished a springhole while I went to see Willard Jalbert, the Old Guide, as he likes to call himself, having become a bit of an institution. His description of fighting rearing bears with a double-bitt ax sounded as if he'd been looking at *Field and Stream* covers, but last fall at eighty-three he had shot a deer, and still could wend his way through the rapids with an outboard full-throttle, or hold his canoe where he wanted it with his pole while casting with his free hand. He once rode a log over the fourteen-foot drop of the Long Lake Dam, and used to play tricks on the ospreys, throwing out chub for them —a fish that is the butt of many river jokes—attached by a line to a log. "Everybody for himself and God for us all," he would call, going into the rips. But it has all somehow ossified now that the wilderness is gone.

At dusk we went for a joyride on the windy water. A

thin-lipped bright sunset, a loon's giddy titter like a police whistle with water in it. Rain with thunder during the night.

From before sunrise, hard logging was going on at Round Pond, all by Canadian labor, the logs being trucked to St. Pamphile. The truth is the Yankee big-timber-logger has been a myth for several decades, and old-timers like the Jalberts disguise their dismay at the fall-off in gumption among young Americans by grumbling that the hunting is tailing off because these Canadian woodsmen must be shooting the deer, tucking their carcasses among the logs and smuggling them out of the country.

We got started at 6 A.M., a sailing hawk peering down at us. A mist almost the color of snow lay between the lines of trees, so that although the weather was warm it was a wintry scene. In the Round Pond Rips a couple of ducks babbled in the thick of the fun, the water reverberating around them. Next, the Musquacook Rips and islands. King's echoing voice in the quietness irritated me exceedingly because this was not *my* sixtieth trip, but as he spoke of his "walking stick," which was his pole, and his "rain shirt," his poncho, exclaiming resoundingly, "Bubbles mean troubles," I had to remember that this was real history he was reliving, that he was a link with the boisterous rivermen whose intent was to knock down the forests and let the light in.

A buckskin-colored deer exploded with springy bounds. We saw a merganser family, a ridge scalped by a tornado. In a dead water we looked down and saw grasses growing on the bottom, while a whole populace of insects bounced in the air. The sun streamed through the morning vapors in warm yellow combinations on the west bank, but on the east the view was still snowy-looking. The black-growth forest humped into low hills. We floated past grassy islands, then sibilant stretches, the water combing through the rocks, turning the big ones yellow with reflected light and leaving a platter of calm downstream of each. There's a disastrous-sounding crunch when a canoe hits a rock and the floor lifts under one's feet, but the sound is worse than the results. We passed an old shack with a sod roof, now burgeoning with raspberries, and saw Savage Brook debouch through its delta, and Five Finger Brook. The water itself looked like running gravel, and we passed several old cabins that used to belong to characters like Sporty Jack (so called because of a birthmark he sported), and the Cunliffe Depot, the abandoned headquarters of a logging boss who rivaled Michaud. Michaud's hay farm was two miles below, now devoid of buildings but spacious after so many miles of woods. Then beaches and finally a slough called Finlay Bogan, where we saw kingfishers, fish jumping, islands foliaged with willows and silver maples, ice-scarred. It became a still, rainy day with some occasional neighborly thunder. We ran by a few gentle rapids and shoals, seeing huge waterlogged stumps that were shaped like moose. The river here was a dream—rustling, windy, wild-looking and lush—chipper with birds, overhung with sweepers, dense with slow channels forking between the islands. It was beautiful and remote. The pioneers chose inter-vale land such as this whenever they could because the river had already partially cleared it for them and laid down topsoil in which the natural wild grasses had seeded, so that their stock could browse.

At the approach to Allagash Falls the water grew deep, the bottom rocky and the forest black. Fred began to hum as we entered the rips that led to the lip, and we squeezed over to the east bank and camped in the crook of land where the portage begins. The water is churned butter-yellow as it goes over, and it spouts off the rocks below like the wake of a ship. I swam in the bombast below the falls, in deep potholes where the water was warm. It's a fat, plentiful falls, not notably high; once some daredevils went over in a bateau and survived. Looking down from above at the charade of destruction, suddenly I missed my wife. It was so lonely watching the water go over and smash that the mosquitoes began to seem friends. Fred, who was turning ornery now that the responsibilities of the trip were nearing an end, shouted from the supper fire, "Beavertail sandwiches" (Spam).

In scratchy places the channel generally stuck close to the outside bank. We'd try to go where the water went but not where it was making a fuss. Below the falls the Allagash achieved its maturity. It was plump, and the birds were dashes of white overhead, singing from every side. In a dead water, a large tributary, Big Brook, flowed in. Then McGargle Rocks, two short rapids with a pool between. We saw various map-eater parties in bang-bang canoes. Between McGargle and Twin Brooks is a nondescript stand of fifth-growth white birch and knobby

313

pulpwood, not showing the logging industry at its best. As usual, Fred's voice scared off the moose in front of us; once we saw a stream of fresh pee on the gravel where one had fled.

The Twin Brooks enter the Allagash directly opposite each other in the midst of a rapids. There was a roar, and the channel was first on the left and then crossed over while we hopped about in the swells. "'I'm lost!' the Cap'n shouted," Fred yelled in the fastest turbulence amid the rocks, before we slid into a pool where a seagull sat. We'd covered eight miles in two hours.

The water got moving again. The government-owned wild area ends at Twin Brooks, and soon we saw log trucks alongside the bank, and a ramshackle structure, the Allagash Inn, at Eliza Hole. The Allagash Inn was One Eye Michaud's jumping-off point on the river, where he kept his successive wives. Two of the four were mail-order floozies who decamped with his assets, but when he was old and pitifully sick and poor, the first of them came back and nursed him.

One expects to arrive at some signs of civilization at the mouth of a river. Ahead we could see the ridge carved by the St. John. The Allagash makes an S-turn to delay joining it, through Casey Rapids. We saw two last deer, smelled a skunk, an animal that prefers a civilized habitat, and heard new bird calls—field and song sparrows, bobolinks, meadowlarks. Crows had replaced the wilderness ravens.

Then the jukebox of the Allagash Pool Hall. Allagash proper is a sad shantytown, a sleeping shell of the Moosetowners' settlement, with everyone drawing food stamps now, but there are canoes on the lawns. It's ragged, not even quite right for potato country, backed smack up against New Brunswick. The old-timers, lame with arthritis after so many years of exposure to rain and cold, when often they slept in the snow next to a small fire, have become supersensitive to the cold. They find it torturing, tack up insulation everywhere, or pray for the money to winter in Florida.

I had a butterscotch sundae and a strawberry milkshake. Fred King departed like a boy let out of school: no more entertaining or catering to us, no more wincing at the bumps delivered to his canoes. He would drive south until he got tired and sleep by the side of the road. Our vehicles had been brought around from Chamberlain Lake, but Jim and Audrey's new Chrysler had not weathered the trip well. The two of us left them changing a tire, putting gas into the empty tank from a one-gallon can and reminding each other that no minor mishap should spoil such a fine trip.

A RUN

OF

BAD LUCK

Bad ions in the air, bad
stars, or bad luck: call it what you will—a run of bad
luck, in fact. I was driving down the Thruway in Vermont
to consult a doctor in New York, and hit a deer. Didn't see
the deer till the impact, sharing its surprise. Deer, unlike
domestic animals, are afraid of cars and leap as you pass,
either into you or away. It lay in the deep grass, heaving
like a creature stranded on the beach.

Sure enough, as befitted the omen, in New York City the
doctor's news was bad. Then within a day or two, Pier 50,
a huge ramshackle structure across the street from where I
live, caught fire and burned hectically for seven hours,
although surrounded by fireboats, as only an abandoned
pier can. The neighborhood was layered in smoke for a
couple of days—for me, acrid testimony to what the doctor
had said. There were also a few of the usual New York
hang-up phone calls, and then, as if to push me into a sump
of depression, somebody—a vandal aroused by the fire, or
someone who thought I had parked in his parking space—

316

poured sugar into the gas tank of my car, not enough to destroy the engine but enough so that I returned to Vermont in relief.

In the meantime, my mother, in another city, had gone into the hospital for surgery, and one evening that week my daughter and I were out walking along a wooded road (I was carrying her on my shoulders), when a car passing another car bore down on us at high speed, its roar not easy to distinguish from that of the slower one; I barely heard it in time. This, in the context of the other incidents, particularly shook me because it seemed to bear a hint of malevolence; I felt very small. Then, within days, my next-door neighbor there, an old man as close as a relative to us, died of a stroke. Another good friend and country mentor went into the hospital after a heart attack. News came from New York as well that a friend in the city had killed herself. I marshaled a motley assortment of tranquilizers and sleeping pills left over from the past— divorce, career crisis, other bad occasions. I had that feeling of luck running out, that I must be *very careful*, although, on the contrary, I was becoming deadened, not alert. At such a time, the opposite of invulnerable, one must take care to move in a gingerly fashion and not get so rattled that an accident happens. I had considered myself a sort of a Sunday's child much of my life, but suddenly intimations of death and calamity were all about.

I remembered talking to a woman who had survived a snowslide by swimming along on the surface while whooshing downhill for a hundred yards—as people caught in an undertow or even in quicksand save themselves by flattening out and floating if they can. Just so, I should ride the current until it turned. The best advice I have heard on bearing pain is to fix one's mind upon the idea that the pain is in one place—the other side of the room—and that you are in another; then, where you are, play cards or whatever. Cooking, fooling with my daughter, I realized more distinctly than at any time in years that although in fact my life was not at stake right now, I believed in some form of reincarnation or immortality—this a conviction, not a wish. I pray in airplanes during takeoff, but it is with a sense of praying *pro forma*, as if the location of my belief weren't really there, but were more generalized, in a bigger God. There are ideas central to society which we seldom question in order that society will hold together— as, for instance, the notion basic to medical care that everybody has a contribution to make, or "a right to life." But there are other conceptions, such as the idea of God, which we disparage and scarcely consider, until later, smiling sheepishly in our mind's eye as if we had disputed the fact that the moon moves in the sky, we admit to having been wrong, and to having known all along that we were wrong.

Once, highborn ladies would flee to a convent if some unnerving sequence of events overtook them, not necessarily taking orders, but resting, collecting their wits. And when they strolled in the cloister around a bubbling fountain, the walkway itself possessed a soothing, perpetual quality, with each right-angle turn leading straight to another. Walking for many hours, they looked at the lindenwood saints, the robust faces—at the Virgin's implacable

verve, or else at a dolor portrayed with an equally saving
exaggeration. Coincidentally, I went to New York's own
Cloisters, and because the reality of each bad event had
been dulled by the others, it was for me one of those queer
times when people recognize how much they can adjust to
—how quickly, for example, they could settle into the routine of life in a prison camp.

Of course I had my daughter to entertain, and in the
country I walked in the woods, watching the aspens quake
(said by legend to occur because Christ's cross was of
aspen). I have an old army siren, hand-cranked, that I
climbed with up on the mountain at twilight, to persuade
a family of coyotes nearby to answer. I was relieved that
the random incidents seemed to have ended. I thought of
two friends in the city who had recently suffered crises—
heart attacks at forty. One fellow, as the pain surged
through him, found himself muttering stubbornly, "No
groveling, Death!" When he was out of danger he wrote
seventy-some letters to friends from his hospital bed, each
with a numbered series of thoughts directed to the recip-
ient. The other man is that rare case where one can put
one's finger exactly on the characteristics of which one is
so fond. He married the same woman twice. Although it
didn't work out either time, she was well worth marrying
twice, and to my way of thinking this showed that he was
at once a man of fervent, rash, abiding love, and yet a
man of flexibility, ready to admit an error and to act to
correct it.

Both my mother and country mentor were now on the
mend, and my own doctor reported good news. Prospects

began looking up. What I'd gained from the period, besides a flood of relief, was the memory of how certain I'd been that the intricacy and brilliance of life cannot simply fold up with one's death—that, as in the metaphor of a fountain, or the great paradigm of rain and the ocean, it sinks down but comes up, blooms up and sinks down again.

BEARS,
BEARS,
BEARS

Bears, which stopped being primarily predatory some time ago, though they still have a predator's sharp wits and mouth, appeal to a side of us that is lumbering, churlish and individual. We are touched by their anatomy because it resembles ours, by their piggishness and sleepiness and unsociability with each other, by their very aversion to having anything to do with us except for eating our garbage. Where big tracts of forest remain, black bears can still do fairly well. The grizzly's prickly ego is absent in them; they are unostentatious woodland animals that stay under cover and do not expect to have everything go their way.

Grizzlies never did inhabit the forested East. They lived on the Great Plains and in the Rockies and Sierras, much of it open or arid country; apparently they are more tolerant than black bears of hot, direct sun. In such surroundings no trees were at hand for the cubs to flee to and the adults developed their propensity for charging an intruder. For their own safety too, the best defense was an assault, and until we brought our rifles into play they didn't trouble to make much distinction between us and other predators. They still are guyed in by instinct to an "attack distance," as the biologists call it, within which their likely first reaction is to charge, whereas if they perceive a man approaching from farther off, they will melt away if they can.

Bears have a direct, simple vegetarian diet supplemented by insects and carrion or fish, so they need less operating space than a wolf, which weighs only about one-fourth what a black bear weighs but must obtain for itself a classy meat meal. Nevertheless, according to several studies, black bears require from one to five square miles apiece just to gather their food, and units of at least fifty square miles of wilderness for their wanderings and social relations. In this day and age such a chunk has other uses too. Loggers will be cutting on parts of it, and boy scouts holding encampments, canoeists paddling the rivers, and hikers and hunters traipsing across. Black bears were originally found in every state but Hawaii, and still manage to survive in about thirty, if only in remnant numbers, so that they seem able to coexist. They are coated for living up on the windy ridges or down in the swamps and hollows, where even the snowmobilers can't get to them during the winter because they are under the snow, and they give promise of being with us for a long while.

Probably the most ardent investigator of black bears right now is Lynn Rogers, a graduate student at the University of Minnesota. He's thirty-four, red-bearded, crew-cut with a wife who used to teach English and two children, and he is another one of David's Mech's protégés. He works in Isabella (once called Hurry Up, until a leading citizen renamed it after his daughter), which is a logging village, a tiny crossroads with more bars than grocery stores, settled by "Finlanders," as they are called, in the Arrowhead region of northern Minnesota, now the Superior National Forest. The logging is fading as aspen grows up in place of the old stands of big pine, but the Forest Service plants red or white pine where it can (there is more jack pine, however), and the swamps are forested with black spruce. The lakeshores are pretty, with birch, cedar, red maple, fir and white spruce, and the whole place is bursting with bears. On a seven-mile stretch of highway near Rogers' headquarters thirty were shot in one year. This was before the townspeople became interested in his work; now they let the bears live.

Rogers is a two-hundred-pounder with a rangy build and a small-looking head, no more bearish than Mech's is wolfish. Though there are scientists who come to resemble the animals they study, more often they look like athletic coaches, animals being in some sense our behind-hand brothers and these the fellows who watch out for them. Rogers could well be a coach, except for the streak in him that makes him extraordinary. In the woods he moves at a silent trot, as only the rarest woodsmen do. His thoughts, insofar as they could be elicited in the week I lived with him, seemed almost exclusively concerned with bears— catching them, amassing more data on them. He seldom reads a newspaper or watches television, and likes to kid his wife about the "fairy tales" of literature which she taught in school. When he takes a day off, it's to snap pictures of beaver or to wait half the day in a tree for an osprey to return to its nest. He's lived only in Minnesota and Michigan—grew up in Grand Rapids—but once he did stop off in Chicago, when driving between the two states, to go to the natural history museum. If you ask what he'd like to do when his achievements are properly recognized, he says he'd want to stay in Isabella and study lynx or else fisher.

As he sits in a brooding posture at the kitchen table, his body doesn't move for long periods and he thinks aloud, not so much in actual words as with a slow series of ums and ahs that seem to convey the pacing of his thoughts. But he lectures nicely, full of his subject, and in the woods whatever is lummoxy drops away in that quickness, the dozen errands he's running at once— searching for a plant whose leaves will match the unknown leaves he has been finding in a given bear's scats, examining a local bear-rubbing tree for hairs left on the bark since his last check. If he's lost in his jeep in the tangle of old logging roads, he gets a fix on the closest radio-collared bear and from that figures out where he is. If he's near one of them and wants a glimpse, he lifts a handful of duff from the ground and lets it stream lightly down to test the wind before beginning his stalk. When he's radio-tracking from the plane that he rents, he watches his bears hunt frogs, or sees one surprise a wolf and pounce at it. If a bear in a thicket hasn't moved since his previous fix and is close to a road or a house, he may ask the pilot to land, if they can, to see whether it has been shot. Then, on the ground again, suddenly he'll climb an oak tree to taste the acorns on top, spurting up the branchless trunk without any spikes, his hands on one side pulling against his feet on the other. Lost in the yellow fall colors, munching bear food, he shouts happily from the tree, "What a job this is, huh?"

Wildlife biology as a profession interests me. Like the law, my father's vocation, it's one I follow. It's a stepchild among the sciences, however—badly paid, not quite respected, still rather scattered in its thrust and mediocre in its standards, and still accessible to the layman, as the most fundamental, fascinating breakthroughs alternate with confirmation of what has always been common knowledge—akin to that stage of medical research that told us that cigarettes were, yes, "coffin nails," and that frying foods in fat was bad for you. Partly because of its romantic bias, as a science wildlife biology has a tragic twist, since the beasts that have attracted the most attention so far are not the possums and armadillos that are thriving but the same ones whose heads hunters like to post on the wall: gaudy giraffes and gorillas, or mermaid-manatees, or "same-size predators," in the phrase ethologists use to explain why a grizzly bear regards a man thornily. It's not that the researchers have hurried to study the animals which are disappearing in order to glean what they can, but that the passion that activates the research in the first place is the passion which has helped hound these creatures off the face of the earth. Such men are hunters *manqué.*

Game wardens are also that way, but have the fun of

stalking, ambushing and capturing poachers, while so often the biologist sees his snow leopards, his orangutans, his wild swans and cranes, vanishing through change of habitat right while his study progresses—wondering whether his findings, like other last findings, invulnerable to correction though they soon will be, are all that accurate. Anthropology can be as sad a science when limited to living evidence and a primitive tribe, but the difference is that woodcraft itself is guttering out as a gift, and apart from the rarity now of observers who can get close to a wilderness animal which has not already been hemmed into a reserve, there is the painful mismatch of skills involved in first actually obtaining the data and then communicating it. Scientific writing need only be telegraphic to reach a professional audience, but again and again one runs into experts who have terrible difficulties in setting down even a small proportion of what they know. Eagerly, yet with chagrin and suspicion of anybody with the power to do the one thing they wish they could do (suspicion of city folk is also a factor), they welcome television and magazine reporters and interrogators like me, sometimes in order to see their own stories told, but sometimes to try to help save the animals dear to them—as if our weak words might really succeed.

But we observers have a piece missing too; maybe we put on our hiking boots looking for it. Like some of the wildlife experts—or like Lady Chatterley's gamekeeper, who was in retreat when he went into the woods—we don't entirely know why we are there. Not that an infatuation with wild beasts and wild places does us any harm or excludes the more conventional passions like religion or love, but if I were to drive by a thicket of palmettos and chicken trees way down South and you told me that a drove of wild razorback hogs lived back in there, I'd want to stop, get out, walk about, and whether or not the place was scenic, I'd carry the memory with me all day. It's said of a wilderness or an animal buff that he "likes animals better than people," but this is seldom true. Like certain pet owners, some do press their beasties to themselves as compresses to stanch a wound, but others are rosy, sturdy individuals. More bothersome to me is the canard that *when I was a man I put away childish things,* and I can be thrown into a tizzy if a friend begins teasing me along these lines. (A sportswriter I know has gone so far as to consult a psychiatrist to find out why a grown man like him is still so consumed by baseball.) Rooting around on riverbanks and mountain slopes, we may be looking for that missing piece, or love, religion and the rest of it—whatever is missing in us—just as we so often are doing in the digging and rooting of sex. Anyway, failure as a subject seems more germane than success at the moment, when failure is piled atop failure nearly everywhere, and the study of wildlife is saturated with failure, both our own and that of the creatures themselves.

Rogers is a man surpassingly suited to what he is doing. Like me—it linked us immediately—he stuttered and suffered from asthma when he was a child, and he's still so thin-skinned that he will talk about suing a TV station because it has edited his comments before airing them.

But with these thick-skinned bears—pigs-of-the-woods—
he is in his element. Just as it was for me while I stayed
with him, each day's busy glimpses and face-offs fulfilled
his dream as a boy twenty or twenty-five years ago: to
track and sneak close to, capture and fondle a noisy, goofy,
gassy, hairy, dirty, monstrous, hot, stout, incontrovertible
bear.

For their part, the bears have been *engineered* to survive.
Whereas wolves have their fabulous legs to carry them
many miles between kills, and a pack organization so
resilient that a trapped wolf released with an injured
paw will be looked after by the others until it is able to
hunt again, a bear's central solution to the riddle of how
to endure is to den. Denning does away with the harsh
months of the year and concentrates the period when a
bear needs to eat a lot in the harvest months when food
is at hand. Although its breathing and heart rate slow
by one half, and its metabolism subsides so that it loses
only about five percent of its weight a month (half the
rate at which it would shed weight during ordinary
sleep), its temperature doesn't fall much while it is in the
den. This distinguishes bears from bona-fide hibernators
like bats and woodchucks, and means that they can give
birth in the security of the den and can defend themselves if attacked. The bear's sense of danger is reduced,
so that the carefully surreptitious visits Rogers makes in
midwinter go off with a minimum of fuss, but in its easily
defended hole it can deal even with a pack of wolves.

Males sleep alone, but a sow has the company of her
cubs—generally two or three. They are born around the

end of January and den with her again the following winter; then in June, when they are a year and a half old, she permits a brawly big male, often several in sequence, to disrupt the close-knit life that she and the cubs have enjoyed since they were born. He or she drive them off and roam a bit together for a week or two, but by the device of delayed implantation of the ova her new cubs are not born till the middle of winter, which gives her a respite. The cubs are exceedingly little when they do arrive, weighing just over half a pound apiece—half what an infant porcupine weighs. The porcupine possesses quills, open eyes and other faculties to meet the world, whereas a bear cub has a great deal of developing to do in the dark den. Its eyes won't open for forty days, and small as it is, it isn't a drain on its fasting mother when suckling. Like a baby ape, it has a long interlude ahead of intimate association with her, an intimacy that will help make it far more intelligent than most animals.

Bears scrape out a depression for themselves under a pile of logs, a ledge or fallen tree, usually pulling in a layer of dead grass and leaves for insulation (paying a high price in heat and weight loss if they don't—one of the facets of denning that Rogers is studying). Some woodsmen claim that bears will position the entrance to face north in order to postpone the moment in the spring when meltwater chills them and forces them outside before the snow is gone and much food has become available. Emerging in mid-April, the adults look in fine shape; with their winter fur they even appear fat, though they shrivel rapidly during those first weeks as they tramp about trying to find something to eat—as if the fat cells are already empty and simply collapse. In Minnesota they break a path to the nearest aspen stand and climb or ride down the young trees to bite off the catkins at the tips of the limbs. They sniff out rotten logs under the snow and bash them apart, licking up the insects that have been hibernating there. A mother will take her cubs to a tall tree, such as a pine, and install them on the warm mound of earth at its base in a resting spot which she scrapes on the south side, nursing them and sending them scurrying up the trunk whenever she goes off in search of a meal. Then when the horsetails and spring grass sprout, the family begins to thrive.

The coating of fat that bears wear most of the year—and which was the frontiersman's favorite shortening—is of indirect use to them if they are shot, blocking the flow of blood, making them difficult to trail. Their flat feet, too, leave less of a track than the sharp feet of other game. Altogether they are excellently equipped, and if they don't insulate their dens or choose a sensible location for themselves, they'll probably come through the winter all right anyhow; the snow, melting to ice from the heat of their bodies, freezes into an igloo around them, complete with a breathing hole. If the complicated physiology by which they are supposed to fatten at an accelerated rate in the fall doesn't take hold (sometimes a mother gives so much milk that she stays thin), they muddle through even so, just as orphaned cubs do if they must winter alone without any denning instruction. The only dead bear Rogers has ever found in a den was a nineteen-year-old female, which despite this exceptionally advanced age, had given birth to two cubs. They had milk in their stomachs but apparently had been killed during her death throes.

In the past four years* Rogers has visited a hundred and six dens, first observing the bears' autumn rituals and later crawling inside. He has an advantage over his friend Mech simply because bears do den; he can head right for any bear wearing a functioning radio—in 1972 there were twenty-seven of them—and, after tranquilizing it, attach new batteries, which with luck are good till the following winter. He can outfit the yearlings with radios before they leave their mothers, and the habit of denning makes bears of any age easier to trap. His traps consist of two 55-gallon barrels welded together and baited with meat; far from finding the contraptions claustrophobic, the bears crawl comfortably in. Occasionally, when an animal is too bulky for the trap—as happened last summer when Rogers was trying to recapture a 455-pound bear whose collar had been torn off in a mating-season imbroglio—he sets foot snares at its favorite dump. This involves choreographing where the bear should place its feet by putting tin cans and other junk and branches close about the trap along its path. The snares are an unerring type developed in Washington State, where for some unfathomed reason

---

* I.e., as of 1972. I have not tried to incorporate his more recent findings, partly not to steal any thunder from his own presentation of them. My account here is deliberately anecdotal, incomplete and imprecise, so as to be scientifically useless whenever it does not cover fairly familiar ground.

(they seldom do it elsewhere) bears tear apart young trees to eat the cambium lining the inner bark, and the timber companies have declared war on them.

By comparison, Mech's wolves are will-o'-the-wisps. From an airplane a frustrated Mech may see one of them wearing a collar whose radio went dead years ago. Even Maurice Hornocker, the mountain-lion man, who works in Idaho, has a simpler time of it because his subjects, while they would be just as hard as a wolf to catch with an ordinary steel trap, obligingly leap into a tree in the winter, when snowed into a valley and pursued by hounds, where he shoots them with a tranquilizing dart and, climbing up, lowers them gently on the end of a rope as the drug takes effect. The best that can be said for wolves in this respect is that at least they do howl morning and evening in certain seasons, and are sociable souls, so that to keep tabs on one is to know the activities of five or ten others.

A heat scientist who is collaborating with Rogers in studying the biology of denning hopes to insert a scale underneath a wild bear so that a continuous record can be obtained of the rate at which it loses weight, to be collated with the winter's weather—weight loss being heat loss in this case, since the bear neither eats nor excretes. Another scientist in Minneapolis, a blood chemist, is creating from the unprecedentedly wide sampling of bears' blood that Rogers has sent him a profile of its composition, by season and in relation to sex, age, body temperature, sickness or behavioral peculiarities. In concert, they are studying particularly the breakneck conversion of food to fat during the late summer, and a nutritionist will analyze the many foods the bears eat. Rogers has charted their diet through the year, drawing on the evidence of scats, his walks and sightings from the air and their radioed locations. The scats he sifts in a pan of water. Leaves, wasp heads and carrion hair float to the top; seeds, tinfoil and twigs sink to the bottom. He's also investigating the fine points of telling an animal's age by counting the rings in a cross section cut from a tooth. Like the rings in a tree, a dark annulus is deposited in the cementum every winter while the bear sleeps and a light one during the bright part of the year. The live-bear biologists pull out a lower premolar and the dead-bear biologists take a canine, but there are also false annuli to confuse the count.

Wildlife biology used to be rather hit-or-miss. Rogers' predecessors would hogtie a trapped bear once in a while and clap an ether cone on it, then proceed to take weights and measurements. From dead bears they catalogued parasites, and looked for placental scars on the uterus. Sometimes a bear was caught and tagged to see where it would travel before a hunter shot it, or it might be color-marked so that it could be recognized at a distance, and transported and released somewhere else to see whether it "homed." To maintain sovereignty, every state's game department insisted on going over much the same ground with these prankish experiments; more seriously, a study of bear depredations on livestock, if any, would be made, because the stereotype of bears as menacing varmints had to be discredited before the legislature could be persuaded to remove the bounty on them, forbid killing them in their dens and give them the spring and summer protection that animals regarded as game receive. In state after state it would be pointed out that back in 1943 California had declared the grizzly its "state animal," but by then twenty years had already elapsed since the last grizzly had vanished from the state. Arkansas and Louisiana set out to right the violence of the past by importing several hundred Minnesota black bears at a cost of up to six hundred dollars apiece. A few have sneaked into neighboring states to delight the outdoorsmen and give the pig farmers the willies (for it's no legend that bears relish pigs), and so Mississippians have had cause to wonder and whoop at the sight of bear prints in the mud, for the first time since back in the era when Faulkner wrote his masterpiece *The Bear*.

In the late 1950s tranquilizers began to be employed, then radio collars. A woodchuck in Maryland bore the first such device; now even turtles and fish are saddled with transmitting equipment, and there is talk of substituting a microphone for the beep signal in the case of certain outspoken creatures like wolves, to record their life histories vocally. Some experts distrust such tools, suspecting that the hallucinogen in the tranquilizer, the obtrusive handling of the animal while it is immobilized, and having to wear an awkward collar may alter its personality and fate. But Rogers is a believer. In Minnesota he has captured a hundred and eighty-three different bears, some many times—one a day during the peak of the summer. Earlier, in Michigan, he had assisted in catching about a hundred and twenty-five. Flying four hundred hours in 1972, as much as his budget allowed, he totted up more than three thousand fixes on his bears. Of the thirty-seven he had put radios on during the previous winter, he could still monitor eighteen in late September and locate nine others whenever he wished to pay his pilot extra for a longer search. One of the travelers, a three-year-old male he had first tagged in its mother's den, went clear to Wisconsin, nearly a hundred and fifty miles, before it was shot.

To place all this in perspective, the State of New Hampshire, for instance, until recently had only one bear trap, a converted highway culvert that was trundled out three or four times a year. The game wardens got so excited when it was used that two of them would sleep overnight in a station wagon parked close by so as to be there when the door clanged. Before Rogers' program began, the most sophisticated telemetric figures on black-bear territoriality had been drawn from the State of Washington, where seventeen bears had been radio-located four hundred and eighteen times from the ground.*

At Rogers' cottage the phone rings with reports of sightings, friends recognizing his ear tags and collars; everybody keeps an eye out the window in the evening for bears crossing the fields around Isabella. He likes these neighbors and talks endlessly—bears, bears, bears—and

* The Craighead brothers, however, who began their grizzly studies in Yellowstone Park in 1959, have captured altogether more than five hundred and fifty grizzlies.

his wife Sue loyally wears shirts with big bear tracks painted on them. She's witty, slightly conspiratorial, and a great help to him, pushing him as she might urge on a student of hers who was talented but disorganized. The data keeps pouring in because he has such a network of methods set up to collect it, and he's out gathering more every day besides. One has the feeling that without her the study might strangle in congestion. He mentions an expert he knew in Michigan who in the course of a decade had collected more information on bears than any other man there, but who, as the years went on, could never write down what he'd learned and get credit for it. Finally, to cushion his disappointment, his chief transferred him to the task of collecting a whole new raft of raw data on deer.

Rogers has received a modicum of funding from the state's Department of Natural Resources, the federal Forest Service, the National Rifle Association and other disparate groups. Mostly, though, it is some Minneapolis magnates who call themselves the Big Game Club who have backed him, and particularly a poker-faced department-store owner named Wally Dayton, who will drive up, go along on a tour with the enthusiastic Rogers, see a few bears, and head back toward the Twin Cities without a hint of his own reactions, except that shortly thereafter the university will get a contribution earmarked for his work. At first, in my time with him, it had seemed sadly chancy to me that he had been afforded so little official support for a project I knew to be first-rate. But soon such a sense evaporated; rather, how lucky it was that this late-blooming man, who creeps through the brush so consummately that he can eavesdrop on the grunting of bears as they breed, had discovered at last, after seven long years as a letter carrier in his hometown, what it was that he wanted to do! In his blue wool cap, with Santa Claus wrinkles around his eyes because of the polar weather he's known, shambling, blundering, abstracted at times, he is an affecting figure, a big Viking first mate proud of the fact that he can heft a 240-pound bear alone. He kisses his wife as he starts out, one pocket full of his luncheon sandwiches, the other with hay-scented packets of scats he forgot to remove after yesterday's trip (they smell pleasant enough, and he likes carrying them as boys like carrying snakes).

In grammar school, with his breathing problems, he couldn't roughhouse and was kept indoors—the teacher would give him a chance to tell the rest of the class what birds he had spotted out the window while they had been playing. As his asthma improved, he and a friend named Butch used to jump from tree to tree or swing on long ropes like Tarzan, until Rogers took a bad fall and was hospitalized. They swam in the summer, plunging into deep ponds and kicking their way underwater along the turtle runways on the bottom to go after snappers, whose meat they sold in Grand Rapids for a dollar a pound. They would never leave off exploring any pond where the fishermen told them there was an oversized fish until they'd determined whether or not it was a great six-foot pike. He still laughs remembering the times when it turned out to be nothing more than a carp.

In adolescence his stutter was the difficulty and he took extended solitary fishing trips. Boyish, he once went through an entire winter in Michigan without wearing an overcoat to see whether he could tough it out, having read of a man who went into the woods stark naked one fall to find out if he could clothe himself with skins and prevail. He was a colorful postman not only because of stunts like this but because hordes of dogs congregated about him on his rounds, following him for hours; in the afternoon sometimes he carried the little ones home in his pouch. He did some judo and boxing in gyms and got into street fisticuffs; he still likes to step into a fight where the odds are three or four against one and knock all the bullies out. Even after he had returned to college and met his wife and started studying bears, Rogers almost lost a finger when some bear feces got into a cut and he refused to go to a doctor at first. Only recently he inflicted what he is afraid may have been a permanent strain on his heart by racing through a swamp after an athletic bear scientist who makes it a point to always keep up with his hounds.

One might speculate that like Jack on the Beanstalk, he *has* to be boyish to be so indefatigable at sneaking up next to these furry ogres. He speaks proudly of his two plane crashes while out spotting bears; his one mishap when a bear chewed him occurred when he was working in front of a high school class with an underdosed bear that climbed to its feet and staggered off, and he was so embarrassed that he tried to wrestle it down. Like a denizen of the woods, he seems full of anomalies to an outsider. He was a Vietnam hawk and hippie-hater during the war, but was glad not to serve in the army himself when his asthma offered him a chance to stay out. He's a member of Zero Population Growth and is thinking of getting a vasectomy, yet kept asking me what it was like to live in New York; didn't the girls smoke an awful lot and wear too much makeup? Though he is working on his doctoral thesis, only lately has he entered what he calls a transitional stage away from his parents' fundamentalist beliefs. He went to a Baptist parochial school and junior college, and not till he went to Michigan State, after the mail-carrying years, did he encounter a serious argument against the theory of life propounded in Genesis. Taught Darwinism for the first time, he had to learn to stop raising his arm in astonishment in biology class and quoting the Bible. The teacher was nonplussed and would suggest "See me afterwards," but then would avoid the meeting, and the students naturally thought he was funny. Offended, Lynn also postponed matching up his parents' ideas with the rest of the world's. He was superb at bear-catching, after all, and felt he was working at real biology, not bookish stuff, and because he was keeping his thoughts to himself, when he did argue about evolution it was usually just as a doubting Thomas with a more convinced fundamentalist, not with a scientist who might have had it out with him. He still seems to be waiting for the rejoinders which never came when they should have, to explain things for him.

"Darwin is full of holes too, you know," he said to me in the jeep, looking to see whether I'd answer, but I smiled and shrugged. For years he and his friend Butch, swimming, leaping from tree to tree, had lived with the dream of Tarzan in their minds, but it was just Butch who had been allowed to go to the movies. He would come back after the show and tell Lynn about Tarzan's feats.

On one of our mornings together, a caller notified Lynn that a bunch of grouse hunters had pumped enough birdshot into a bear caught in one of his foot snares to kill it, so he went out to do an autopsy. It was a mother with milk in her udders and two surviving cubs which had run away. She was brownish compared to an Eastern black bear but blacker than many Western bears. Her feet were cut from stepping on broken glass while garbage-picking, and years before her right ear had been torn off. While he worked, the hunters who had shot her showed up, hoping to claim the skin. They were rough, heavyset customers, one a battered-looking Indian, and the witnesses to the killing, who were also grouse hunters and were standing around in hopes that *they* might get the skin, were too scared to speak up until after the culprits had left—which they did just as soon as they heard Rogers talking about getting the law after them. Then when the witnesses, two St. Paul men, after he'd helped tie the gutted bear onto their car, felt safe enough to enlighten him, Rogers could scarcely believe his ears, that people were so chicken-hearted. He hollered at them, threatening to take the bear back, went to a phone and called all the game wardens around.

We drove to several other dumps—perhaps a desolate sight to most people, but not to him. Gazing up at the white gulls and black ravens wheeling above, he imitated how his bears weave their heads, looking up at the birds. He told cheery stories, wretched stories. Somebody in Isabella had gutshot a bear with a .22, and the beast took five months to die, at last going from den to den in the middle of winter, in too much pain to be able to sleep. It died in the open snow, its belly bloated with partly digested blood, having shrunk down to ninety pounds.

That afternoon David Mech's crew from Ely delivered one of his radioed bears, #433, which had been caught in one of their wolf traps. They'd already tranquilized it, and he treated its banged paw; "Poor 433, poor 433." He marked down the latest data on it and drove it back to its home territory. Sometimes he howls to a pack of Mech's wolves for the fun of it until they answer him, and has caught about twenty wolves in bear snares, enjoying his own mystic moments with them. He uses a choker on the end of a stick while he tapes their jaws and wraps a weighing rope around their feet, careful not to let them feel actually in danger of strangling, however, or they go mad. Crouched over them, he achieves an effect similar to that of a dominant wolf; the thrashing animal gives up and lies quietly. Sometimes a possumlike catatonia slips over it and it loses consciousness for a while.

The next day, because one of the newly orphaned cubs had been caught in a snare, he had a chance to tag it in order to keep track of its fortunes. Thanks to the marvelous alimentary system bears have, young orphans tend to

341

stay fat, and they hang together through their first winter, but with no mother to defend a territory for them, many questions remain about how they eventually fit into the pecking order of the area. All summer he had been in radio contact with two cubs a poacher had orphaned in June, when they were not long out of their mother's den. They'd been keeping body and soul together, traveling cross-country in a haphazard fashion, presumably scuttling up a tree if a wolf or another bear materialized, until a Duluth, Missabe and Iron Range Railway train killed them. They had begun by eating their mother; maybe could not have survived otherwise, since they were unweaned. One can imagine them at first simply scratching at her udder in order to reach the milk curdling inside.

In a barrel trap Rogers had caught a three-year-old male, blowing like an elephant because of the resonance of the barrels. Bears really can huff and puff enough to blow the house down. While it chuffed at him through one vent he injected the drugs Sernylan and Sparine into its shoulder through another, then lifted the door and rubbed the bear's head as it went under, boyishly showing me that he could. This was unfortunate because the bear's last waking image was of that dreaded hand. Licking its nose and blinking and nodding while the shot took effect, it kept its head up, straining, sniffing as though it were drowning, or like a torture victim struggling for air. Once Rogers live-trapped seven bears in a single day, and once in the winter he handled five bears in one den—four yearlings and their mama. He says that in his experience

all really large bears are males, though a hunter sometimes thinks he has shot a "big sow" because the males'
testicles retreat into their bodies after the breeding
season.

Later he shot a grouse for his supper, and showed me a
few empty dens, of the ninety-four he has located so far.
We drove to a bleak little hamlet called Finland to check
on bear #320, a sow he had already pinpointed more than
two hundred times in his studies of territoriality. She goes
there every fall to eat acorns, staying till the snow is
thick before hurrying twenty-odd miles back to her home
stamping ground to dig her den. "What a job!" he said
again, exuberantly showing me balm of Gilead, climbing
an oak tree or two, pointing out a dozen different kinds of
birds, and halting by the road to jump up on the roof of the
jeep and do a sweep with his antenna to see whether
another bear was near.

In a typical day for as much as six hours he will jounce
along abandoned logging trails, then go up with his
pilot for another four hours, the plane standing on one
wing most of the time in tight circles over a succession
of bears. Cautious pilots cost the project money, but he
has found a young man who is paying for his plane with
bear-study money and is daring enough. Wearing a head-
set, homing in according to the strength of the beeps entering each ear, Rogers directs him by hand signals.
Sometimes the beeps sound like radar chirps, sometimes
like the *pop-pop-pop* of a fish-tank aerator. On the ground
they are still more accurate, to the point where he can

343

distinguish not only a bear's movements across humpy terrain but its restlessness during a thunderstorm, its activity pawing for ants, or digging its den.

These bears produce more cubs than the mothers of Michigan, which ought to signify that they eat better; yet the cubs seem to grow slower. Rogers tabulates the temperatures for each week of the summer, believing that the weather may be as important a factor as the availability of food. At the end of a hot summer with plenty of blueberries, the first-year cubs he was in touch with weighed only an average of thirty-two pounds, but another year, when there were practically no blueberries but the temperature was cooler, another group had managed to fatten to an average of forty-seven pounds. An older bear once expanded from eighty-nine to two hundred and fifty-five pounds in a year, and another gained ninety-five pounds in forty-two days, ending up at three hundred and eighty, and nevertheless crawled into a barrel trap, getting so stuck that Rogers had to stand the barrels on end and lift them off to free the poor fatty.

Despite these gourmand triumphs and the fact that his bears face little hunting, Rogers finds that the average age of the population is only about four and a half—just about the same as biologists calculate for much more severely hunted places like Vermont, where almost a quarter of the bears are shot every fall. Even without the attrition from hunting, the mortality among cubs, and more especially among yearlings and two-year-olds, is high. Nobody has quite figured out what happens to them. G. A. Kemp, a researcher at Cold Lake, Alberta, has theorized that the population is regulated mainly by the adult boars, which kill the subadults if there is a surplus. The Craigheads, working with the grizzlies of Yellowstone, have suggested that dominant bears—grizzlies that occupy themselves principally with being king of the hill around a dump or other gathering point, rather than with eating—seem to lose the will to live when defeat comes, and fade from the scene.

Bears don't mature sexually until they are four, which, combined with the circumstance that the sows only breed every other year, and plenty of eligible sows not even then, gives them one of the lowest reproductive capabilities of any animal. Now that his research has extended through several years, however, bears that Rogers handled as infants, then watched play on their mothers' backs, are themselves giving birth. Occasionally he tracks them for a full twenty-four hours, using student assistants, discovering when they travel and how far and fast. In this wild region, they do most of their sleeping in the dark of the night, from midnight to five.

From his plane in the fall he photographs the terrain in color so as to delineate the zones of vegetation, mapping these to compare with his radio-marked bear ranges for the same area. Keying the bears to the vegetation indicates the feed and habitat they prefer, and also which logging practices of the past have benefited them. Logging, like a forest fire or a tornado, brings in new growth, and even in the primitive section of the national forest, where cutting is not allowed, bears haunt the openings where vetch and pea vine have had an opportunity to sprout and where the windfallen trees are dry from the sun and teem with bugs. On the other hand, clear-cutting does them no good because, like other game animals, they are uncomfortable without hideouts nearby. Sometimes the Forest Service, adding insult to injury, sprays on a herbicide to kill the young aspens and birch—the trees here which are most palatable to wildlife; Rogers is on the watch for any birth defects in his new cubs that may result.

In the spring and early summer the bears' diet is salady —early greens in shady places, and clover, grass, plantains, pea vine and vetch. They dig out grubs, chipmunks and burrowing hornets, clean up wolf kills, eat dandelions, strawberries (the first of the berries), juneberries, bilberries, thimbleberries, chokeberries, chokecherries, rose hips, haw apples, wild plums, hazelnuts and osier dogwood. Raspberries, although abundant, are not eaten in the quantities one might imagine, perhaps because they grow singly on the cane, but bears do feast on blueberries in midsummer, pausing only for a week or two to give closer attention to the berries of the wild sarsaparilla plant. In Michigan and New England they stay above ground into November, munching nuts in the hardwood forests and apples in derelict orchards, but in Rogers' wilderness the last crop eaten is the fruit of the mountain ash—red, berrylike clusters. By October most of the bears have chosen their dens and are puttering around—they excavate less than grizzlies—sleeping more and more, gradually letting their bodies wind down, except for a few savvy males which journey to Lake Superior to visit the dumps at the resorts there, eating until the snow covers their food before making tracks back. The Craigheads, indeed, think that grizzlies may possess an instinct to enter their pre-dug dens during a storm, when the snow will cover their tracks. When a bear stops eating and its intestines are empty, a seal of licked fur, pine needles and congealed digestive juices forms across the anus, putting a period to the year.

Usually they are tucked in their dens before the first harsh cold snap. The cold itself doesn't affect them except to put hair on their chests, but once the food supply is blanketed over, their interests are best served by going to sleep. During the winter their tapeworms starve to death and their cubs have maximum protection, and, for the rest of the year, they generally give every evidence of invulnerability to natural disaster because of the array of foods that suit them. In 1972, for example, when a June frost had ruined both the blueberry and mountain-ash crops, the Isabella bears needed to improvise an unsugary diet of salads right into the fall, then ran out of fodder entirely a month earlier than usual; yet when they denned they wore the same good belting of fat.

Disease, too, like malnutrition, is uncommon among bears; their preference for solitude helps ensure that. One of the mysteries that have intrigued biologists, therefore, is how predators or quasi-predators, especially such redoubtable beasts as bears and wolves, regulate their own numbers. Most prey animals are kept within bounds by being hunted—if not, they pop like popcorn until an epidemic combs through them—but what natural force rides herd on the hunters? Among bears, the burly males unquestionably pluck out and kill a proportion of the wandering young if an area becomes thick with them— as will a sow with cubs of her own kill other cubs—and the device of delayed implantation of the ova probably offers a kind of hormonal "fail-safe," by which some of the bred mothers simply do not wind up pregnant by autumn, if conditions are bad during the summer. The complexities of fertility and sterility operate as a balance wheel for wolves and mountain lions also. Several studies on these other animals are coming to fruition now, and more and more evidence points to sterility in conjunction with territoriality as the answer. To compare the findings is fascinating.

Mountain lions are geared for a life alone, and each inclines so sedulously to solitude that they rarely fight one another. The toms, in particular, according to Maurice Hornocker, don't overlap in their ranges. The females are slightly more tolerant; besides accepting some overlap among neighbors, they make adjustments of range from year to year so that those with big yearling cubs to provide for and train occupy more space than does a mother with newly born kittens. In the snowy country of central Idaho the females each have a winter range of from five to twenty square miles, and a male will encompass the home territories of two or three females, like smaller geometric figures within his own bailiwick, though he steers clear of actual contact with them except to consort briefly to breed. Mountain lions neither cooperate nor directly compete in hunting, and their scent-marking, which seems to be done mostly by the toms and which takes the form of periodically scratching with the hind feet a shovel-shaped scrape in the soil or in needles and leaves under a tree, compares with the punctilious, gossipy sort of urination male wolves indulge in and the regular round of rubbing-trees boar bears maintain. The lion is different, though, in that he doesn't pursue a rival to punish him if he is trespassing. Instead, his territoriality has been likened by Hornocker to a system of "railway signals," which, merely by notifying one cat of the presence of another, effectively "closes" that track to him. Since male mountain lions will sometimes kill kittens they come across, as boar bears kill cubs, it makes ethological sense for the species to insist upon a territoriality that is exclusive—only one dangerous male is regularly in the vicinity. On the other hand, the females, upon whom falls the responsibility of feeding the young, benefit by being willing to allow some overlap in their ranges; they can follow the game as it drifts about.

A newly grown lion setting out in its third summer from its mother's abode rambles along in an easy fashion with, in effect, a safe conduct through the territories of older lions but no desire to settle in and try to rub shoulders with them, until eventually it locates a vacant corner of the world to call its own. This impulse to clear off, which is present in young wolves and young boar bears as well, discourages inbreeding and helps to ensure that a lion lost from the population anywhere is likely to be replaced, that no plausible lion habitat goes undiscovered for long. The reclusive temperament of mountain lions befits their solitary techniques in hunting—based on the ambush, the stalk—and the way that they hunt, in turn, dovetails naturally with the abrupt, broken country they are partial to—terrain not so suited to the convivial, gang-up manner of pursuit which wolves, living usually at a lower, flatter elevation, prefer. But as is true of wolves, lions feel the urge to breed only after they have managed to establish a territory; or to put it the other way around, they do not take up permanent residence, even if they find an empty niche, until they locate scent signs and symbols around indicating that here they will be able to breed.

Despite Mech's discovery that lone wolves, dispensing with territoriality, roam more widely and often eat better than wolves in a pack, those in the prime of life do pair up and live in packs within a territorial discipline if they can. They put up an outright fighting defense once they have plumped upon ground of their own. Perhaps the fact that they fraternize so freely contributes to their readiness to fight; being sociable, they want company, but place a strict limit on how much they want. Hornocker speculates that such gregarious predators can afford the luxury of an occasional test of strength (though their howling and scent posts allay much of the need), whereas a solitary cat cannot. A mountain lion, depending wholly upon itself, must keep fit, and so as an economy measure the race has evolved a gentlefolk's way of spacing its populace about.

Individually too, bears have no other creature to lean on

except themselves, but grazing the forest meadows as they do, they can nurse an injury along when necessary, and aggressiveness toward their own kind has a biological function for them. The bullying of the weak by the strong first puts good virile genes in the cubs, then weeds out the dullards among the yearlings and two-year-olds. The ladder of dominance in a wolf pack is a matter of still greater importance, because in the relatively level country wolves frequent, where game is easier to find than in a lion's convoluted topography and where there is more of it to go around, they must have no last-minute doubts as to who is boss; they must all streak after the same beast, swarm upon it, dodge its front hooves and bring it down. The bickering and the spurting of pee on each other's piss that they like to do is not just boundary-marking, but reaffirms which one—to judge by that tangy thermostat deep inside the body (and even a dog can distinguish one unit of urine in sixty million parts of water)—will lead the charge.

Wolves and bears are fastidious in their sexual clocking, breeding only so that the bear cubs will be delivered during the denning period and the wolf puppies into the lap of the spring. If a female lion loses her kittens, however, she may come into estrus again almost immediately. She has the onerous task of killing food for the litter, as sow bears do not and a bitch wolf need not, and is more likely to lose some of them, and so is equipped for another try. But like the bear, once her young are developing, she does not breed again for two years because no pack structure surrounds them to nurture them in the meantime. (The bitch wolf can go right at it the next February.)

Both bear and wolf scientists remark on how many of the females they study are barren in years when, to judge by the calendar, they ought to give birth. When an animal requires several square miles to stretch its legs and its psyche and to forage for food, inhibition assumes an importance. The creature must not simply be physiologically ready for offspring; it must have a great spread of land at its disposal, a competence, a self-confidence, and a wolf pack is wonderfully elastic in regulating this sort of thing. The strongest youngsters, with the wherewithal of nerve, fan out at the age of two to colonize new territory, but the old pack—parents, pups of the spring and yearlings of the year before, and sometimes older shrinking violets who haven't yet made the transition to independence, or an adopted senior widowed wolf—continues to hold the fort.

If the hunting is good in winter it's very good, with deer floundering in deep bogs of snow, but if it's bad, there are no summer beaver moseying about to be ripped up and no baby animals for hors d'oeuvres. When faced with starvation, a pack will evaporate rapidly from eight or ten or twelve to the single primary pair, as the others, barred from eating the sparse kills, head away in desperation to try their luck elsewhere. Then, from the odds and ends of packs that have disintegrated, a new apportioning of the countryside occurs. Sometimes a big pack will coalesce for a season if two former littermates, each

leader of a family on ranges that adjoin, meet affectionately again, maybe after weeks of howling to each other,
and throw in their lot together. In a pack, although several
females may be nubile, only one of them conceives, as a
rule. The lid is on unless the dominant animals are put
out of commission, whereupon all sorts of pairings become possible.

Like other recent studies (Jonkel and Cowan's in Montana, for instance), Lynn Rogers' investigations suggest
an almost equally ingenious instinctual realpolitik for
bears. No pack exists—though grizzlies occasionally are
prone to live in a loose sort of pack arrangement—but the
boar black bears of Minnesota each roam over a chunk
of geography averaging more than sixty square miles
during the June–July breeding season. This is about the
same freehold that a small wolf pack would use, but since
the bear does not need even remotely as much land for
food, he merely bestirs himself to be certain that no other
male is around where he is at the same time. Males overlap, in other words, and Rogers thinks that two miles is
about the buffer they insist upon, scratching, rubbing
against so-called bear trees for the purpose of warning
lesser males to beware. In his experience, sows seldom
make use of these signposts, but do, by contrast, appear
to enforce a severe territoriality upon each other, driving
other sows, including large ones, beyond distinct boundaries that they lay out. Although Rogers hasn't figured
out the method of marking that they employ, because the

area involved is usually less than ten square miles,* it is easier for them to exclude a trespasser than it would be for a boar to try to do the same. The boar is excellently situated, since six or eight or more sows live within his stamping grounds. Though each will be receptive to him for only a few weeks every couple of years, he doesn't have to depend on the mood and good health of any one of them in order to breed. They don't wait upon his welfare either, because each lives within the roaming range of several boars—the smaller specimens giving way before the fearsome bruisers, but skulking back. Boar bears are more likely to come to grief than sows because of their wandering disposition, yet whenever one is killed, others are on the scene—the whole uncanny setup being just the reverse of how mountain lions live.

June is an ideal month for bears to breed. They have had about three months to flesh out and recover their aplomb after the winter's sleep and plenty of opportunity remains for serious fattening before they slip below ground again. Wolves court and breed in the most grueling month instead—February, just when they should need to save their energy—but their love life goes on year-round and culminates extravagantly on the midwinter hunt. It's a time when all prudent bears are hoarding up their fat

* A. M. Pearson of the Canadian Wildlife Service gives a grizzly density of one bear per 10 square miles in a study area in the Yukon Territory, with the average sow's range being 27 square miles and the average boar's range 114 square miles, figures influenced by the local food supply as well as by the nature of the beasts involved.

and their newborn young under the ice and snow; the cubs grow from half a pound to five pounds before they even see the sun.

Bears hoard, wolves spend. Under the circumstances it's no wonder that scarcely half of the bitch wolves conceive, that though a wolf gives birth to at least twice as many pups as the sow does cubs, half of them probably won't survive for a year. Even the five or ten square miles the sow defends against other females would be more land than she needs for herself, if she weren't also defending nourishment for her cubs and for those of previous years. The winter of their first birthday, they den with her, then in the following summer are driven off as she keeps company with her paramours, but they are not driven outside her territory; they are still welcome there. They split up and den separately from her that fall, weighing maybe eighty pounds. In their third summer the mother appears with a new brace of cubs, and now they must keep severely clear of her. The males, not yet sexually capable, are full of urges and strike off on free-lance jaunts, as wolves and mountain lions of the same age do, each trying to light upon an empty space among the crazy quilt of bear bailiwicks that intersect throughout the forest. One young bear may travel thirty miles and set up shop, only to have a close shave with a resident bear, after which he will dash straight back to his mother's domain to recuperate for a little while before sallying forth on a different tack. Because he's slower to mature than a wolf or mountain lion, when he does find a neighborhood that suits him he has a couple of years to explore the district before committing himself. By scent he makes the acquaintance of the various sows he will pursue and the boars he must rival, eventually reaching at sexual maturity a weight of perhaps two hundred and twenty-five pounds when fat in the fall or a hundred and seventy-five pounds in the hungry spring.

Young males are the pioneers when bears resettle an area such as grown-over farmland. But they must cool their heels until a food shortage or some more arcane pressure pushes the sows toward them. Their sister cubs tend to linger in the mother's realm, living in isolation but protected from molestation by other sows because of the territorial right which they retain. One obvious effect of this procedure is that whenever a new sow does breed, her partner will probably have originated in another region, but as long as her mother remains sexually active, it appears that she will not do so. She lives there in reserve—in limbo, as it were, like an unhatched egg—in a section of her mother's territory as small as a single square mile, against the day when the elder sow meets with a disaster, whereupon the range will pass to her. Then her turf may shrink a bit, as the sows on the borders challenge her boundaries, but sooner or later she blossoms to the task of defending it.

When Rogers was starting his study, he almost ran out of funds in August when the bears he was tracking left their haunts after the agitations of the mating season, and went for trips he hadn't expected—vacations, the impulse might be called. The males sometimes travel substantial distances and mingle festively without much quarreling, and he was paying his pilot to chase them. The sows don't wander so far, but may go ten or twenty miles, as if to eat new plums and cherries, or merely ramble into an unfamiliar loop of land adjacent to their regular duchy, which for the time being they stop patrolling. This custom is another means by which bears discover gaps left by mishaps and exploit them so as to keep the countryside producing bears at full capacity. It is also a kind of relaxation which wolves could not afford because the territoriality of a wolf pack is based on the exigencies of hunting.

These are exciting discoveries, and of the several authorities engaged in zeroing in on the details, I didn't doubt that Rogers was the best. I liked his rushing way of driving and hiking and his enormous hunger for data. I liked his enthusiasm for the unfashionable black bear (there are many more scientists studying the wolf), and as we toured, enjoyed being in the shadow of a man larger and more vivid than myself—though with his bigness, as with the bigness of big women, went an affecting vulnerability. His ums and ahs annoyed me, yet I was saying um and ah myself by now. We kept remarking how we had each spent hours after school alone, daydreaming of seeing wild animals in the woods and searching out their hideouts and handling them—not imagining that such good fortune might ever really be ours. Here we were, he said, in woods that many people drive a thousand miles to camp in, people who felt that if they could happen upon a bear it might make their whole summer excursion—and we could see one at any time.

Rogers has actually put radios on seventy-two over the years, and when he's trying to enlist somebody's support or testing a student who wants to help him, he generally goes to a den. The kids (or me, or Wally Dayton) crouch down on their hands and knees, peering into the troll-like crevice where mushrooms grow. Whether or not the smell of the bear actually persists inside, it *seems* to, and one is reminded of humble caves that a boy might run away to, and of digging to China, and of bottomless cracks in the earth. In the fall, after the bear has gone to sleep in its new hole, Rogers will tie a thread across the mouth so that on his next visit he will know whether it has woken up and scrambled outside for an interlude.

Whenever he gets near a bear in the flesh, as in mixing with them in their dens, he comes into his own—decisive, direct. Where other biologists explode the tranquilizer into an animal with a dart gun, leaving a wound, perhaps knocking the bear out of a tree so that it is killed, he does almost all his injecting by hand. The sows stand chuffing at him, slamming their paws on the ground to scare him, but he runs at them, stamping *his* feet, and stampedes both sow and cubs into separate trees. Then he climbs up and sticks the needle into their round rear ends, before lowering them one by one on a rope as the drug takes effect. Approaching a bear denned under the snow, he slips off his parka so it won't squeak as he crawls. Wriggling forward underground, he carries a flashlight in one hand and the syringe in the other, fastened to the end of a stick. If the bear is awake and panics and begins to come out, he rolls quietly to one side of the entrance and hunches there, poking it with the drug as it lumbers past; it can't get far. Sometimes bears make a blowing sound, like a man loudly cooling soup, which he listens to, not taking the warning to heart unless it is accompanied by a lifted upper lip—this being a true giveaway of belligerence. "It's like driving in town. You've got a traffic light to tell you when to stop." Usually, though, the bears stay becalmed, resting in their nests, merely sniffing the syringe when it is presented to them, making no more objection to the prick than they would to an insect's bite. He takes his time; the air inside the den is dead and hardly carries his scent.

Weather causes worse problems. Some days Rogers has to break trail on snowshoes for his snowmobile for miles, and must put the needles and vials of drugs in his mouth to warm them; the tubes of blood that he collects go in his shirt. For his blood-tapping and temperature-taking he must haul the bear outside, and if there are cubs he deals with them, squeezing into the furthest recesses but finding them unresisting once the mother has been subdued. Newborns have blue eyes and pink noses, and the smell left by his hands does not make the mother abandon them. He listens to their hearts, measures the length of their fur and wraps them in his parka until he is finished examining the mother. Even knocked out, the bears are all right in the cold, although in the summer they sometimes need to be bathed in cool water after panting in a metal trap; he washes off the matted mud if they've been struggling in a snare. After he's through, he replaces the family just as it was—wriggling inside the den, dragging the cubs and mother in after him, adjusting her posture and limbs so that she'll wake up feeling natural.

On September twenty-second we spent a red-letter day together, starting at a dump where gulls and ravens whirled above us and Rogers scanned the line of trees for any fat rear end that might be beating a retreat. He flew for four hours, locating all the bears whose radios were functioning; then back on the ground, as a check on his methods he went to three of the fixes to confirm that the bears were where he'd marked them. He inspected seven denning places, showing me how he discovers the hole itself by the raking that bears do as they collect insulation. This is while the ground is clear of snow, so he memorizes how to find it later on by lining up the nearby trees. Number 414's chamber last winter was under a clump of boulders, fifteen feet back through a passage. Number 320's was under a bulldozed pile of birch that the loggers had left. A few miles away we watched a female preparing a small basket-shaped sanctum under the upturned roots of a white pine, from which she sneaked, like a hurrying, portly child, circling downwind to identify us before clearing out. Another bear, a hundred-pound male, was hollowing a den under a crosshatch of windfalls just above a patch of swamp. He too scrambled silently away downwind ahead of us like a gentleman disturbed in a spot where he's afraid perhaps he shouldn't be.

In a pea-vine clearing Rogers photographed three bears eating and obtained some scats. He tasted bear delicacies as he walked, spitting out prickly or bitter leaves. In one of his traps was a young male, chopping its teeth, clicking its tongue, with a strong ursine smell of urine. Rogers answered with the same sounds, and when he let the bear loose it bounded toward the woods like the beast of a children's fairy tale—a big rolling derrière, a big tongue for eating, and pounding feet, its body bending like a boomerang

We ate rock tripe off the rocks, saw moose tracks, wolf scats, two red-tailed hawks, three deer and a painted turtle. The dogwood was turning purple now, the aspens golden, the plum bushes red, the pin cherries brown, and the birches and hazel and thimbleberries yellow. There was pearly everlasting, and blue large-leafed aster still blooming in the woods, and sweet fern that we crushed in our hands to smell. Alders had grown up higher than the jeep on some of the roads we followed. "Doesn't have too much traffic," said Rogers.

There is sometimes a sadness to David Mech's work, when he knows in advance from the blood tests he does which of his wolf pups is going to die. But Rogers' cubs are hardier, the winter hold no terrors for them, and when they do disappear it is not due to the sort of anemia which an investigator can foresee. I thought very highly of him—this admirable animal-catcher, this student of wild foods and smells, this scholar of garbage dumps. Because his bears like dumps, so does he.

A
LOW-WATER
MAN

Leave the astronauts out
of it, and the paratroop teams that free-fall for 10,000
feet or skate down by means of those flattish, maneuverable new parachutes. Leave out the six people who have
survived the 220-foot fall from the Golden Gate Bridge,
and the divers of Acapulco, who swan-dive 118 feet, clearing outcrops of 21 feet as they plunge past the sea cliff.
Leave out even the ordinary high diver, who enters the
pool rigid and pointed after a comely jackknife. Come
down from such lofty characters to Henri LaMothe—who
on his seventieth birthday last April dove from a 40-foot
ladder into a play pool of water 12 inches deep.

The high diver in his development first increases his
height, then crowds more gainers and twists into his drop,
but LaMothe's progress in middle age and since has not
involved ascending higher. Rather, he has provided himself with less and less water to land in: an ambition oddly
private and untheatrical. Three feet, two feet, twenty
inches, sixteen inches, fourteen inches. He strikes, not

headfirst or feetfirst, which would be the finish of him, but on the arched ball of his belly. Inevitably, his endeavor over the years has been to manage somehow to jump into no water at all in the end. Since this is impossible, he is designing a break-away plastic pool whose sides will collapse as he hits, so that except for the puddles remaining on the pavement, he will at least experience the sensation of having done just exactly that.

It's as if LaMothe hasn't heard that during his lifetime man has learned to fly, or that he knows that the flying we do is not really flying. In the meantime his posture resembles a flying squirrel's. Apparently nobody else entertains similar ambitions, although one of the old-time carnival thrills was for a stunt man to jump feetfirst from a platform into a very considerably deeper hogshead of water, doing what divers describe as a tuck as he entered, then partly somersaulting and scooping madly. As the person dropped, he could steer just a bit by tilting his head—the head being the heaviest mass in the body—but like Henri's feat, this one was gilded with none of the nifty, concise aesthetics of fancy diving: no "points" to be scored, no springboard to bound from, no Hawaiian plunge after the mid-air contortions into a sumptuous, deep-blue, country-club pool, with a pretty crawl stroke afterwards to carry him out of the way of the next competitor. Such a performer lived on hot dogs and slept with the ticket seller and often received an involuntary enema through the two pairs of trunks that he wore; got sinus and mastoid infections and constant colds from the water forced into his nose.

LaMothe dives, however—doesn't jump—into water that

scarcely reaches his calves as he stands up, his hands in a Hallelujah gesture. His sailor hat never leaves his head, his back stays dry unless the wash wets him, and yet so bizarre is the sight of a person emerging from water so shallow that one's eye sees him standing there as if with his drawers fallen around his feet. As he plummets, his form is as ugly and poignant as the flop of a frog—nothing less ungainly would enable him to survive—and, watching, one feels witness to something more interesting than a stunt—a leap for life into a fire net, perhaps.

He wears a thin white-sleeved bodysuit that looks like a set of long johns (the crowd is likely to titter), and, up on his jointed ladder, huddles into a crouch, holding onto the shafts behind him. Like a man in the window of a burning building, he squats, stares down, hesitating, concentrating, seeming to quail, and finally letting go, puts out his arms in what seems a clumsy gesture, creeping into space between gusts of wind. He sneaks off the top of the ladder, spreading his fingers, reaching out, arching his back, bulging his stomach, cocking his head back, gritting his teeth, never glancing down, and hits in the granddaddy of all bellywhoppers, which flings water twenty feet out.

Though one's natural impulse when falling is to ball up to protect one's vitals, he survives precisely by thrusting his vitals *out*. He goes *splat*. And when a microphone is put to him—"How do you do it?"—Henri says, "Guts!" grinning at the pun. "Why do you do it?" asks the reporter. "I get a *bang* out of it!" sez LaMothe, sez that he is "a low-water man." In his long johns, white-haired, in that tremulous hunch forty feet up a guyed-out magnesium ladder that he folds up and wheels about for fees of a few hundred dollars, he's anything but an Evel Knievel. He's from vaudeville, a fire victim, his career a succession of happenstances.

In Chicago, growing up pint-sized with the nickname Frenchy—his father, a South Side carpenter, was from Montreal—he dove off coal tipples, bridges and boxcars, swimming and swaggering at the 76th Street Beach, doing the Four-Mile Swim off Navy Pier. In the winter he swam indoors with a gang that included Johnny Weissmuller, who was already swinging from the girders over the pool. But Henri's hands were too small, his build too slight for competitive swimming. To make a living he drove a cab and posed at the Chicago Art Institute, where he began to draw too. He stayed up late, speeding around town to neighborhood Charleston contests, four or five in a night —this being the Roaring Twenties—winning up to a hundred dollars an evening. He quit modeling in order to Charleston full time, closing his act with handstands, back bends and a belly-flop, sliding and rolling across the waxed floor. His girlfriend's specialty was the split; she'd kick him into his belly-flop, do the split over him and "lift" him up with two fingers and dance on his stomach as he leaned over backwards, balancing on his hands. They were local champions, and by and by he invented an Airplane Dance, his arm the propeller—"the Lucky Lindy," for Lindbergh—which he claims was adapted into the Lindy Hop. June Havoc and Gypsy Rose Lee's famously stingy stage mama took him to New York City as one of six "Newsboys" in their hoofer show, but he quit to dance in a musical called *Keep It Clean*. By 1928 he was dancing at the Paramount as "Hotfoot Henri" ("Hotpants" backstage), usually planted among the ushers or as a dummy sax player in the orchestra pit when the show began. The clowning, pat repartee and belly-busters were right up his alley; on occasion he still will flop on his breadbasket into a puddle of beer at home to startle guests, or lie flat and lift his wife Birgit by the strength of his stomach muscles.

Although he'd been thankful to dancing for whisking him away from the Windy City and the life of a commercial artist drawing pots and pans for newspaper ads, after the 1929 crash he had to scratch for a job. He designed Chinese menus to pay for his meals, did flyer layouts for theaters and bands, and painted signs. He was art editor of the *Hobo News*, later the *Bowery News*, and tinkered, streamlining the stapler used everywhere nowadays, and inventing a "Bedroom Mood Meter" to post on the wall, like the ones sold in Times Square novelty shops. He got work drawing advertising for a Long Island plastics company, and actually prospered; even flew his own plane. Mushing down for a landing, he would think of the pratfalls he had performed in the Charleston contests and his belly-flops back on Muscle Beach, clowning his way to popularity.

Clowning on the board at the swimming club for the executives, he heard the suggestion that he ought to do it professionally, and so after a stint in a shipyard during World War II he went swimming with Johnny Weissmuller's troupe in Peru. Then he went to Italy with his own water show, the "Aquats," in partnership with two girls, one of whom, a Dane called Birgit Gjessing, became his wife. Birgit had been an actress in Germany during the war, a swimmer before that, and a puppeteer back home in Denmark, marking time after fleeing the collapse of the Reich. She's a lean lady of fifty-seven with a quick expressive face, a school counselor now, but she remembers playing chess in a wine cellar near Mainz during the worst of the bombing. At one point in 1944 she traded her winter coat for a bicycle, thinking to swim the Rhine while holding it over her head and then peddle on home.

Henri would emulate the dives the girls did and mess everything up, or get into a race and be towed through the water, roped to a car. He dressed as Sweet Pea or Baby Snooks with a curl painted on his forehead. Wheeled to the pool in a buggy by Birgit, dressed in a starchy costume, he would scramble up on the high diving board while his nurse underneath pleaded with him to climb down. She would fall in, and he would pancake on top of her, landing crisscross. He used break-off boards to make his dive doubly abrupt, or wore a pullover sweater fifteen feet long, which would still be unraveling as he stumbled backwards into his fall. In a beret, with his French mustache, he'd put on blue long johns with rolled-up newspapers over his biceps and a great cape and, calling himself Stupor Man, bend "iron" bars and launch himself on a mission of mercy from a high place, only to crash on his belly into the water. He would "drown" and need artificial respiration, but as the girls bent over him, would squirt water at them from his mouth. Then, running to apologize to Birgit, he would trip, belly-whop, and skid into her.

He wore low-necked bathing suits through which he could push his bay window, and sometimes to publicize the show would stand on his elbows on a building ledge, drinking coffee, eating a doughnut. Unfortunately it wasn't until both he and the century were into their fifties that his agent had sense enough to tip him off that the dive he was doing anyway as a water comedian would earn more money if done straight, so he speaks of those first twenty years of diving as "wasted." Then it was maybe another two thousand leaps before his seventieth birthday provided a gimmick to get him a *Daily News* centerfold and a spot on a David Frost show. For part of this long period he practiced commercial art in New York, but New Year's Eve would find him in Miami Beach dressed as the Baby New Year, poised in a third-floor hotel window as the clock tolled twelve, diving into "Lake Urine," the kiddie pool. He sprang out of trees, from flagpole yardarms and roofs—once from the ensign standard forty-seven feet up into two feet of water in the Westchester Country Club wading pool. Touring the country clubs, they "ate lentils," says Birgit. And always Henri looked a bit silly as he stood up, the water lapping at his shins: the less water the sillier.

Water shows are lumped with ice shows in the lower echelon of show business. The very term has a kiddie ring. Indeed, Birgit still shivers, remembering a week in Quebec when they had to perform in a hockey rink, paired with a skating follies, in water poured into a tank right on top of the ice. She wore a fish costume and executed finny undulations to the *Basin Street Blues*, but otherwise, as always, tried to get herself and the rest of the ballet swimmers out of the water at frequent intervals to remind the audience that they were really human, not fishy, in shape. Ice skaters have no such identity problem. Water, on the other hand, elemental, deep, somber, healing as it is, imparts a nobility to swimming which no ice show can match. With the mysterious oceans behind it, stretching around the world, water can be a powerful ally.

But Henri, leaping into a thin film of water, has sacrificed the majesty of the ocean to the bravery of his frog dive. Landing as he does, on the paunch, the craw, the crop, he loses the pretensions to dignity of mankind as well. It's raw, realer than drama, and tremendously poignant; it's his masterpiece, he says, in a life of inventing, which, even when he's been shabbily treated on the show-business scene, nobody has been able to steal away from him. He talks now of diving from the Eiffel Tower or the Leaning Tower of Pisa, combining this with his dream of diving at last into no water at all.

He's a short, plump, pigeonlike man who rubs his stomach continually, bends his back and bulges his chest. His look is matter-of-fact, like a man calculating practicalities, yet self-preoccupied, like one who knows pain and catastrophe. Though he dives on an empty stomach with lungs half filled, he lives by the bulge of his stomach. Clapping his hands, he will demonstrate how his arched back is the key to surviving. If air is trapped between the hands the clap is loud, but if one hand is convex the impact is muted. Just so, he explains, an air pocket under his belly would "split me right open." His belly is holding up fine, but his back is decidedly less limber; his scrapbook of photographs testifies to what a bend he could bring to his work only a decade ago. Offstage he looked the dare-devil then, and back in the fifties, his two lady partners would give him a rubdown after his feat. Now, because of the slackening that old age effects on the best of bodies, except for his stern mouth and nose he looks more like a health nut maintaining his youth.

He has a fluffy ring of white hair around his bald head, and likes being up on his ladder—says that he's happy up there. His beloved round pool glows like a globe be-low him, even seeming to expand. He says that a power goes out from him to intimidate the water. "That water is going to take the punishment, not me." Kids always ask whether it hurts. "Why do you care if it hurts?" he asks them. At the Hampton, Virginia boat show, where I watched him leap, his dressing room was the aisle be-tween the showers and toilets. Among other exercises he did his stretching drill holding on to a sink and swing-ing from the top of a toilet stall. "Coffee's working," he said, because emptying his bowels was part of the ritual so he would feel "clean," ready for the impact. He drank a cup half an hour before he climbed up the ladder, both as a laxative and to bring an alive feeling to his stomach. Women sometimes ask if he wears a jock strap, but "I just put my tail between my legs and go." After the evening act he celebrated with a swig of whisky, rippling his stomach anatomy to help it down as he used to do to amuse the students at the Chicago Art Institute. For five or six hours afterwards in his room at the Holiday Inn he let his nerves unwind with the aid of beer, while concocting a vegetable-fruit mix in his blender and soup pot, the day's one big meal.

Once when he was a young man LaMothe swam the St. Lawrence—something his father before him had done —fetching up at a convent, where the nuns hid their eyes. And once he was paid three-thousand dollars for a week at the San Antonio HemisFair, "banging my belly." Working shopping malls and sports shows, he carries his pool in a shopping bag; it's a flimsy low roll of fencing with a plastic liner which sways with the waves of the blow. (Again, Henri's agent had to wise him up to the hammy fact that the sides ought to be down as low as the water.) On his ladder he lets all other sights and sounds except the bull's-eye blur out. He crouches, "hoping for" rather than aiming for it, and lets go, putting his froggy arms out as his body falls. A team of accident experts from General Motors has tested him and concluded that he hits with the force of gravity multiplied seventy times; or, with his weight, 10,500 pounds.

So he does what the bigger kids couldn't do, long after they have given up their own specialties. And since the death wish of a daredevil who is seventy years old must be fairly well under control, perhaps the best explanation for why he continues is that this is what he is good at. Humiliation is a very good school for clowns, and, watching him, as with certain other notable clowns, one is swept with a tenderness for him as he lands, God's Fool, safe

371

and sound and alive once again. As with them, our fascination is enhanced because at the same time that he has sought our applause, he has seemed to try to obscure our appreciation, make the venture difficult for us to understand, and thereby escape our applause—a "low-water man."

THOUGHTS ON RETURNING TO THE CITY AFTER FIVE MONTHS ON A MOUNTAIN WHERE THE WOLVES HOWLED

City people are more supple than country people, and the sanest city people, being more tested and more broadly based in the world of men, are the sanest people on earth. As to honesty, though, or good sense, no clear-cut distinction exists either way.

I like gourmets, even winetasters. In the city they correspond to the old-timers who knew all the berries and herbs, made money collecting the roots of the ginseng plant, and knew the taste of each hill by its springs. Alertness and adaptability in the city are transferable to the country if you feel at home there, and alertness there can

373

quickly be transmuted into alertness here. It is not necessary to choose between being a country man and a city
man, as it is to decide, for instance, some time along in
one's thirties, whether one is an Easterner or a Westerner.
(Middle Westerners, too, make the choice: people in
Cleveland consider themselves Easterners, people in Kansas City know they are Western.) But one can be both a
country man and a city man. Once a big frog in a local
pond, now suddenly I'm tiny again, and delighted to be
so, kicking my way down through the water, swimming
along my anchor chains and finding them fast in the
bottom.

Nor must one make a great sacrifice in informational
matters. I know more about bears and wolves than anybody in my town or the neighboring towns up there and
can lead lifelong residents in the woods, yet the fierce,
partisan block associations in my neighborhood in New
York apparently know less than I do about the closer drug-
peddling operations or they surely would have shut them
down. This is not to say that such information is of paramount importance, however. While, lately, I was tasting
the October fruit of the jack-in-the-pulpit and watching
the club-moss smoke with flying spores as I walked in the
woods, my small daughter, who had not seen me for
several weeks, missed me so much that when I did return,
she threw up her arms in helpless and choked excitement
to shield her eyes, as if I were the rising sun. The last
thing I wish to be, of course, is the sun—being only a
guilty father.

But what a kick it is to be back, seeing newspaperman

374

friends; newspapermen are the best of the city. There are new restaurants down the block, and today I rescued an actual woodcock—New York is nothing if not cosmopolitan. Lost, it had dived for the one patch of green in the street, a basket of avocados in the doorway of Shanvilla's Grocery, and knocked itself out. I'd needed to drag myself back from that mountain where the wolves howl, and yet love is what I feel now; the days are long and my eyes and emotions are fresh.

The city is dying irreversibly as a metropolis. We who love it must recognize this if we wish to live in it intelligently. All programs, all palliatives and revenue-sharing, can only avail to ease what we love into oblivion a little more tenderly (if a tender death is ever possible for a city). But to claim that the city is dying, never to "turn the corner," is not to announce that we should jump for the lifeboats. There are still no better people than New Yorkers. No matter where I have been, I rediscover this every fall. And my mountain is dying too. The real estate ads up in that country put it very succinctly. "Wealth you can walk on," they say. As far as that goes, one cannot live intelligently without realizing that we and our friends and loved ones are all dying. But one's ideals, no: no matter what currently unfashionable ideals a person may harbor in secret, from self-sacrifice and wanting to fall in love to wanting to fight in a war, there will continue to be opportunities to carry them out.

My country neighbor is dying right now, wonderfully fiercely—nothing but stinging gall from his lips. The wolves' mountain bears his name, and at eighty-six he is dying almost on the spot where he was born, in the one-room schoolhouse in which he attended first grade, to which he moved when his father's house burned. This would not be possible in the city. In the city we live by being supple, bending with the wind. He lived by bending with the wind too, but his were the north and west winds.

You New Yorkers will excuse me for missing my barred owls, ruffed grouse and snowshoe rabbits, my grosbeaks and deer. I love what you love too. In the city and in the country there is a simple, underlying basis to life which we forget almost daily: that life is good. We forget because losing it or wife, children, health, friends is so awfully painful, and because life is hard, but we know from our own experience as well as our expectations that it can and ought to be good, and is even *meant* to be good. Any careful study of living things, whether wolves, bears or man, reminds one of the same direct truth; also of the clarity of the fact that evolution itself is obviously not some process of drowning beings clutching at straws and climbing from suffering and travail and virtual expiration to tenuous, momentary survival. Rather, evolution has been a matter of days well-lived, chameleon strength, energy, zappy sex, sunshine stored up, inventiveness, competitiveness, and the whole fun of busy brain cells. Watch how a rabbit loves to run; watch him set scenting puzzles for the terrier behind him. Or a wolf's amusement at the anatomy of a deer. Tug, tug, he pulls out the long intestines: ah, Yorick, how *long* you are!

An acre of forest will absorb six tons of carbon dioxide in a year.

Wordsworth walked an estimated 186,000 miles in his lifetime.

Robert Rogers' Twenty-first Rule of Ranger warfare was: "If the enemy pursue your rear, take a circle till you come to your own tracks, and there form an ambush to receive them, and give them the first fire."

Rain-in-the-face, a Hunkpapa Sioux, before attacking Fort Totten in the Dakota Territory in 1866: "I prepared for death. I painted as usual like the eclipse of the sun, half black and half red."

OTHER
LIVES

Often there seems to be a playfulness to wise people, as if either their equanimity has as its source this playfulness or the playfulness flows from the equanimity; and they can persuade other people who are in a state of agitation to calm down and manage a smile. If they believe in God and an afterlife, then the parts of life we are not responsible for are naturally rather a game. If they don't believe, they find that generally it is more sensible to be amused than miserable. But what used to surprise me and make me a good deal less judging of people was to realize how vulnerable nearly all of them are, including these grown-up types. Unless he craves to straddle the world, there may be just a kernel of basic reassurance that each person needs. He needs some friends, some modest success in love or love life, a reasonable sense of accomplishment in the work that he does, and a home. Yet these benefits, in competition, are not so easily obtained. If our needs seem relatively simple, the psyches with which and the circumstances from which we must win satisfaction are not, and we live a long while, besides, seldom able to rest on our laurels.

So one discovers that everybody's equilibrium is surprisingly shaky, that you can't with impunity criticize someone, and that if you do criticize him you may rattle him more than you had intended. More to the point, though, I began to grasp that snap judgments are incomplete, unjust, that the complex of emotion and difficulty in which another man lives cannot be quickly ascertained. Of course, the glory and luck of it is that running counter to all that shakiness is a resilience: you can't shake up the fellow for long. Most of us have a way of riding out assaults or disappointments of even the toughest variety, an animal salubrity that somehow takes over and that we trust in, that makes us begin to grin a little again after a night's sleep, a long walk in the sunshine, a good meal or two.

The great leveler nowadays is· divorce; almost everybody thinks about it, whether because we expect to be happy all the time—daily, weekly—or because we want the smell of brimstone in lives made too affluent and easy. Maybe some of us will end up back with the same wives and husbands again at the end of our lives (we sometimes hope so), but in the meantime it's as if marriage had become a chancy, grim, modern experiment instead of an ancient institution. *We have other lives to lead,* we say to ourselves, casting about for more freedom or erotic sizzle, more simplicity, leisure, "integrity" at work, or money, or whatever. Physiologically men reach their sexual peak at nineteen, an appropriate age for their original life span of thirty years, but now they have forty more years to go, and the expectation is that every year should be terribly straightforward or terribly crowded in every respect. To be original is to be lonely, we've always been told, and for that reason, too, we may feel the need for some form of hazard to enter our lives, especially if it was not in our diet when we were young. Many divorces are not really the result of irreparable injury but involve, instead, a desire on the part of the man or woman to shatter the setup, start out from scratch alone, and make life work for them all over again. They want the risk of disaster, want to touch bottom, see where bottom is, and, coming up, to breathe the air with relief and relish again.

It's not easy. The public effort to look harmonious may help hold some couples together. After sitting in silence going to a party, they will hold hands in the taxi when they come home; they make love rarely, but do so with pleasure if they have company staying over. Moreover, some of their differences are disconcertingly homely ones. She wants to sell the house, he wants to keep it, and they disagree about the children's school. He resents the fact that she got herself pregnant "accidentally" for each of the children, but she is sick and tired of battling his timidity, which, among other things, would have meant that he'd never have had any children at all if she hadn't taken matters in hand. He resents almost as a betrayal her quick abandonment of most of the sex games—what she calls "Krafft-Ebbing" now—that so pleased him during their courtship and drew him on, but she is tired of holding him to a maturity that should befit the head of a household; it doesn't seem to come naturally to him. Bachelors fall into two types, as she sees them—the "glassies," who reflect back what they encounter, and the thickset, blocked, sad fellows, to whom passivity is a pain and a blight—and he probably would have been one of the latter if she hadn't turned up, had their first child and settled down into family life, exchanging her rakish black boots for shoes. She wants to go to Europe this summer, whereas he wants to bask at the beach. She thinks he treats his mother and father badly and that his behavior in their own fights is a continuation of hangups he has with them, but he makes no bones at all about his contention that her affection for *her* parents is livelier than what she feels for him, that even her preoccupation with motherhood is partly an attempt to give to the world her mother all over again.

They're at swords' points; grotesqueries come to the fore. He carries a portable radio everywhere, even to the dinner table, the bathroom, and she constantly plays with the dog. He's sick of the hack of her nervous cough and she of his scratching his ass. In bed, when they argue late into the night or lie rigid, unable to speak, she crosses her arms on her chest and he holds his balls as if to keep them intact for life later on. Apprehension and exhaustion make them postpone separating, but they take to fighting via notes left in prominent spots about the house, bulletins to be read in silence and answered by the same method, which cuts down the talk. Yet neither really wants this disaster; their nerves and their stomachs beg them to have a care.

For a poor boy, just earning a lot of money used to be plenty. Now moneymaking is seldom sufficient—*we have other lives to lead.* On the contrary, the higher the wages, the more wildcat strikes there are; a malaise afflicts the assembly lines. It's their time off that people are concerned with. Hitchhiking has had a new vogue for its dramatization of rootlessness, and a good many young men and women brought up comfortably in the suburbs have plunged into bucolic living, the men immediately confronting the extraordinary question of whether or not they could build a house for themselves. To do so seemed essential to them, and a surprising proportion did manage somehow. As one visits among the communes, one finds the woods full of houses—sheepherders' cabins, Japanese hutches, alpine chalets, airy, belvedered, summery bowers —that often are empty. The fellow, hastily beginning the job, worrying about that formidable scatter of sawmill lumber—the footing and sills and studs and siding—forgot to think about locating water, or built uphill from his spring. Or maybe the site is so woodsy-lovely that his girlfriend finds it frightening at night; they're sleeping instead in a Volkswagen van parked next to the central farmhouse. Isolated shacks dispersed about may have come to seem in conflict with the overall experiment in living. Or perhaps the builders merely moved on, leaving these homes like dated bomb shelters.

Some communes are for homesteading, others are rest homes or pleasure domes. Some are loose neighborly arrangements not unlike pioneer settlements where the people pitched in to help one another; others have a religiosity about them, though it may rather smack of the Children's Crusade. In Vermont, close by the subsistence existence that with some difficulty can still be achieved—outhouse, staked pig—is the fact of Boston or New York a few hours away. Even though the choice of living this way has been deliberate, a communard would have to be unusual to shut himself up on a mountain slope as if the contemporary world didn't exist at all. So these people make trips out, dipping into the maelstrom of the city every few months, working locally in town if they need cash, a rhythm that can be precise. Movies, restaurants, traffic, then home to a brook they can drink from: silence, noise, silence and noise.

Because it's a bad time for ideology, the communes are fading in favor of families who live private lives on a separate but cooperative basis. The problem remains that a place where land is cheap enough for the simple life is also a depressed area, where even the natives don't find much work, and so the women tend to do better than the men as the months become years. Not feeling obliged to come up with the mortgage money, the women set about doing what they might do anywhere—taking care of the kids, being ameliorative, homemaking. Particularly if they are the earth-mother sort to begin with, they thrive, while the men are dishwashers during the tourist season or carpenters or mechanics or set up a bakery, do leatherwork, carve salad bowls, drive a truck, until the limitations to earning a living in such a parched economy may come to seem not worth the candle.

I don't believe this rural activity is only a footnote to

the divisiveness of the Vietnam war. People are going to keep choosing a manner of living to suit themselves, and there are going to be different ways: we forget what miracles we are. On summer holidays some of the long-haired couples and communes in my town in Vermont get together for a big softball game, everybody contributing food for the meal that follows. The lush grass is high except where they've knocked it down, the outfield is full of extra fielders, and each team tries to run up the score. Watching the playing, the smiles people wear as they swing, I think it must be as gleeful a time as any, these late twenties that most of them are in. Sometimes I feel as though I'm looking at snapshots taken today of one or another of them, young, happy, at a kind of peak, on the best afternoon of their twenty-eighth summer. It's so American a scene that nearly everyone must be represented here, the lank hair only a disguise. I wonder where they will be, what will have happened to them, what changes their faces will show in twenty-eight more. Smiling in the sun, a girl takes a strong swing, and I feel perhaps some of the same painful tenderness she herself would feel years from now, holding pictures from today in her hands, pictures such as old men and women will show you to indicate that they too were graceful once and had happy times.

Afterwards, when the crowd is gone, my friend who owns the ballfield calls in his herd of goats for milking. "Goatee! Goatee!" The goats with their bland farmer faces run in a bevy of white bobbing heads, mild-looking. The unfinished new barn is a competent cross-hatch of joists and roof beams, taller than it will seem when it is completed. We are friends because recently we walked forty-five miles together, cooking over wispy fires, eating from the same pot, hunching under a canvas fly in the rain. He is so well settled here after eight years that it took me almost the whole hike to see him in the other guise that I always look for: what he would have been like if he hadn't left New York City. Finally, in the rain when he was tired, I did recognize the New York face he would have worn, and it was darkly confused and sad. Often behind the communard's veil of hair one sees a man who is just marking time, sliding past forks in the road that he should take, but here was my friend, with his fields and his garden and goats, in the midst of life.

During the Black Power period of the late 1960s in New York City, one babysitter who came to our apartment looked at our baby's blond head, and when she thought that they were alone, said to her, "How would you like to be thrown out the window?" But another babysitter caught my hand when I paid her and tried to kiss it and lay it against her cheek, while her knees bent as if she were going to kneel—this not "camp," you understand; her boyfriend was a white policeman, and it was actually what she most wished to do. There is no accounting for individuality. Hairdressers at the same time were costuming themselves as if for service under the Jolly Roger, with hanging the penalty if they were caught. Their savage mustaches would have fit them to ride with a bandit band in the massifs of Afghanistan.

In New York if I go out my door and turn left I'm at the federal holding penitentiary almost immediately. Loudspeakers, guards with carbines, men in fetters taking a last look at the street before being led inside. There are attorneys, and the rigmarole of bread deliveries, and visiting wives, mothers and babies—"ten years!" in the snatches of conversation. It's said not to be a harsh place and probably would not have the facilities to handle much trouble, in any case. The guards who do look like ugly customers are the out-of-staters from prisons like Lewisburg who have driven in vans to transport the sentenced prisoners for a longer stay. They play with their chains as they wait—long waist and leg chains.

Turning right on the street, I'm soon at a drug peddlers' location, a slithy spot at midnight, where two dozen trucks are kept closely parked in a narrow lot and the very moonlight is blocked off by railroad tracks running above. Over by a single bulb at the far corner a mechanic, as a cover, is leaning into an engine, making some repairs, while the sellers, several of them, pace in and out between the tight trucks, quickly disappearing in the darkness to reappear at another spot. A series of Dickensian starvelings scutter up, each one palavering furtively and then moving off, while other addicts await their turn in the gloomy doorways down the block. They are mostly so thin that they remind me of the poverty of another continent, casting desolate-looking faces backward as they come, to see whether anybody is following them. But some drive up and park; and there's a courier service for wholesale deals, because every few minutes an off-duty taxi swings slowly past to make a pickup—if the cabbie is scared he keeps going around the block until one of the peddlers whistles at him. It's a perfect maze, and if all the people transacting business in an evening were scooped up, they would fill the federal detention headquarters. Some will find themselves there rapidly enough anyway. For them it is only a step from being free to being nabbed. They've already largely been nabbed.

The foghorns of this stretch of the waterfront, carried through the window, cause a slippage of resolve in me, just as they must work to demoralize the prisoners and peddlers and addicts nearby—we have other lives to lead. I'm not so sure I know what is permanent any more, although as recently as a year or two ago I thought that I did. The stars, the flowers, and so on—genes, mountains, and even the sore points of love. Picking at the heaps of raspberries growing up from the ruins of an old barn— sweet from the manuring of twenty years—I'd find a quietude in that. And our choreography, too, outlives us. A porcupine pushes its head around the corner of the house, and with weak bulging eyes cautiously sits up on its hindquarters before venturing onto the lawn. Porcupines chew holes in houses, so I slide inside for my gun. When my dog sees me loading he thinks his time may have come. He knows there is no escape, if so, having seen other men shoot other dogs, and he cringes as our eyes meet. The porcupine, which had retreated alongside the house, heads for the woods when I reappear, its waddle suddenly transformed into a flight for life. It is a primitive animal that when wounded still only waddles, cannot limp, but die it does, holding its wound with one hand and bracing itself with the other, sighing as a person would. Yet during this sad episode I've felt larger, quicker, hardly myself, augmented as though by the fact that each of us has moved along tracks older than our own time and place.

Most people enjoy some sense of permanence, even rather approving of the circumstance that old people eventually die (part of the permanence), until they themselves grow old. Children represent immortality, supposedly, and, to look at their scooting energy, they probably do. Their shouts are sufficient proof of that—shouts as harsh as a crow's cry that the next generation picks up at the age of five. Our image of ourselves throughout later life remains that of a person in his early twenties, old people say, and this may be part of the meaning of the vivid, monotonous schoolyard shouts. But much of my own feeling of permanence has been grounded in the wildness of the natural world. Wildness is permanence because it is what is unaltered, an infinity of particulars which are changing only very slowly without special reference to man. That the sun shines just as brightly on somebody who is dying in the desert of thirst is our good luck, because if he could turn out the sun for himself it would go out for us as well. Now, however, "wildness," instead of being infinity and superabundance, has a different reference: often simply the sniper gone haywire up in the bell tower. The glass panel in a taxicab that used to be there to protect the toffs from the unblanched opinions of the cabdriver is now intended to shield him from the violence of the toffs.

We don't know enough about what has been destroyed of the natural world even to take inventory; and though there should be other reasons besides what we call nature to believe in the permanence of the world, if nature in health and wealth and variety is to be permitted to exist only for its recreational value to man, then we must base our convictions about the world's permanence in the meanwhile, on the permanence of him. That wouldn't be so hard to do, when one considers people to be more good than bad, except for the exceptional power at hand nowadays in those brutal moments, even just to the local vandal. Ten years of good intentions can't match one night of cruelty; what we watch is the dangerously balanced duality. Where the Indians were spellbound by the succession of thunderheads in their sky—which was so much bigger than ours—we eye ourselves; or when we do turn our attention away from our own psyches, we watch our leaders, who have become bigger than the sky.

Looking at clergymen in the street, I notice the same inward stitching of worry in their faces that was characteristic of the profession when I went to church as a boy. It's like the face of a man at a sickbed when the patient has turned aside to his basin. The profession is in eclipse, almost in disrepute. First the civil-rights people wanted to know where the clergy had been for the past century or more; then the environmentalists wondered whether the clergy's sense of continuity extended only as far back as Christ's time. But clergymen have never claimed to be particularly prescient. They knew they weren't visionaries, but conventional fellows—good men at a sickbed—who tried to practice what everybody else preached, and who sorrowed about the same things a little bit more. They had not been much concerned with the lot of Negroes or the carnage in Vietnam until a larger constituency was; so, with the vulnerability of individuals who are both conventional and conscientious, they are quite rattled and feel blameworthy now.

The people with the fewest qualms are the evolutionists —those who remain evolutionists. Against most of the evidence of instability and disorientation, they proffer the same serviceable idea: that we have other lives to lead. Which is just what we always wished. To be married, yet take a vacation from marriage; to work and to loaf; to be kind and yet tough, rich yet idealistic; to live and to die.

We have our freedom and miraculous variance, and lately I've tried to discover which is the wildest mountain left in Vermont, from scouting as well as map-reading and talking to people. I think that I have. A jeep could bump to within a mile or two of the east or west base, but nobody happens to climb it. The mountains round about are encountered first, and it's an intricate, broad-topped, low little mountain, a confusion of starfish ridges and high swamps thick with windfalls. Nothing spectacular, no cliffs, waterfalls or fifty-mile views, just lots of forest. Its only distinction is its wildness, and moose, bear, lynx and coyotes make their homes there. I'm drawn to it and frequently wind toward it in walks, tasting the creeks that run off its sides, getting to know the valleys below, spending the night on mountains nearby so as to look at its contours at dusk and at dawn. Old log-skidding trails go

halfway up, and I soft-foot up some of these, watching
for animal prints, but though it seems like a low little
mountain, hiding its higher complexities, eventually I turn
back, postponing climbing clear to the top. Such an important event should not be rushed. If this indeed is the
most remote mountain in Vermont, I hope to explore it
gradually for many summers and never really climb it.
Wildness is indifference, wildness exists without any
knowledge of whether or not it will be destroyed. Its
survival on this last mountain matters not to the mountain,
nor to the attributes that define wildness, but only to me.

Half the battle is knowing what matters, and if we are
prepared to make up our minds, an almost unlimited number of choices exists; in a way, the world is less crowded
than it used to be. Alongside the closeness and safeness
and sameness of modern living is a frightening roominess
—cheap instant travel, swift risk and misery, old-fashioned
loneliness and poverty, wars marbled with primeval terror,
yet scholarship leading straight toward the roots of life,
and so many experiments in pleasure in progress that it
takes only a minimal gift for adventure for somebody to
live several lives in the space of one. What is scandalous
or impermissible now? Kicking a child in the street; maybe
a few other odd taboos. So, what is happening is that we
come to face the decision: do we want to explore ourselves in several marriages or in only one? Do we want
one life to lead, or more? And how much does our own
ambivalence really interest us? Is our self-concern the best
focus in life? No doubt there aren't single answers; nor
will our private answers necessarily have much to do with

how we behave. Instead, as always, we trust that when we make a mistake we will land on our feet. What we know, as social sea changes come roaring at us, is that human beings are extraordinarily adaptive.

I stand on a pier near my house, looking at the river and south toward the larger harbor. If I were feeling glum it might seem an escape route, but I'm simply watching the sunlight jiggle on the wide currents, which are refreshingly broader than the yardsticks of distance that one is used to in the city. The water's jiggling and skittering establishes a parallel lightness in me, and though the weather happens to be cold, the sun's warm sheen brings out from within me, besides my good spirits, the lizards, snakes, turtles that I sprang from—all the creatures that merged to make me and that loved the sunlight, depending upon it so much that even if I no longer need it myself as imperatively, I can't feel it on my skin without slowing my thoughts and my feet, stopping and closing my eyes for a moment to *bask*.

So the day is lovely: there's sunshine that I turn my throat to slowly, the water hopping and sparkling, and many moiling dogs. Out of doors, the dogs too arouse a level of existence that is usually sleeping in me. It's as if I had grown from them and my feet were still linked to them, as if I were dangling my legs in the spaciousness of them. Fortunately for my own safety, however, I'm neither lizard nor dog, because this is the center of the city and two or three hundred people besides me are taking their ease on the pier. An inventory of what they look like could encompass the history of the world, which, needless to say, I'm not up to; but I'm at home with them. Without sparing much attention from the boats and the children, the lovers and girls and old people whose stories I'd like to hear, I can pretty well spot people in trouble or those who spell trouble, and can get a handle on anybody who ambles near. Schizophrenia, diabetic collapse, belt-between-the-teeth for epilepsy—subway things. There are encroachers and trapped people and people here before they go home to dress for a party. One can place them in their apartments and with their friends.

Hundreds of people, and a freighter steaming grandly by, and barges, tugboats, police boats, sightseers' launches. The West Side Highway provides constant engine static; and two private planes are crossing overhead, and now a 707, big, flat, gray as the newest invented metal, on a descent pattern, sweeping around toward LaGuardia Airport. A helicopter, too, is sliding downtown, very low and arrested-looking above us, with another angling in from New Jersey. From every direction aircraft are converging, it seems—I suddenly notice a third helicopter— and the trucks on West Street, and the roar of the cars on the highway over them, and some stunting guy in a powerboat making waves down where we are, and these crowds of wrought-up people here to relax for an hour. Lizard though I am, dog that I am, I am able to absorb it all. Somehow the more the merrier. I'm grinning. It's like swimming in the ocean, and suddenly Lake Superior is dumped in, then the Danube and Nile, then the Caspian Sea. One bobs above them. Whether one will always bob above them is a question. But, grinning, one finds that somehow each increment is adjusted for; one rides above it. It can all be absorbed.

AN
EDWARD HOAGLAND
CHECKLIST

BOOKS

Cat Man (Houghton Mifflin, 1956)

The Circle Home (Thomas Y. Crowell, 1960)

The Peacock's Tail (McGraw-Hill, 1965)

Notes from the Century Before: A Journal from British Columbia (Random House, 1969)

The Courage of Turtles (Random House, 1971)

Walking the Dead Diamond River (Random House, 1973)

Red Wolves and Black Bears (Random House, 1976)

African Calliope: A Journey to the Sudan (Random House, 1979)

SHORT STORIES

"Cowboys," *The Noble Savage,* No. 1 (February 1960), pp. 176–91

"The Last Irish Fighter," *Esquire,* August 1960, pp. 99–114

"The Witness," *The Paris Review,* Summer–Fall 1967, pp. 141–78

"The Colonel's Power," *New American Review,* No. 2 (January 1968), pp. 230–51

CHECKLIST

"Kwan's Coney Island," *New American Review*, No. 5 (January 1969), pp. 106–16

"A Fable of Mammas," *Transatlantic Review*, No. 32 (Summer 1969), pp. 106–14

"The Final Fate of the Alligators," *The New Yorker*, October 18, 1969, pp. 52–57

ESSAYS

"The Big Cats," *Esquire*, April 1961, pp. 92–95

"The Draft Card Gesture," *Commentary*, February 1968, pp. 77–79

"Notes from the Century Before," *The Paris Review*, Winter 1968, pp. 142–85

"On Not Being a Jew," *Commentary*, April 1968, pp. 58–62

"The Threshold and the Jolt of Pain," *The Village Voice*, October 17, 1968, p. 5

"The Courage of Turtles," *The Village Voice*, December 12, 1968, p. 32

"The Elephant Trainer and the Man on Stilts," *The Village Voice*, April 17, 1969, p. 8

"Why This Extra Violence," *The Village Voice*, May 8, 1969, p. 5

"Knights and Squires: For Love of the Tugs," *The Village Voice*, May 29, 1969, p. 21

"The Problem of the Golden Rule," *Commentary*, August 1969, pp. 38–42

"Blitzes and Holding Actions," *The Village Voice*, October 16, 1969, p. 28

"Books, Movies, the News," *Book World*, November 9, 1969

"Home Is Two Places," *Commentary*, February 1970, pp. 70–76

"The Circus in 1970," *The Village Voice*, April 9, 1970, p. 11

CHECKLIST

"The Moose on the Wall," *New American Review*, No. 9 (April 1970), pp. 166–74

"Americana by the Acre," *Harper's*, October 1970, pp. 109–19

"Meatcutters Are a Funny Bunch," *The Village Voice*, December 17, 1970, p. 35

"The Portland Freight Run," *The Atlantic*, February 1971, pp. 26–38

"The War in the Woods," *Harper's*, February 1971, pp. 96–103

"Splendid, with Trumpets," *The Village Voice*, April 8, 1971, p. 5

"Two Clowns," *Life*, April 25, 1971, p. 70A

"The Assassination Impulse," *The Village Voice*, May 27, 1971, p. 5

"Of Cows and Cambodia," *The Atlantic*, July 1971, pp. 33–39

"The Soul of the Tiger," *Esquire*, July 1971, pp. 88–92, 126–34

"Hailing the Elusory Mountain Lion," *The New Yorker*, August 7, 1971, pp. 26–33

"Jane Street's Samurai," *The Village Voice*, November 25, 1971, p. 3

"Nobody Writes Stories about Unicorns," *The Village Voice*, December 16, 1971, p. 9

"Passions and Tensions," *The Village Voice*, February 2, 1972, p. 11

"On the Question of Dogs," *The Village Voice*, March 30, 1972, p. 15

"City Rat," *Audience*, March–April 1972, pp. 61–71

"Women Aflame," *The Village Voice*, April 27, 1972, p. 8

"Marriage, Fame, Power, Success," *The Village Voice*, May 18, 1972, p. 9

"In the Toils of the Law," *The Atlantic*, June 1972, pp. 53–58

"Looking for Wilderness," *The Atlantic*, August 1972, pp. 35–41

CHECKLIST

"Heart's Desire," *Audience,* November–December 1972, pp. 82–89

"Howling Back at the Wolves," *Saturday Review,* December 1972, pp. 5–12

"Wall Maps and Woodpeckers," *The Village Voice,* January 25, 1973, p. 11

"Fred King on the Allagash," *Audience,* January–February 1973, pp. 30–41

"Mountain Towers," *The Village Voice,* February 15, 1973, p. 9

"At Pinkham Notch," *The Village Voice,* March 15, 1973, p. 17

"Wildlands in Vermont," *The Village Voice,* March 22, 1973, p. 11

"In a Lair with a Bear," *Sports Illustrated,* March 26, 1973, pp. 32–40

"Tricks, Innocence, Pathos, Perfection," *The Village Voice,* May 10, 1973, p. 11

"The Young Must Do the Healing," *New York Times Magazine,* June 10, 1973, pp. 19, 44–45

"Other Lives," *Harper's,* July 1973, pp. 20–28

"A Run of Bad Luck," *Newsweek,* July 30, 1973

"Writing Wild," *New York Times Book Review,* September 23, 1973

"That Gorgeous Great Novelist," *The Village Voice,* November 15, 1973, p. 29

"But Where Is Home," *New York Times Book Review,* December 23, 1973

"A Mountain with a Wolf on It," *Sports Illustrated,* January 14, 1974, pp. 74–86

"Where Have All the Heroes Gone," *New York Times Magazine,* March 10, 1974, pp. 20, 92–95

397

"Where the Action Is," *New York Times Book Review*, October 13, 1974

"Nine Home Truths about Writing," *The Village Voice*, January 20, 1975, p. 41

"The Tug of Life at the End of the Leash," *Harper's*, February 1975, pp. 26–32

"Big Frog, Very Small Pond," *Sports Illustrated*, March 3, 1975, pp. 36–43

"The Survival of the Newt," *New York Times Magazine*, July 27, 1975, p. 6

"Apocalypse Enough," *Not Man Apart*, July 1975, pp. 1, 8, 9

"A Paradox among Us," *Harper's*, January 1976, pp. 18–20

"Southern Mansions," *Travel & Leisure*, February 1976, pp. 42–44, 66–69

"What I Think, What I Am," *New York Times Book Review*, June 27, 1976

"Cairo Observed," *Harper's*, June 1976, pp. 65–78

"At Large in East Africa," *Harper's*, August 1976, pp. 64–68

"The Fragile Writer," *New York Times Book Review*, December 12, 1976

"The Ridge-Slope Fox and the Knife-Thrower," *Harper's*, January 1977, pp. 41–60

"Do Writers Stay Home," *New York Times Book Review*, May 22, 1977

"Without American Express," *New York Times Book Review*, June 4, 1978

"Into Eritrea: Africa's Red Sea War," *Harper's*, July 1978, pp. 39–54

"Gabriel, Who Wanted to Know," *The New England Review*, Summer 1979

"Nature Watch," *The Nation*, May 26, 1979

CHECKLIST

Commencing from March 12, 1979, unsigned editorials in *The New York Times:* "The Price of Fur," "In the Spring," "Hang-ups," "Mountain House," etc.

BOOK REVIEWS

In *The New York Times Book Review,* May 9, 1971; June 13, 1971; February 6, 1972; October 7, 1973; October 21, 1973; December 2, 1973; April 14, 1974; May 19, 1974; June 1, 1975; June 22, 1975; November 9, 1975; December 7, 1975; April 11, 1976; April 18, 1976; May 9, 1976; August 15, 1976; September 5, 1976; November 14, 1976; January 9, 1977; June 19, 1977; August 14, 1977; September 11, 1977; November 27, 1977; December 11, 1977; November 19, 1978; November 26, 1978; January 21, 1979; February 4, 1979; June 1979
In *Book World,* April 12, 1970; June 6, 1970; October 30, 1972
In *The Village Voice,* December 30, 1971; October 24, 1974
In *The Boston Herald,* December 20, 1970
In *The Chicago Daily News,* December 1, 1974
In *Life,* October 14, 1971; April 21, 1972; October 27, 1972
In *Harper's Book Letter,* May 12, 1975; in *Harper's,* July 1977
In *Saturday Review,* April 28, 1979
In *New York* magazine, May 28, 1979

ABOUT THE AUTHOR

EDWARD HOAGLAND was born in New York City in 1932. He graduated from Harvard in 1954, and published his first novel two years later, devoting the first ten years of his career to fiction. His novels are *Cat Man, The Circle Home* and *The Peacock's Tail.* In the late 1960's he wrote short stories, and also a book-length journal of travels in northern British Columbia, *Notes from the Century Before.* Other direct narratives followed, in essay form. Altogether, he has published more than a hundred essays and reviews, collecting many of these in three books, *The Courage of Turtles, Walking the Dead Diamond River* and *Red Wolves and Black Bears.* He lives with his wife and daughter in New York City, teaching or traveling intermittently, and spending his summers in northern Vermont. His new book is *African Calliope: A Journey to the Sudan.*

ABOUT THE EDITOR

GEOFFREY WOLFF has written the novels *Bad Debts* (1969), *The Sightseer* (1974) and *Inklings* (1978). He is the author of a biography of Harry Crosby, *Black Sun* (1976), and his most recent book is *The Duke of Deception* (1979), memories of his father.